The Time-Life Book of
Hearty Home Cooking

Time-Life Books Inc.
is a wholly owned subsidiary of
THE TIME INC. BOOK COMPANY

TIME-LIFE BOOKS INC.

EDITOR: George Constable
European Editor: Ellen Phillips
Design Director: Louis Klein
European Design Director: Ed Skyner
Fresh Ways Series Director: Dale M. Brown
Series Designer: Herbert H. Quarmby
Book Manager: Blaine Marshall
Production Manager: Prudence Harris
Editorial Assistant: Karen Goettsche

PUBLISHER: Joseph J. Ward

THE COOKS

Adam DeVito
Henry Grossi
John T. Shaffer
Lisa Cherkasky
Pat Alburey
Joanna Farrow
Carole Handslip
Rosemary Wadey
Jane Suthering
Anthony Kwok
Nigel Slater
Janice Murfitt

THE CONSULTANTS

Carol Cutler
Janet Tenney
Patricia Judd
Pat Alburey
Mary Jo Feeney
Norma Macmillan

Library of Congress Cataloging in Publication Data
The Time-Life book of hearty home cooking / by the editors of
Time-Life Books.
    p.   cm.
    Includes index
    1. Cookery.   I. Time-Life Books
TX714.T56 1990   641.5—dc20   90-11293 CIP
ISBN 0-8094-6704-6
ISBN 0-8094-6705-4 (lib. bdg.)

BOMC offers recordings and compact discs,
cassettes and records. For information and a
catalog write to BOMR, Camp Hill, PA 17012.

The Time-Life Book of Hearty Home Cooking

BY

THE EDITORS OF TIME-LIFE BOOKS

TIME-LIFE BOOKS / ALEXANDRIA, VIRGINIA

Contents

Eating Wisely and Well

To eat wisely is to eat well—and the recipes in this cookbook amply demonstrate that point. Here you will find hearty homestyle food at its best, food to be savored and enjoyed, but food that is also healthful and well balanced.

As you begin turning the colorfully illustrated pages (almost every recipe comes with a photograph of the finished dish), you will see cooking that is pleasing to look at and even better to eat. Each dish has been thoughtfully created and tested in the American and British kitchens of Time-Life Books' latest food series, *Fresh Ways,* by imaginative cooks working under the guidance of several nutritionists. The teams have paid particular attention to limiting fat in the 262 dishes that are proudly presented here. Beside every recipe you will find a nutritional analysis that lists not just the calories, protein, sodium, and cholesterol in a single serving, but the amounts of saturated and other fats that it contains.

The book may emphasize calorie-conscious, healthful eating—but it is still food to warm the heart. Happily, the recipes included do not shy away from old favorites like beef and pork. But taking into account modern concerns about cholesterol, there is an emphasis on lean cuts cooked in little additional fat that are served in three-ounce portions (based on four ounces of trimmed raw meat). And to ensure moist, agreeable dishes, the book employs a variety of gentle cooking methods. Thus you will find a wide selection of recipes for enticing beef, veal, lamb, and pork dishes.

The good news about red meat

Beef and lamb are considered nutrient-dense foods. Three ounces of cooked lean beef—which has just 181 calories—supplies 46 percent of the protein, 76 percent of the vitamin B_{12}, 20 percent of the niacin, and 40 percent of the zinc that an adult male should have in his daily diet. That portion of beef also provides 27 percent of his iron requirement. And because 40 to 60 percent of the iron is heme iron, which the body readily absorbs, beef has particular importance to a woman, for whom iron ranks high among essential minerals.

Contrary to what most people currently believe, red meat is not overloaded with cholesterol. A three-ounce serving of beef, for example, contains an average 73 milligrams of cholesterol, a quarter of the amount that a healthy individual may have in the course of a day's eating. Most meats and some fish have cholesterol levels comparable to those of beef.

Pork offers pleasant surprises, too. This has partly to do with the fact that today's pig is bred more for its lean meat than for its fat. Still, a pig's carcass consists of about 32 percent fat. Once the surface fat has been trimmed, however, the lean meat that remains contains an average of 7 percent fat (compared with 9 percent in lean lamb and 4.5 percent in lean beef). And because it is rich in protein, minerals, and B vitamins—especially thiamin (vitamin B_1), which is necessary for the release of energy from carbohydrates—lean pork has much to contribute to the healthful diet.

The meat dishes in this book are prepared from the least fatty parts of the animals. If cooked improperly, the cuts could be tough, but care has been taken to ensure that they won't be. Carefully worked out cooking times, given along with the instructions, prevent the meat from turning leathery. And such moist-cooking methods as braising and stewing help guard against this as well. The eternal appeal of such methods lies in the culinary alchemy by which the flavor of the meat, and the flavor of any supporting vegetables and herbs, is drawn into the surrounding fluid.

The most commonly used liquids are stock, wine, and water. But there are no hard-and-fast rules. Beer might be employed, or tomatoes, puréed or chopped. While some of the recipes call for unsalted brown or chicken stock that you can prepare in volume from instructions at the front of the book, you can substitute canned stock. But if the commercial product is salted, be sure to eliminate the salt from the recipes in order to keep the sodium level down.

In recipes for roasting, broiling, and grilling lean beef and lamb, it is best to cook the meat medium rare. You can gauge readiness by inserting a meat thermometer into the thickest part of the meat and letting it register 140° F., a temperature that guarantees that any harmful organisms that might be present will be killed. Pork calls for a higher temperature. Insert the thermometer into the meat's thickest part, avoiding any bones, and cook until the internal temperature reaches 160° F. This is enough to safeguard against trichinosis. Gone are the days when the one method of cooking pork was to overcook it.

As well as avoiding fatty cuts, the meat section also looks to supporting ingredients to play a part in keeping the calorie count low. Missing are the excess of flour, egg yolks, and cream that were used to thicken cooking liquids. Many of the sauces are thickened instead by cooking down the liquids in which the meat and other ingredients simmered. This has the additional benefit of preserving nutrients and intensifying flavor. Because the recipes ask for scant cooking oil, the cooks recommend the use of nonstick skillets, saucepans, and roasting pans wherever possible. They urge, too, that any melted fat be skimmed or otherwise removed before a sauce is prepared.

Poultry and fish's healthful pluses

Everyone's favorite, poultry, does not go ignored in the book. Indeed, it receives full play in 36 original recipes. Surely poultry is one of nature's greatest gifts to cooks the world over. No food can be treated more variously in the kitchen and brought to table in more delicious ways; nor is there meat with more innate goodness than chicken. When skinned, chicken and that other ever-popular bird, turkey, are wonderfully low in fat and therefore in calories, yet they are high in protein. Even duck and goose, long considered so rich as to be indulged in only at holidays or other festive occasions, can be eaten year round when certain measures—as explained in the recipes—are taken to relieve them of much of their fat.

Like poultry, fish has its own virtues as healthful food and receives the attention it deserves in these pages. It is one of the most concentrated sources of high-quality protein, with an average four-ounce serving yielding up to half the daily dietary requirement of this nutrient. Fish delivers an uncommonly rich supply of vitamins and minerals as well, and it is easily digested.

At the same time, most varieties of fish recommend themselves to weight-conscious diners. A four-ounce portion of haddock or cod, for example, has fewer than 100 calories. Even their fattier cousins, such as king salmon and shad, have fewer than half the calories of a T-bone steak. Moreover, nearly all fish and shellfish (for which you will also find recipes in the book) are low in cholesterol. Certain highly polyunsaturated fatty acids called omega-3s occur almost exclusively in seafood and marine animals. Polyunsaturated fats have been shown to lower the level of cholesterol in some humans. (Only squid, octopus, shrimp, razor clams, blue crab, and black abalone have more than 100 milligrams of cholesterol per 3½-ounce portion; people on low-cholesterol diets should be wary of them, along with fish roe, which is also high in cholesterol.)

Shellfish, fish, poultry, and meat are usually entrées and do not themselves constitute a whole meal, and so this book is generous with recipes for starters and for vegetable and pasta dishes. There are plenty of salads represented too, several of which are served warm. Soups and stews, time-honored comfort foods, receive their due here as well. Prepared more often than not in a single pot, they can incorporate all kinds of ingredients in combinations that are as nutritious as they are flavorful. They make wonderful cold-weather fare.

Magic desserts

Not to be forgotten are the desserts. You may think they look sinful when you see them, but they aren't. You can enjoy them guilt free—especially if you prepare and serve them in the portions recommended, which average just 200 calories. Indeed, nutritionists acknowledge that refined sugar in modest quantities (no more than 10 percent of one's daily caloric intake) is not harmful to a normal person's health.

The desserts presented here, although delicious, have little fat. A custard can delight with fewer egg yolks than usual when the number of egg whites is increased. A small amount of heavy cream, whipped to twice its original volume, adds a rich look and taste, but relatively few calories. And low-fat, low-calorie ingredients such as yogurt and buttermilk yield desserts that are every bit as delectable as those made with heavy cream. A similar stratagem can reduce the sugar in recipes. Even for some cakes, cookies, pastries, and frozen desserts, where sugar plays a crucial role, quantities can be cut without compromising taste or texture. The results, as the desserts section demonstrates, are still sweet, but never cloyingly so.

As a special bonus, the book presents recipes for outstanding breakfasts and brunches. Indeed, the ones for breakfast will do a lot to take the boredom out of that meal. Nutritionists recommend that breakfast provide a quarter of the day's calories— some 500 for the average woman and 675 for a man. By telescoping two meals into one, brunch can account for an even bigger bite—800 calories for a woman and 1,080 for a man. The brunch menus and recipes have been developed taking these maximums into account, and they are designed to provide as much as 40 percent of the day's calories. In these hurried times, you may find one of the complete brunches a perfect way to entertain friends on a quiet Sunday and to share the good news about the new, healthful cooking.

The Key to Better Eating

Better eating is an achievable goal for everyone. This book makes it possible by addressing the concerns of today's weight-conscious, health-minded cooks with recipes that take into account guidelines set by nutritionists. The secret to eating well, of course, has to do with maintaining a balance of foods in the diet. The recipes thus should be used thoughtfully, in the context of a day's meals. To make the choice easier, the book presents an analysis of nutrients in a single serving, as at right. The counts for calories, protein, cholesterol, total fat, saturated fat, and sodium are approximate.

Interpreting the chart

The chart below shows the National Research Council's Recommended Dietary Allowances of calories and protein for healthy men, women, and children, along with the council's recommendations for the "safe and adequate" maximum intake of sodium. Although the council has not established recommendations for either cholesterol or fat, the chart does include what the National Institutes of Health and the American Heart Association consider the daily maximum amounts of these substances for healthy members of the general population.

The book does not purport to be a diet book, nor does it focus on health foods. Rather, it expresses a common-sense approach to cooking that uses salt, sugar, cream, butter, and oil in moderation while including other ingredients that also provide flavor and satisfaction. Herbs, spices, and aromatic vegetables, as well as fruits, peels, juices, wines, and vinegars are all employed toward this end.

The recipes make few unusual demands. Naturally they call for fresh ingredients, offering substitutes when these are unavailable. (Only the original ingredient is calculated in the nutrient analysis, however.) Most of the ingredients can be found in any well-stocked supermarket. The presence now in

Calories **180**
Protein **21g.**
Cholesterol **65mg.**
Total fat **8g.**
Saturated fat **4g.**
Sodium **230mg.**

many communities of farmers' markets, health-food stores, and gourmet shops enlarges the range of choice and adds new dimensions of excitement to cooking.

In order to simplify meal planning, most of the recipes offer accompaniments. These accompaniments are intended only as suggestions, however; cooks should let their imaginations be their guide and come up with ideas of their own to achieve a sensible and appealing balance of foods.

In the test kitchens where the recipes were developed, heavy-bottomed pots and pans were used to guard against burning the food whenever a small amount of oil was called for and where there was danger of the food adhering to the hot surface, but nonstick pans can be utilized as well. Both safflower oil and virgin olive oil were favored for sau-

téing. Safflower oil was chosen because it is the most highly polyunsaturated vegetable fat widely available in supermarkets, and polyunsaturated fats reduce blood cholesterol. Virgin olive oil was used because it has a fine fruity flavor lacking in the lesser grade known as "pure." When virgin olive oil is unavailable, or when its flavor is not essential to the dish, "pure" may be substituted.

About cooking times

To help the cook plan ahead, the book takes time into account in its recipes. While recognizing that everyone cooks at a different speed and that stoves and ovens differ, it provides approximate "working" and "total" times for every dish. Working time stands for the minutes actively spent on preparation; total time includes unattended cooking time, as well as time devoted to marinating, steeping, or soaking ingredients. Since the recipes emphasize fresh foods, they may take a bit longer to prepare than "quick and easy" dishes that call for canned or packaged products, but the payoff in flavor, and often in nutrition, should compensate for the little extra time involved.

Recommended Dietary Guidelines

		Average Daily Intake		Maximum Daily Intake			
		CALORIES	PROTEIN grams	CHOLESTEROL milligrams	TOTAL FAT grams	SATURATED FAT grams	SODIUM milligrams
Children	7-10	2000	22	240	67	22	2000
Females	11-14	2200	37	220	73	24	2200
	15-18	2200	44	210	73	24	2200
	19-24	2200	44	300	73	24	3000
	25-50	2200	44	300	73	24	3000
	50+	1900	44	300	63	21	3000
Males	11-14	2500	36	270	83	28	2500
	15-18	3000	56	280	100	33	3000
	19-24	2900	56	300	97	32	3000
	25-50	2900	56	300	97	32	3000
	50+	2300	56	300	77	28	3000

1 Thinly sliced sautéed mushrooms float lightly in a sherry-enriched soup that contains just 140 calories per serving (recipe, page 14).

Soups and Openers

Homemade Stocks: Foundations of Flavor

The elixir that is stock comes from humble beginnings indeed — inexpensive cuts of meat, fish bones, or chicken wings and backs. Attention to details will reward you with a rich and beautifully limpid stock: Any large fat deposits should be trimmed away beforehand; large bones, if they are to cede the treasured gelatin that gives body to a stock, should be cracked first. During cooking, remove the scum that collects occasionally atop the liquid. Scum consists of protein particles released by meat and bones; these float to the surface, where they gather in a foam. As nutritious as it is, the foam must be removed lest it cloud the stock. Skim off the scum as it forms at the start of cooking; skim thereafter only as the recipe directs. After its initial rapid cooking, a stock must not be allowed to return to a full boil; the turbulence would muddy the liquid. As a final cleansing, the stock should be strained through a fine sieve or a colander lined with cheesecloth.

To prepare stock for storage, divide it among containers surrounded with ice water. Wait until the stock has cooled to cover the vessels; otherwise, it may sour. Refrigerated in covered containers, any of these stocks will keep for up to three days. Because the fat atop the stock will form a temporary seal, helping to keep it fresh, you need not degrease the stock until shortly before you are ready to use it. To prolong the life of a refrigerated stock, first remove and discard the congealed fat, then boil the stock for five minutes; either freeze the stock or boil it again every two or three days. As always, cool it quickly — and uncovered — before storing it once more.

Fish stock and vegetable stock may be frozen for two months; the other three may be frozen for as long as four months. Stock destined for the freezer must first be degreased; frozen fat can turn rancid.

The recipes that follow yield differing amounts of stock. Brown stock and veal stock, for example, are made from large bones, which require more water for cooking. But like any stock, these two freeze well, meaning an abundance is never too much.

Vegetable Stock

Makes about 2 quarts
Working time: about 25 minutes
Total time: about 1 hour and 30 minutes

4 celery stalks with leaves, cut into 1-inch pieces
4 carrots, scrubbed and cut into 1-inch pieces
4 large onions (about 2 lb.), coarsely chopped
3 large broccoli stems (optional), coarsely chopped
1 medium turnip, peeled and cut into ½-inch cubes
6 garlic cloves, crushed
½ cup coarsely chopped parsley leaves and stems
10 black peppercorns
4 fresh thyme sprigs, or 1 tsp. dried thyme leaves
2 bay leaves, crumbled

Put the celery, carrots, onions, broccoli if you are using it, turnip, garlic, parsley and peppercorns into a heavy stockpot. Pour in enough cold water to cover the contents by about 2 inches. Bring the liquid to a boil over medium heat, skimming off any scum that rises to the surface. When the liquid reaches a boil, stir in the thyme and the bay leaves. Reduce the heat and let the stock simmer undisturbed for one hour.

Strain the stock into a large bowl, pressing down lightly on the vegetables to extract all their liquid. Discard the vegetables.

Chicken Stock

Makes about 2 quarts
Working time: about 20 minutes
Total time: about 3 hours

4 to 5 lb. uncooked chicken trimmings and bones (preferably wings, necks and backs), the bones cracked with a heavy knife
2 carrots, cut into ½-inch-thick rounds
2 celery stalks, cut into 1-inch pieces
2 large onions (about 1 lb.), cut in half, one half stuck with 2 cloves
2 fresh thyme sprigs, or ½ tsp. dried thyme leaves
1 or 2 bay leaves
10 to 15 parsley stems
5 black peppercorns

Put the chicken trimmings and bones into a heavy stockpot; pour in enough water to cover them by about 2 inches. Bring the liquid to a boil over medium heat, skimming off the scum that rises to the surface. Reduce the heat and simmer the liquid for 10 minutes, skimming and adding a little cold water to help precipitate the scum.

Add the vegetables, herbs and peppercorns, and submerge them in the liquid. If necessary, pour in enough additional water to cover the contents of the pot. Simmer the stock for two to three hours, skimming as necessary to remove the scum.

Strain the stock, discard the solids, and degrease the stock.

EDITOR'S NOTE: *The chicken gizzard and heart may be added to the stock. Wings and necks — rich in natural gelatin — produce a particularly gelatinous stock, ideal for sauces and jellied dishes.*

Turkey, duck or goose stock may be prepared using the same basic recipe.

Veal Stock

Makes about 3 quarts
Working time: about 30 minutes
Total time: about 4½ hours

3 lb. veal breast or shank meat, cut into 3-inch pieces
3 lb. veal bones (preferably knuckles), cracked
2 onions, quartered

2 celery stalks, sliced
1 carrot, sliced
8 black peppercorns
3 unpeeled garlic cloves (optional), crushed
1 tsp. fresh thyme, or ¼ tsp. dried thyme leaves
1 bay leaf

Fill a large pot halfway with water. Bring the water to a boil, add the veal meat and bones, and blanch them for two minutes to clean them. Drain the meat and bones in a colander, discarding the liquid. Rinse the meat and bones under cold running water and return them to the pot.

Add the onions, celery, carrot, peppercorns, and garlic if you are using it. Pour in enough water to cover the contents of the pot by about 3 inches, and bring the water to a boil over medium heat. Reduce the heat to maintain a simmer, and skim any impurities from the surface. Add the thyme and bay leaf, and simmer the stock very gently for four hours, skimming occasionally.

Strain the stock into a large bowl; allow the solids to drain thoroughly into the bowl before discarding them. Degrease the stock.

EDITOR'S NOTE: *Any combination of veal meat and bones may be used to make this stock; ideally, the meat and bones together should weigh about six pounds. Ask your butcher to crack the bones.*

Brown Stock

Makes about 3 quarts
Working time: about 40 minutes
Total time: about 5½ hours

3 lb. veal breast (or veal-shank or beef-shank meat), cut into 3-inch pieces
3 lb. uncooked veal or beef bones, cracked
2 onions, quartered
2 celery stalks, chopped
2 carrots, sliced
3 unpeeled garlic cloves, crushed
8 black peppercorns
3 cloves
2 tsp. fresh thyme, or ½ tsp. dried thyme leaves
1 bay leaf

Preheat the oven to 425° F. Place the meat, bones, onions, celery and carrots in a large roasting pan and roast them in the oven until they are well browned — about one hour.

Transfer the contents of the roasting pan to a large pot. Pour 2 cups of water into the roasting pan; with a spatula, scrape up the browned bits from the bottom of the pan. Pour the liquid into the pot.

Add the garlic, peppercorns and cloves. Pour in enough water to cover the contents of the pot by about 3 inches. Bring the liquid to a boil, then reduce the heat to maintain a simmer and skim any impurities from the surface. Add the thyme and bay leaf, then simmer the stock very gently for four hours, skimming occasionally during the process.

Strain the stock; allow the solids to drain thoroughly into the stock before discarding them. Degrease the stock.

EDITOR'S NOTE: *Thoroughly browning the meat,*

Quick Stocks from Supplies at Hand

Canned stocks are no substitute for homemade, but they can be used in a pinch. A handful of readily available ingredients will invigorate them. Similar treatment will transform bottled clam juice into a creditable fish stock.

To enliven canned beef stock (called broth or bouillon), combine several tablespoons each of minced onion and carrot and a tablespoon or two of minced celery with 2 cans of stock. Next pour in ½ cup of red or dry white wine and 2½ cups of water, then add two sprigs of parsley, a small bay leaf and a pinch of dried thyme. Simmer the mixture for 20 to 30 minutes, then strain and degrease it.

To add spark to two cans of low-sodium chicken broth, use vegetables and herbs in the same proportion as for beef stock, but do not add water; instead use ¼ cup of white wine. If you wish, toss in a few celery leaves. Simmer the stock for 20 to 30 minutes, then strain it. In the case of beef stock, a good low-sodium stock is unavailable, so reduce or omit the salt in the recipe.

To every 2 cups of clam juice, add 1 cup of water, ½ cup of dry white wine, a sliced onion and four black peppercorns. (Be sure to reduce or omit the salt in the dish.) Simmer the stock for 10 minutes, then strain it.

---

bones and vegetables should produce a stock with a rich mahogany color. If your stock does not seem dark enough, cook 1 tablespoon of tomato paste in a small pan over medium heat, stirring constantly, until it darkens — about three minutes. Add this to the stock about one hour before the end of the cooking time.

Any combination of meat and bones may be used to make the stock; ideally, the meat and bones together should weigh about six pounds. Ask your butcher to crack the bones.

Fish Stock

Makes about 2 quarts
Working time: about 15 minutes
Total time: about 40 minutes

2 lb. lean-fish bones, fins and tails discarded, the bones rinsed thoroughly and cut into large pieces
2 onions, thinly sliced
2 celery stalks, chopped
1 carrot, thinly sliced
2 cups dry white wine
2 tbsp. fresh lemon juice
1 leek (optional), trimmed, split, washed thoroughly to remove all grit, and sliced
3 garlic cloves (optional), crushed
10 parsley stems
4 fresh thyme sprigs, or 1 tsp. dried thyme leaves
1 bay leaf, crumbled
5 black peppercorns

Put the fish bones, onions, celery, carrot, wine, lemon juice, 2 quarts of cold water, and the leek and garlic if you are using them, in a large, nonreactive stockpot. Bring the liquid to a boil over medium heat, then reduce the heat to maintain a strong simmer. Skim off all the scum that rises to the surface.

Add the parsley, thyme, bay leaf and peppercorns, and gently simmer the stock for 20 minutes more.

Strain the stock; allow the solids to drain thoroughly before discarding them. If necessary, degrease the stock.

EDITOR'S NOTE: *Because the bones from oilier fish produce a strong flavor, be sure to use only the bones from lean fish. Sole, flounder, turbot and other flatfish are best. Do not include the fish skin; it could discolor the stock.*

Mushroom Soup with Sherry

Serves 4 as a first course
Working (and total) time: about 45 minutes

Calories **140**
Protein **5g.**
Cholesterol **15mg.**
Total fat **8g.**
Saturated fat **3g.**
Sodium **355mg.**

½ tbsp. unsalted butter
½ tbsp. safflower oil
1 onion, thinly sliced
1 lb. mushrooms, wiped clean, trimmed and thinly sliced
4 cups unsalted chicken stock
¼ cup dry sherry
½ tsp. salt
freshly ground black pepper
¼ cup light cream
1 to 2 tbsp. chopped fresh parsley

Melt the butter with the oil in a large, heavy-bottomed or nonstick skillet over medium-high heat. Add the onion and sauté it, stirring often, for four minutes. Add the mushrooms, reduce the heat to medium, and cover the skillet to help the mushrooms release their moisture. Cook the mixture for two minutes, stirring it several times.

Uncover the skillet and increase the heat to medium high. Sauté the mushrooms and onions, stirring from time to time, until all of the moisture has evaporated — about 10 minutes. Continue sautéing, stirring the mixture frequently to prevent sticking, until the mushrooms and onions are golden brown all over — five to 10 minutes more.

Transfer the mushroom mixture to a large saucepan; add the stock, sherry, salt and some pepper. Simmer the soup for 15 minutes. Stir in the cream and the parsley, and allow the soup to heat through before serving.

The soup is better reheated after a mellowing period in the refrigerator. It will keep refrigerated for as long as three days.

Bread Soup

Serves 4
Working time: about 35 minutes
Total time: about 1 hour

Calories **275**
Protein **10g.**
Cholesterol **6mg.**
Total fat **11g.**
Saturated fat **2g.**
Sodium **605mg.**

1 ½ cups 1-inch bread cubes, cut from day-old French or Italian bread
2 tbsp. olive oil
1 large leek, trimmed, split, washed thoroughly to remove all grit, and thinly sliced
2 garlic cloves, finely chopped
1 small Belgian endive, trimmed, split lengthwise and sliced crosswise
1 oz. prosciutto (about 2 thin slices), julienned
1 bunch arugula, or 8 oz. fresh kale, washed and stemmed
6 cups unsalted chicken or veal stock
2 boiling potatoes, peeled and diced
5 drops hot red-pepper sauce
½ tsp. salt
½ tsp. crushed black peppercorns

Preheat the oven to 350° F. Arrange the bread cubes in a single layer on a baking sheet and bake them until they are toasted — about 15 minutes.

Heat the oil in a large, heavy-bottomed pot over medium heat. Add the leek and cook it, stirring frequently, until it begins to brown — about 10 minutes. Stir in the garlic, endive and prosciutto, and continue cooking, stirring occasionally, until the endive softens — approximately five minutes. Add the arugula or kale and cover the pot; cook the mixture until the arugula or kale wilts — about three minutes more.

Stir in the stock, potatoes and red-pepper sauce. Reduce the heat, cover the pot and simmer the soup until the potatoes are tender — about 15 minutes.

Stir in the salt, pepper and toasted bread cubes; allow the bread cubes to soak up some of the broth before serving the soup.

Tomato Purée with Yogurt-Ricotta Stars

Serves 6 as a first course
Working time: about 25 minutes
Total time: about 45 minutes

Calories **95**
Protein **4g.**
Cholesterol **5mg.**
Total fat **4g.**
Saturated fat **1g.**
Sodium **155mg.**

1 tbsp. virgin olive oil
3 onions, chopped (about 2½ cups)
1 carrot, thinly sliced
1 tsp. chopped fresh thyme, or ¼ tsp. dried thyme leaves
3 garlic cloves, chopped
freshly ground black pepper
28 oz. canned unsalted tomatoes, seeded and coarsely chopped, with their juice
1¼ cups unsalted chicken or vegetable stock
¼ tsp. salt
⅓ cup part-skim ricotta cheese
2 tbsp. plain low-fat yogurt
1½ cups watercress sprigs, stems trimmed

Heat the oil in a large, heavy-bottomed pot over medium heat. Add the onions, carrot, thyme, garlic and some pepper, and cook the mixture, stirring it often, until the onions are translucent — seven to 10 minutes. Add the tomatoes and their juice, the stock and the salt. Reduce the heat and simmer the vegetables for 30 minutes.

While the soup is cooking, purée the cheese and yogurt together in a food processor, blender or food mill. Set the purée aside.

Now purée the soup in batches, processing each batch for about one minute. Return the puréed soup to the pot, bring it to a simmer over medium heat and add the watercress. Simmer the soup just long enough to wilt the watercress — about one minute — then ladle the soup into warmed serving bowls.

Gently spoon 1 heaping tablespoon of the ricotta-yogurt mixture into the middle of each bowl. With the tip of a knife, make a star pattern by pushing a little of the mixture out from the center in several directions. Serve the soup at once.

Scallion Soup

COOKED SCALLIONS HAVE THE MILDNESS
AND SWEETNESS OF LEEKS.

Serves 8 as a first course
Working time: about 15 minutes
Total time: about 50 minutes

Calories **75**
Protein **4g.**
Cholesterol **2mg.**
Total fat **3g.**
Saturated fat **1g.**
Sodium **150mg.**

1 tbsp. virgin olive oil
4 bunches scallions, trimmed, white parts cut into 1-inch lengths, green parts sliced into ¼-inch pieces
8 cups unsalted chicken stock
1 tarragon sprig, leaves stripped and chopped, stem reserved, or 2 tsp. dried tarragon
¼ tsp. salt
freshly ground black pepper

In a large, heavy-bottomed pot, heat the oil over medium-high heat. Add the white parts of the scallions and sauté them until they are soft — about two minutes. Then pour in the stock and add the tarragon stem or 1 teaspoon of the dried tarragon, the salt and some pepper. Reduce the heat and cook the mixture at a strong simmer, uncovered, for 30 minutes. If you used a tarragon stem, remove and discard it.

Add to the pot the tarragon leaves or the remaining teaspoon of dried tarragon, and the green parts of the scallions. Cook the soup until the scallion greens are tender — about four minutes more. Serve at once.

Cabbage and Caraway Soup

Serves 10 as a first course
Working time: about 45 minutes
Total time: about 1 hour and 45 minutes

Calories **75**
Protein **3g.**
Cholesterol **1mg.**
Total fat **4g.**
Saturated fat **0g.**
Sodium **165mg.**

2 tbsp. safflower oil
one 3-lb. cabbage, cored, quartered and thinly sliced
1½ tsp. caraway seeds
1 tsp. mustard seeds
½ tsp. salt
¼ cup red wine vinegar or white wine vinegar
4 cups unsalted chicken or veal stock
4 garlic cloves, finely chopped
14 oz. canned unsalted tomatoes, puréed with their juice
¼ to ½ tsp. cayenne pepper
2 tbsp. finely cut fresh dill, or 1 tbsp. dried dillweed

Heat the safflower oil in a large, heavy-bottomed pot over medium heat. Add the cabbage, caraway seeds, mustard seeds and salt. Cover the pot, and cook, stirring occasionally, until the cabbage is wilted — about 25 minutes.

Add the vinegar and cook the mixture, stirring, for one minute. Pour in the stock and 3 cups of cold water, then stir in the garlic, the tomato purée and the cayenne pepper. Reduce the heat and slowly bring the liquid to a simmer. Cook the soup gently for 45 minutes. Stir in the dill and serve immediately.

Hot and Sour Soup

THE LILY BUDS CALLED FOR HERE ARE THE DRIED BUDS
OF COMMON DAY LILIES. AVAILABLE AT ASIAN MARKETS, THEY
ADD UNUSUAL TEXTURE AND FLAVOR TO THE SOUP.

Serves 8 as a first course
Working (and total) time: about 30 minutes

Calories **80**
Protein **5g.**
Cholesterol **1mg.**
Total fat **2g.**
Saturated fat **0g.**
Sodium **190mg.**

6 cups unsalted chicken stock

¼ cup rice vinegar

2 tbsp. Chinese black vinegar or balsamic vinegar

1 to 2 tsp. chili paste with garlic, or 5 to 10 drops
hot red-pepper sauce

1 tbsp. low-sodium soy sauce

1 tbsp. dry sherry

½ tsp. finely chopped garlic

1 to 2 tsp. finely chopped fresh ginger

1 carrot, julienned

6 dried shiitake or Chinese black mushrooms,
covered with boiling water and soaked for 20 minutes,
stemmed, the caps thinly sliced

¼ cup cloud-ear mushrooms (optional), covered with
boiling water and soaked for 20 minutes, thinly sliced

16 lily buds (optional), covered with boiling water and
soaked for 5 minutes, trimmed, each bud tied in a knot

¾ cup bamboo shoots (optional), rinsed and julienned

2 tbsp. cornstarch, mixed with 3 tbsp. water

8 oz. firm bean curd (tofu), cut into thin strips

3 scallions, trimmed and sliced diagonally into ovals

Heat the stock in a large pot over medium-high heat.
Add the vinegars, chili paste or hot red-pepper sauce,
soy sauce, sherry, garlic, ginger, carrot and shiitake
or Chinese black mushrooms, and, if you are using
them, the cloud-ear mushrooms, lily buds and bamboo
shoots. Bring the liquid to a boil, then stir in the cornstarch mixture. Reduce the heat and simmer the soup,
stirring, until it thickens slightly — two to three minutes. Gently stir in the bean curd. Ladle the soup into
bowls and garnish each serving with the scallion slices.

Couscous Soup
with Harissa

HARISSA IS A HOT, SPICY MIXTURE USED TO FLAVOR NORTH
AFRICAN DISHES; IN THIS RECIPE, SOME PIMIENTOS ARE ADDED.

Serves 8
Working time: about 40 minutes
Total time: about 1 hour and 15 minutes

Calories **360**
Protein **25g.**
Cholesterol **51mg.**
Total fat **15g.**
Saturated fat **4g.**
Sodium **750mg.**

1 tbsp. olive oil
1 tbsp. unsalted butter
1 large onion, coarsely chopped (about 1½ cups)
½ tsp. cayenne pepper
½ tsp. ground cumin
½ tsp. cumin seeds
1 tsp. salt
½ tsp. cracked black peppercorns
½ tsp. ground allspice
4 tsp. chopped fresh thyme, or 1 tsp. dried thyme leaves

2 tsp. chopped fresh oregano, or ½ tsp. dried oregano
2 bay leaves
2 or 3 garlic cloves, finely chopped (about 1 tbsp.)
2½ lb. ripe tomatoes, peeled, seeded and chopped, or 28 oz. canned unsalted tomatoes, drained and chopped
8 cups unsalted chicken stock
1 large boiling potato, peeled and cut into ½-inch cubes
5 celery stalks, cut into ½-inch lengths (about 1½ cups)
3 carrots, sliced into ¼-inch-thick rounds (about 1½ cups)
1 lb. boneless chicken breast meat, cut into 1-inch cubes
4 oz. chorizo or other spicy sausage, cut into ½-inch-thick rounds
2 cups cooked and drained chick-peas
1 yellow squash and 1 zucchini, each cut lengthwise into 8 strips, the strips cut into 1-inch pieces (about 3 cups)
½ green pepper, seeded, deribbed and cut lengthwise into ¼-inch strips
½ sweet red pepper, seeded, deribbed and cut lengthwise into ¼-inch strips
¼ cup couscous

Harissa
6-oz. jar pimientos, drained
1 garlic clove
1 tsp. hot red-pepper sauce
2 tsp. chili paste
2 tsp. ground cumin
¼ tsp. salt

Heat the oil and butter together in a large, heavy-bottomed pot over medium-high heat. Add the onion and sauté it, stirring frequently, until it is translucent — about eight minutes.

Meanwhile, combine the spices with the thyme, oregano and bay leaves in a small bowl.

Add the garlic to the onions and cook the mixture, stirring constantly, for two minutes more. Add the combined spices and herbs, tomatoes and stock, then increase the heat, and bring the liquid to a boil. Stir in the potato, celery and carrots. Reduce the heat, cover the pot, and simmer the mixture until the potato cubes are tender — about 20 minutes.

Add the chicken, sausage, chick-peas, squash, peppers and couscous, and continue to simmer the soup for 20 minutes more.

While the soup finishes cooking, purée the harissa ingredients in a food processor or blender. Transfer the mixture to a small bowl to be passed at the table.

Serve the soup hot; allow each diner to add a dab of harissa if desired.

Crab, Fennel and Tomato Soup

Serves 4
Working time: about 45 minutes
Total time: about 2 hours

Calories **245**
Protein **9g.**
Cholesterol **31mg.**
Total fat **8g.**
Saturated fat **1g.**
Sodium **420mg.**

2 lb. live blue crabs (4 to 8 crabs)
2 tbsp. virgin olive oil
1 onion, thinly sliced
1 small fennel bulb, trimmed, cored and thinly sliced (about 2 cups), several stems and leaves reserved for the court bouillon and for garnish
3 garlic cloves, finely chopped
1 lb. ripe plum tomatoes, peeled, seeded and chopped, or 14 oz. canned unsalted tomatoes, drained and chopped
½ tsp. salt
cayenne pepper
Court bouillon
1 large onion, thinly sliced
1 celery stalk, thinly sliced
several parsley stems (optional)
2 cups dry white wine
8 to 10 peppercorns

To make the court bouillon, pour 8 cups of water into a large pot and add the onion, celery, reserved fennel stems and a few of the reserved fennel leaves, and the parsley stems if you are using them. Bring the liquid to a boil, then reduce the heat and simmer it for 15 minutes, skimming off any foam as it rises to the surface. Pour in the wine and return the liquid to a boil. Simmer the liquid for 10 minutes; add the peppercorns and simmer five minutes more.

Bring the court bouillon to a full boil and drop the crabs into it. Cover the pot until the liquid returns to a boil. Skim off any foam that rises to the surface, then reduce the heat and simmer the crabs, covered, for 20 minutes.

Strain the cooking liquid into a bowl. Set the crabs aside and discard the remaining solids. Return the

cooking liquid to the pot and boil it until it is reduced to about 4 cups.

Heat the oil in another large pot over medium-low heat. Add the onion, fennel and garlic. Cover the pot and cook the vegetables, stirring occasionally, until they are soft — 10 to 15 minutes. Stir in the tomatoes, salt and a pinch of cayenne pepper. Pour in the reduced cooking liquid and bring the mixture to a boil. Reduce the heat and simmer the mixture, covered, until the fennel is very soft — about 45 minutes.

Remove the flesh from the crabs (there should be about 1 cup) and set it aside.

Purée the fennel-tomato mixture in batches in a blender or food processor until it is very smooth. Return the purée to the pot and add the crab meat. Cook the soup over medium-low heat until it is warmed through; garnish it with the remaining fennel leaves.

Turkey-Lentil Soup

Serves 6
Working time: about 15 minutes
Total time: about 1 hour

Calories **220**
Protein **22g.**
Cholesterol **44mg.**
Total fat **5g.**
Saturated fat **1g.**
Sodium **185mg.**

1½ lb. turkey drumsticks, skinned
freshly ground black pepper
2 tsp. safflower oil
1 small onion, thinly sliced
1 cup lentils, picked over and rinsed
1 small bay leaf
1 small carrot, thinly sliced
1 small zucchini, thinly sliced
1 celery stalk, thinly sliced
1 ripe tomato, peeled, seeded and coarsely chopped
½ tsp. finely chopped fresh sage, or ¼ tsp. dried sage
⅜ tsp. salt

Sprinkle the drumsticks with some pepper. Heat the oil in a large, heavy-bottomed pot over medium heat. Add the drumsticks and cook them, turning them fre-quently, until they are evenly browned — two to three minutes. Push the drumsticks to one side of the pan, then add the onion and cook it until it is translucent — two to three minutes.

Pour 5 cups of water into the pot. Add the lentils and bay leaf, and bring the water to a boil. Reduce the heat to maintain a simmer and cook the lentils, covered, for 20 minutes. Skim off any impurities that have risen to the surface. Continue cooking the mixture until the juices run clear from a drumstick pierced with the tip of a sharp knife — about 20 minutes more.

Remove the drumsticks and set them aside. When they are cool enough to handle, slice the meat from the bones and cut it into small pieces; discard the bones. Remove and discard the bay leaf. Add the car-rot, zucchini, celery and tomato to the soup and sim-mer until the vegetables are tender — about five min-utes. Add the turkey meat, sage and salt, and continue cooking the soup until the vegetables are tender — about two minutes more. Serve hot.

Lamb Broth
with Winter Vegetables

Serves 6
Working time: about 15 minutes
Total time: about 2 hours

Calories **205**
Protein **9g.**
Cholesterol **33mg.**
Total fat **14g.**
Saturated fat **7g.**
Sodium **225mg.**

1 tbsp. safflower oil
1 small onion, thinly sliced, the slices separated into rings
1½ lb. lamb shank, trimmed
¼ cup pearl barley
1 bay leaf
1 tsp. chopped fresh thyme, or ¼ tsp. dried thyme leaves
1 garlic clove, finely chopped
½ tsp. salt
¼ tsp. crushed black peppercorns
1 turnip, peeled and cut into ½-inch cubes
1 small rutabaga, peeled and cut into ½-inch cubes
1 carrot, cut into ½-inch cubes

Heat the oil in a large, heavy-bottomed pot over medium heat. Add the onion rings and cook them until they are browned — about eight minutes. Add the lamb shank, barley, bay leaf, thyme, garlic, salt and crushed peppercorns. Pour in 12 cups of water and bring the liquid to a boil. Reduce the heat and simmer the mixture, partially covered, for one hour and 15 minutes.

Remove the bay leaf and discard it. Remove the lamb shank from the pot; when the shank is cool enough to handle, slice the meat from the bone and cut it into small cubes. Return the lamb cubes to the pot. Simmer the soup, uncovered, over medium heat until it is reduced by half — about 15 minutes. Add the turnip, rutabaga and carrot, cover the pot, and simmer the soup until the vegetables are tender — about 15 minutes more. Serve immediately.

Chicken Soup with Chilies, Cabbage and Rice

Serves 4
Working time: about 20 minutes
Total time: about 1 hour

Calories **285**
Protein **20g.**
Cholesterol **58mg.**
Total fat **11g.**
Saturated fat **2g.**
Sodium **275mg.**

1 tbsp. safflower oil
1½ lb. chicken thighs, skinned, fat trimmed away
1 garlic clove, finely chopped
3 scallions, trimmed and sliced into thin rounds
2 cups unsalted chicken stock
1 tbsp. fresh thyme, or ¾ tsp. dried thyme leaves
freshly ground black pepper
¼ tsp. salt
½ cup rice
2 dried ancho chilies, stemmed, split lengthwise and seeded
1 large carrot, julienned (about 1 cup)
2 cups shredded Nappa cabbage (about 6 oz.)

Heat the safflower oil in a large, heavy-bottomed pot over medium-high heat. Add the chicken thighs and sauté them, turning them frequently, until they are evenly browned — three to four minutes. Push the chicken to one side of the pot; add the garlic and scallions and cook them for one minute, stirring con-

stantly. Pour in the stock and 3 cups of water. Add the thyme and some pepper, and bring the liquid to a boil. Reduce the heat to maintain a simmer and cook the mixture, partially covered, for 20 minutes. Skim any impurities from the surface and simmer the liquid for 20 minutes more.

While the stock is simmering, bring 1 cup of water and ⅛ teaspoon of the salt to a boil in a saucepan. Add the rice and stir once, then reduce the heat and cover the pan. Simmer the rice until all of the water is absorbed — about 20 minutes.

While the rice is cooking, pour 1 cup of boiling water over the chilies and soak them for 15 minutes. Purée the chilies with their soaking liquid in a blender. (Alternatively, pulverize the soaked chilies with a mortar and pestle, gradually adding the soaking liquid until it is incorporated into the chili paste.)

With a slotted spoon, remove the chicken thighs from the pot and set them aside. When the chicken is cool enough to handle, remove the meat from the bones with your fingers and cut it into small pieces; discard the bones. Return the chicken pieces to the pot. Add the carrot, cabbage, rice and the remaining ⅛ teaspoon of salt. Increase the heat to maintain a simmer and cook the soup until the carrot is tender — three to four minutes. Strain the chili purée through a fine sieve into the soup. Stir to incorporate the purée and serve the soup at once.

Black Bean, Bourbon and Ham Soup

Serves 6
Working time: about 1 hour and 30 minutes
Total time: about 3 hours (includes soaking)

Calories **365**
Protein **24g.**
Cholesterol **14mg.**
Total fat **5g.**
Saturated fat **1g.**
Sodium **215mg.**

1 lb. black beans, picked over
1 lb. smoked ham hocks
3 cups chopped onion
5 garlic cloves, chopped
1½ tsp. dried thyme leaves
½ tsp. ground cumin
freshly ground black pepper
3 tbsp. sour cream
⅓ cup plain low-fat yogurt
1 scallion, trimmed and finely chopped
¼ cup bourbon or sour-mash whiskey

Rinse the beans under cold running water, then put them into a large pot and pour in enough cold water to cover them by about 3 inches. Discard any beans that float to the surface. Cover the pot, leaving the lid ajar, and slowly bring the liquid to a boil over medium-low heat. Boil the beans for two minutes, then turn off the heat and soak the beans, covered, for at least one hour. (Alternatively, soak the beans in cold water overnight.)

Place the ham hocks in a large, heavy-bottomed pot. Pour in 14 cups of water and bring it to a boil. Cook the ham hocks over high heat for 20 minutes, skimming off any impurities that collect on the surface.

Drain the beans and add them to the pot with the ham hocks. Return the mixture to a boil and cook it for 15 minutes more, stirring from time to time and skimming any foam from the surface.

Reduce the heat to medium. Add the onion, garlic, thyme, cumin and some pepper. Simmer the soup, stirring occasionally and skimming any foam from the surface, until the beans are tender — one and a half to two hours.

While the beans are cooking, whisk together the sour cream, yogurt and scallion; set the mixture aside.

When the beans finish cooking, remove the soup from the heat. With tongs or a slotted spoon, take out the ham hocks and set them aside to cool. When the ham hocks are cool enough to handle, separate the meat from the skin and bones by hand. Cut the meat into small pieces and return it to the soup; discard the skin and bones.

Whisk in the bourbon or sour-mash whiskey and bring the soup to a boil. Remove the pot from the heat and ladle the soup into bowls; garnish each portion with a dollop of the sour-cream-yogurt mixture.

Tarragon-Zucchini Soup

Serves 8 as a first course
Working time: about 50 minutes
Total time: about 1 hour and 10 minutes

Calories **110**
Protein **5g.**
Cholesterol **7mg.**
Total fat **5g.**
Saturated fat **2g.**
Sodium **230mg.**

1 tbsp. unsalted butter
1 tbsp. safflower oil
3 onions, chopped
1½ lb. zucchini, trimmed and cut into 1-inch pieces
2 carrots, thinly sliced
6 cups unsalted chicken stock
1½ tbsp. finely chopped fresh tarragon, plus several tarragon stems tied in a bundle
1 cup low-fat milk
½ tsp. salt
freshly ground black pepper
pinch of cayenne pepper

Melt the butter with the safflower oil in a large, heavy-bottomed pot over medium heat. Add the onions and cook them, stirring often, until they are golden — 15 to 20 minutes. Add the zucchini, carrots, chicken stock and tarragon stems, and bring the mixture to a boil. Reduce the heat, cover the pot, and simmer the liquid for 15 minutes. Remove the lid, increase the heat, and boil the soup, skimming off any impurities that rise to the surface. Continue to cook, stirring occasionally, until the soup is reduced by about one third — 20 to 25 minutes.

Remove the pot from the heat and discard the bundle of tarragon stems. Pour the soup into a large bowl. Purée about two thirds of the soup in a blender or food processor. Return the purée to the pot. Briefly process the remaining third of the soup to achieve a coarse consistency, and pour it back into the pot. Stir in the milk, salt, black pepper and cayenne pepper. Reheat the soup gently without letting it come to a boil. Stir in the chopped tarragon. Serve the soup either warm or chilled.

Black-Eyed Pea and Collard Green Soup

Serves 6
Working time: about 45 minutes
Total time: about 2 hours and 30 minutes
(includes soaking time)

Calories **130**
Protein **8g.**
Cholesterol **5mg.**
Total fat **5g.**
Saturated fat **1g.**
Sodium **500mg.**

1 cup dried black-eyed peas, picked over
1 tbsp. safflower oil
¾ cup chopped onion
1 oz. Canadian bacon, cut into ¼-inch dice
1 garlic clove, finely chopped
1 bay leaf
¼ tsp. hot red-pepper flakes, crushed
5 cups unsalted brown or chicken stock
8 oz. collard greens, trimmed, washed and coarsely chopped (about 4 cups)
1 tsp. salt
2 tsp. cider vinegar

Rinse the peas under cold running water, then put them into a large, heavy pot and pour in enough cold water to cover them by about 3 inches. Discard any peas that float to the surface. Cover the pot, leaving the lid ajar, and slowly bring the liquid to a boil over medium-low heat. Boil the peas for two minutes, then turn off the heat, cover the pot, and let the peas soak for at least one hour. (Alternatively, soak the peas in cold water overnight.)

Heat the oil in a large, heavy-bottomed pot over medium heat. Add the onion and sauté it, stirring occasionally, until it is translucent — about four minutes. Add the bacon and garlic, and cook them for two minutes, stirring frequently.

Drain the peas and add them to the pot along with the bay leaf, red-pepper flakes and stock. Bring the liquid to a boil, then reduce the heat to maintain a simmer, and partially cover the pot. Cook the mixture for 30 minutes, stirring gently several times. Toss in the collard greens and the salt, and cook until the greens are soft and the peas are tender — about 20 minutes. Remove and discard the bay leaf. Stir in the vinegar and serve the soup immediately.

EDITOR'S NOTE: *Mustard greens or kale may be substituted for the collard greens; either of these vegetables will require less cooking than the collard greens.*

Preparing an Artichoke for Cooking

1 *TRIMMING THE LEAVES. Cut off the stem and small outer leaves from the base of the artichoke with a stainless-steel knife. Rub the cut surfaces with freshly cut lemon to keep them from turning brown. Cut off the top third of the artichoke. Then snip off the sharp tips of the outer leaves with kitchen scissors.*

2 *REMOVING THE CHOKE. With a teaspoon, scoop out the tiny inner leaves and the hairy choke from the center of the artichoke to reveal the smooth, green heart. The artichoke is now ready for cooking. (On large, mature artichokes, the choke may be difficult to remove until after the artichoke has been cooked.)*

Artichokes with an Egg and Herb Vinaigrette

Serves 6
Working time: about 20 minutes
Total time: about 1 hour

Calories **100**
Protein **2g.**
Cholesterol **35mg.**
Total fat **8g.**
Saturated fat **1g.**
Sodium **85mg.**

6 artichokes, trimmed, chokes removed (technique, above)	
1 egg, hard cooked	
1 tbsp. white wine vinegar	
½ tsp. fresh lemon juice	
3 tbsp. virgin olive oil	
¼ tsp. salt	
freshly ground black pepper	
1 tbsp. chopped parsley	
1 tsp. chopped chives	
1 tsp. chopped lemon balm (optional)	
1 tsp. torn summer savory leaves (optional)	

In a large, nonreactive saucepan, bring 6 quarts of water to a boil. Add the artichokes and 1 tablespoon of salt, and boil the artichokes until they are tender—about 40 minutes. Place a colander over a bowl and drain the artichokes, reserving 2 tablespoons of their cooking water.

While the artichokes are cooling, shell the hard-cooked egg and chop it coarsely. In a small bowl, whisk together the vinegar, lemon juice, reserved cooking water from the artichokes, olive oil, salt, and some black pepper. When the dressing is thoroughly mixed, stir in the chopped egg, parsley, and chives, and the lemon balm and summer savory if you are using them.

Place the cooled artichokes on individual serving plates. Divide the herb dressing among the hollowed-out centers, and serve the artichokes.

EDITOR'S NOTE: *The easiest way to eat artichokes presented in this manner is to break off the outer leaves first and use them to scoop out the dressing. When the edible part of all the leaves has been eaten, use a knife and fork to eat the tender artichoke bottoms with the remaining herb vinaigrette. Each diner should be supplied with a finger bowl.*

Artichoke Bottoms Filled with Vegetables Vinaigrette

Serves 4
Working time: about 20 minutes
Total time: about 45 minutes

Calories **110**
Protein **2g.**
Cholesterol **0mg.**
Total fat **10g.**
Saturated fat **1g.**
Sodium **110mg.**

½ lemon, juice only
4 artichoke bottoms (technique, right)
¼ cup baby carrots cut into ½-inch diagonal slices
¼ cup trimmed broccoli florets
¼ cup trimmed green beans, cut into 1-inch pieces
¼ cup baby zucchini, sliced into thin rounds
Walnut dressing
1 tbsp. white wine vinegar
¼ tsp. salt
2 tbsp. walnut oil
ground white pepper
1 tbsp. coarsely chopped walnuts

In a large nonreactive saucepan, bring 1 quart of water to a boil. Add the lemon juice to the water, drop in the artichoke bottoms, and simmer them until they are tender—about 25 minutes.

While the artichokes are cooking, parboil the other vegetables separately in boiling water just until they are tender—the carrots and broccoli for about two minutes each, the green beans and zucchini for about one minute each. Drain the vegetables in a colander, refresh them under cold running water, drain them thoroughly again, and set them aside.

When the artichoke bottoms are cooked, lift them from the water with a slotted spoon, and set them upside down on a clean towel to drain.

Turning an Artichoke Bottom

PREPARING THE BOTTOM. Cut off the stem using a stainless-steel knife. Bend back each outer leaf, snapping the tough upper part from the fleshy base, until you reach the tender, pale inner leaves. Rub the cut surfaces with lemon as you work. Cut off the top two-thirds of the artichoke. Pare away the tough, dark green bases of the leaves (above). Then scrape out the choke (Step 2, opposite).

To prepare the walnut dressing, mix the vinegar and the salt in a small bowl, stirring well until the salt dissolves. Whisk in the walnut oil, add some pepper, and stir in the walnuts. Toss the broccoli, carrots, green beans, and zucchini in the dressing, spoon them into the artichoke bottoms, and serve.

EDITOR'S NOTE: *Any colorful combination of fresh vegetables may be used in the filling for the artichokes. Alternative possibilities to those above include sautéed mushrooms, cooked green peas, diced and parboiled baby turnips, or slivers of blanched snow peas.*

processor or blender and purée it, gradually pouring in the saffron-flavored stock as you work. Pour this mixture into the beaten eggs, add a pinch of cayenne pepper, and beat until just mixed. Butter a 3-cup mold, pour the mixture into it, and cover the top with foil. Set the mold in a deep baking dish and pour in enough boiling water to come halfway up the sides of the mold. Bake the timbale until it sets — 40 to 50 minutes.

Remove the mold from the water bath and let it stand for 10 minutes. In the meantime, warm the sauce over low heat. Remove the foil from the mold, run a knife around the inside edge and unmold the timbale onto a heated serving dish. Pour the red pepper sauce around the border and garnish the timbale with the remaining 2 tablespoons of scallions.

EDITOR'S NOTE: *To give body and texture to the timbale, the chicken stock must be rich and gelatinous. Four small ramekins may be used in place of the large mold, provided the cooking time is reduced to 20 to 25 minutes.*

Onion Timbale with Red Pepper Sauce

A TIMBALE IS A CREAMY VEGETABLE MIXTURE BAKED IN A MOLD.

Serves 4
Working time: about 30 minutes
Total time: about 1 hour and 30 minutes

Calories **101**
Protein **5g.**
Cholesterol **69mg.**
Total fat **6g.**
Saturated fat **1g.**
Sodium **213mg.**

1 large onion, coarsely chopped (about 1½ cups)
1 tbsp. virgin olive oil
¼ cup plus 2 tbsp. finely chopped green scallion tops
¼ tsp. salt
1 cup gelatinous unsalted chicken stock
⅛ tsp. saffron threads
1 whole egg plus 2 egg whites
cayenne pepper
Red pepper sauce
2 red peppers, broiled and peeled
½ cup unsalted chicken stock
cayenne pepper

Heat the oil in a heavy-bottomed skillet over low heat. Add the onion, ¼ cup of the scallions and the salt. Cook the mixture until the onion becomes very soft — 15 to 20 minutes. Remove the pan from the heat and allow the mixture to cool.

While the onion is cooking, make the sauce. Remove the stems and seeds from the peppers. Purée the peppers in a food processor or blender. Transfer the purée to a saucepan, pour in the stock, and sprinkle with a pinch of cayenne pepper. Set the pan aside. Preheat the oven to 350° F.

Warm the cup of stock over low heat and dissolve the saffron threads in it. In a mixing bowl, lightly beat the egg and egg whites until they are just combined but not foamy. Transfer the onion mixture to a food

Onion and Goat Cheese Pizza

Serves 8
Working time: about 40 minutes
Total time: about 2 hours and 30 minutes

Calories **220**
Protein **6g.**
Cholesterol **12mg.**
Total fat **10g.**
Saturated fat **3g.**
Sodium **171mg.**

6 onions, thinly sliced (about 8 cups)
2 tbsp. virgin olive oil
2 tsp. fresh thyme, or ½ tsp. dried thyme leaves
¼ cup red wine vinegar or cider vinegar
¼ tsp. salt
1 tbsp. cornmeal
3 oz. mild goat cheese or feta cheese
2 oz. low-fat cream cheese
Thyme-flavored pizza dough
1 package active dry yeast
¼ tsp. sugar
1¾ to 2 cups bread flour
¼ tsp. salt
2 tsp. fresh thyme, or ½ tsp. dried thyme leaves
2 tbsp. virgin olive oil

To make the dough, pour ¼ cup lukewarm water into a small bowl and sprinkle the yeast and sugar into it. Let the mixture stand for two or three minutes, then stir it until the yeast and sugar are completely dissolved. Allow the mixture to sit in a warm place until the yeast bubbles up and the mixture has doubled in size — about 15 minutes. If the mixture does not double, start over again with another package of yeast.

Sift 1¾ cups of the flour and the salt into a large bowl, and stir in the thyme. Make a well in the center and pour in the yeast mixture, ½ cup lukewarm water and the oil. Mix the dough by hand; it should feel slightly sticky. If it feels too soft and sticky, work in up to ¼ cup additional flour. As soon as the dough is firm enough to be gathered into a ball, place it on a floured board and knead it until it is smooth and elastic — about 10 minutes.

Put the dough in a clean oiled bowl and cover it with a damp towel. Set the bowl in a warm, draft-free place until the dough has doubled in size — about one hour and 30 minutes.

While the dough is rising, make the onion topping. Heat 1 tablespoon of the olive oil in a large, heavy-bottomed casserole over medium heat. Put the onions and thyme in the casserole and cook them, stirring and scraping the bottom frequently, until the onions are well browned — 45 minutes to one hour. Add the vin-

egar and salt, and cook, stirring often, until the liquid has evaporated — about 10 minutes.

Preheat the oven to 450° F. Sprinkle the cornmeal on a large, heavy baking sheet. Punch down the dough, then gather it up into a ball and flatten it with your hands. Stretch out the dough by holding it at the edges with both hands and turning it until it forms a circle about 8 inches in diameter. Put the circle of dough in the center of the baking sheet and pat it out to 12 inches in diameter.

Distribute the onions in an even layer over the pizza dough, leaving a ½-inch border uncovered at the edge. Combine the goat or feta cheese and the cream cheese in a small bowl; dot the pizza with the cheese mixture. Bake the pizza for 10 minutes. Remove it from ▶

the oven and drizzle the remaining tablespoon of oil over the top. Return the pizza to the oven and bake it until the bottom of the crust is browned and the cheese turns golden — four to six minutes. Cut the pizza into wedges and serve at once.

EDITOR'S NOTE: *To prepare the pizza dough in a food processor, put 1¾ cups of the flour, the salt and thyme in the processor and mix it in two short bursts. In a separate small mixing bowl, combine the yeast mixture with ⅔ cup lukewarm water and the oil. While the motor is running, pour the mixture into the processor as fast as the flour will absorb it; process until a ball of dough comes away from the sides of the bowl — about one minute. If the dough is too sticky to form a ball, work in up to ¼ cup additional flour. Remove the dough from the processor, place it on a floured board and knead it for five minutes. Set the dough aside to rise as described above.*

Leeks and Cheese in Phyllo Packets

Serves 6
Working time: about 45 minutes
Total time: about 1 hour and 45 minutes

Calories **275**
Protein **9g.**
Cholesterol **28mg.**
Total fat **14g.**
Saturated fat **6g.**
Sodium **288mg.**

3 large or 4 medium leeks, trimmed, cleaned (technique, below) and sliced into ½-inch pieces
1 tbsp. safflower oil
2 tbsp. unsalted butter
1½ cups chopped onion
1 garlic clove, finely chopped
½ tsp. dried thyme leaves
¼ tsp. salt
freshly ground black pepper
2 tbsp. light cream
⅔ cup grated Gruyère or other Swiss cheese
12 sheets phyllo dough, each sheet 12 inches square

In a large, heavy-bottomed skillet, heat the oil and 1 tablespoon of the butter over medium heat. Add the leeks, onion, garlic, thyme, salt and pepper. Cook, stirring often, for 12 minutes. Stir in the cream and continue cooking until all the liquid is absorbed — about three minutes more.

Transfer the leek mixture to a bowl and let it cool slightly. Stir in the cheese and refrigerate the mixture for 30 minutes.

Preheat the oven to 350° F. On a clean, dry work surface, lay out two sheets of phyllo dough, one on top of the other. Mound about ½ cup of the leek-cheese mixture 3 inches from the lower right corner of the dough. Fold up the dough as shown at right, forming a compact packet. Repeat the process with the remaining filling and dough sheets to form six packets in all. Put the packets, seam sides down, on a lightly buttered baking sheet. Melt the remaining tablespoon of butter in a small saucepan over low heat. Brush the packets with the melted butter and bake them until they are golden — about 30 minutes. Serve them hot.

EDITOR'S NOTE: *These make an excellent luncheon dish when served with a green salad.*

Cleaning Leeks

1 *SPLITTING THE LEEK. Remove any bruised outer leaves from the leek. Cut off the root base and the tough leaf tops. With a paring knife, pierce the leek about 2 inches below the green portion, then draw the knife through to the top to split the leek.*

2 *RINSING OUT THE GRIT. Dip the leafy part of the leek into a bowl of water and swirl it vigorously to flush out the grit. Alternatively, rinse well under running water. Run your fingers along the insides of the leaves to remove any remaining particles of sand.*

Forming a Phyllo Packet

1 MAKING THE FIRST FOLD. Spread out two sheets of phyllo dough, one atop the other. Place the filling in a mound 3 inches from the lower right corner. Lift the corner and fold it over until it touches the far edge of the filling.

2 FOLDING IN THE SIDES. Lift the lower left corner of the dough square and fold it in toward the center of the square. Repeat the procedure with the upper right corner so that the filling is enclosed on both sides.

3 ROLLING THE PACKET. Gently roll the enclosed filling toward the far corner of the dough square to form a compact parcel. Set the packet aside; repeat the process with the remaining filling and dough sheets to form six packets in all.

Three-Mushroom Marinade

ANY COMBINATION OF CULTIVATED OR EDIBLE WILD
MUSHROOMS CAN BE USED IN THIS MARINADE.

Serves 8
Working time: about 30 minutes
Total time: about 5 hours (includes marinating)

Calories **60**
Protein **2g.**
Cholesterol **0mg.**
Total fat **4g.**
Saturated fat **1g.**
Sodium **60mg.**

⅔ cup dry white wine
1 lemon, juice only
1 garlic clove, crushed
½ lb. oyster mushrooms, trimmed, wiped, and sliced
½ lb. button mushrooms, trimmed and wiped
6 oz. fresh shiitake mushrooms, trimmed, wiped, and halved if large
2 tbsp. virgin olive oil
2 tbsp. chopped parsley
¼ tsp. salt
freshly ground black pepper
oakleaf or other lettuce leaves, washed and dried

In a large saucepan, combine the wine, lemon juice, and garlic, and bring the mixture to a boil. Add the mushrooms, lower the heat, cover the pan, and cook gently until the mushrooms are tender but not over-cooked—six to eight minutes.

Place a colander over a bowl and drain the mushrooms, reserving the liquid. Return the mushroom juices to the saucepan, bring them to a boil, and reduce to about ½ cup. Remove the pan from the heat, and whisk in the oil, parsley, salt, and some pepper. Pour this mixture into a bowl and add the drained mushrooms. Let the mushrooms cool in the marinade, then cover the bowl with plastic wrap and refrigerate for at least four hours, or overnight.

Arrange the lettuce leaves on eight plates. Using a slotted spoon, lift the mushrooms from the marinade and transfer them to the plates. Spoon a little of the marinade over them and serve immediately.

SUGGESTED ACCOMPANIMENT: *melba toast.*

Zucchini Filled with Crab

Serves 6
Working time: about 30 minutes
Total time: about 1 hour and 10 minutes

Calories **80**
Protein **2g.**
Cholesterol **35mg.**
Total fat **3g.**
Saturated fat **1g.**
Sodium **180mg.**

6 zucchini, about 4 oz. each, trimmed, washed, and patted dry
1 tbsp. unsalted butter
1 very small onion, finely chopped
2 tbsp. all-purpose flour
⅔ cup dry white wine
6 oz. fresh or frozen crabmeat, picked over
1 tbsp. light cream
1 tsp. fresh lemon juice
¼ tsp. salt
freshly ground black pepper
3 tbsp. fresh white bread crumbs
1 small carrot, finely julienned, for garnish

Preheat the oven to 375° F.

Cut the zucchini in half lengthwise, and score the cut sides lightly with the tines of a fork or a sharp knife. Grease a large, shallow ovenproof dish and place the zucchini halves in the dish, cut side down. Cover them with aluminum foil and bake until they are cooked through—45 to 50 minutes.

About 20 minutes before the zucchini are ready, melt the butter in a saucepan, then add the chopped onion and cook it gently until it is very soft but not browned—three to four minutes. Stir the flour into the onion and cook for one minute. Gradually stir the wine into the saucepan, then bring the mixture to a boil, stirring all the time until the sauce becomes very thick. Remove the saucepan from the heat, and stir in the crabmeat, cream, lemon juice, salt, and some freshly ground black pepper.

Preheat the broiler.

When the zucchini are cooked, turn them over so the cut sides are uppermost. Divide the crab mixture among the zucchini, spooning it neatly on top of the halves. Sprinkle the bread crumbs evenly over the top, and place the dish under the broiler until the crab mixture is heated through and the crumbs are golden brown. Serve the zucchini hot, garnished with the carrot julienne.

EDITOR'S NOTE: *The zucchini may be stuffed in advance. When you are ready to serve them, top with the bread crumbs and heat through under a hot broiler.*

Eggplant, Tomato, and Crab Croustades

Makes 12 croustades
Working time: about 30 minutes
Total time: about 35 minutes

Per croustade:
Calories **90**
Protein **4g.**
Cholesterol **10mg.**
Total fat **4g.**
Saturated fat **1g.**
Sodium **80mg.**

12 thin slices white bread
3 tbsp. virgin olive oil
one ½-lb. eggplant, peeled and coarsely chopped
1 garlic clove, finely chopped
2 medium tomatoes, peeled, seeded and coarsely chopped
½ lemon, strained juice only
½ tsp. salt
freshly ground black pepper
4 oz. crabmeat, picked over
lemon wedges for garnish

Preheat the oven to 400° F. Using a 3-inch round pastry cutter, cut a circle from each slice of bread. Brush both sides of the bread circles lightly with 2 tablespoons of the oil, and press them firmly into 12 muffin cups or small tart pans. Bake in the oven until the bread is golden and has set into shape—about 10 minutes.

Meanwhile, prepare the filling. Heat the remaining oil in a frying pan over medium heat and sauté the eggplant with the garlic. When the eggplant is well browned, stir in the tomatoes, lemon juice, salt, and some pepper. Increase the heat to evaporate all the juices, then spoon the mixture into the croustade cases. Flake the crabmeat and divide it among the cases.

Cover the crab croustades loosely with a piece of aluminium foil and return the tray to the hot oven for five minutes.

Serve hot, garnished with the lemon wedges.

Pissaladière Tartlets

Makes 24 tartlets
Working time: about 1 hour
Total time: about 1 hour and 45 minutes

Per tartlet:
Calories **70**
Protein **2g.**
Cholesterol **trace**
Total fat **3g.**
Saturated fat **trace**
Sodium **45mg.**

1½ tbsp. virgin olive oil
2 large onions (about 1½ lb.), quartered and thinly sliced
1 large garlic clove, finely chopped
6 anchovy fillets, soaked in skim milk for 30 minutes, rinsed in cold water, and patted dry
12 black olives, pitted and quartered
Tartlet dough
1 envelope (¼ oz.) active dry yeast
2 cups unbleached all-purpose flour
¼ tsp. salt
1½ tbsp. virgin olive oil
1 tsp. chopped fresh rosemary, or ½ tsp. dried rosemary

First, prepare the tartlet dough. Dissolve the yeast in ¼ cup of tepid water and set it aside until it foams—about 10 minutes. Sift the flour and salt into a large bowl, make a well in the center, and pour in the yeast solution. Add 1 tablespoon of the oil, the rosemary, and ¾ cup of tepid water, and mix to make a dough that is soft but not sticky. On a floured work surface, knead the dough until it is smooth and elastic—approximately five minutes.

Put the remaining ½ tablespoon of oil into a mixing bowl. Form the dough into a ball and put it into the bowl; turn the dough to coat it all over with oil. Cover the bowl with a damp dishtowel and leave the dough in a warm place to rise until it has doubled in size—about one hour.

While the dough rises, prepare the filling. Heat the oil in a large frying pan, and stew the onions and garlic for 40 minutes over low heat, adding a little water if necessary to prevent them from sticking.

Cut each anchovy fillet lengthwise into four strips, then halve the strips by cutting across them.

Preheat the oven to 400° F.

Punch down the dough, then turn it out onto a lightly floured surface and knead briefly. Cut the dough into 24 portions. Roll out each portion into a circle about 2½ inches in diameter, and use the circles to line 2½-inch-diameter tartlet pans.

Fill each dough case with a heaped teaspoon of the onion mixture and smooth the surface. Cross two anchovy strips on each tartlet and add two olive quarters. Place the tartlet pans on a baking sheet, and bake the tartlets until the dough has risen and is lightly golden—about 15 minutes. Serve hot.

Chickpea and Yogurt Dip

THIS RECIPE IS REMINISCENT OF THE MIDDLE EASTERN
DISH KNOWN AS HUMMUS.

Serves 6
Working time: about 15 minutes
Total time: about 2 hours (includes soaking)

Calories **145**
Protein **9g.**
Cholesterol **2mg.**
Total fat **3g.**
Saturated fat **trace**
Sodium **160mg.**

1 generous cup dried chickpeas
2 tbsp. tahini
½ cup plain low-fat yogurt
3 garlic cloves, crushed
2 lemons, juice only
½ tsp. salt
freshly ground black pepper
paprika for garnish
chopped parsley for garnish

Rinse the chickpeas under cold running water. Put them into a large, heavy-bottomed pan and pour in enough cold water to cover them by about 2 inches. Discard any chickpeas that float to the surface. Cover the pan, leaving the lid ajar, and bring the water to a boil; cook for two minutes. Turn off the heat, cover the pan, and soak the peas for at least one hour. (Alternatively, soak the chickpeas overnight in cold water.)

After soaking the chickpeas, drain them well in a colander. Return them to the pan and pour in enough water to cover them by about 2 inches. Bring the liquid to a simmer; cook the chickpeas over medium-low heat until they are quite tender—45 minutes to one hour. (If they appear to be drying out at any point, pour in more water.) When cooked, drain the peas and allow them to cool.

Place the chickpeas in a food processor with the tahini, yogurt, garlic, lemon juice, salt, and some pepper. Process for about 45 seconds to produce a soft, creamy paste. Transfer the dip to a shallow bowl, and sprinkle with some paprika and parsley before serving.

SUGGESTED ACCOMPANIMENT: *warmed pita bread, cut into fingers.*

Taramasalata

Serves 6
Working time: about 15 minutes
Total time: about 20 minutes

	Calories **80**
3 thick slices white bread (about 3 oz.), crusts removed	Protein **6g.**
3 oz. codfish roe	Cholesterol **0mg.**
2 oz. low-fat ricotta cheese	Total fat **3g.**
½ lemon, juice only	Saturated fat **trace**
1 small garlic clove, crushed	Sodium **120mg.**
freshly ground black pepper	
lemon wedges for garnish	

Place the bread in a small bowl, cover with water, and let it soak for a few minutes.

Remove the bread from the water and squeeze it thoroughly dry, then place it in a food processor with the roe, ricotta cheese, lemon juice, garlic, and some black pepper. Process until smooth.

Transfer the purée to a small bowl and garnish with the lemon wedges.

SUGGESTED ACCOMPANIMENT: *warmed pita bread, cut into fingers.*

2 *First steamed, then roasted, a duck stuffed with garlic, rosemary, and pear is presented with watercress and stuffed tomatoes (recipe, page 79).*

Poultry

the cornstarch mixture and the orange zest, and simmer for five minutes.

Brush the chicken pieces with the glaze and place them under the broiler for a few minutes to brown. Garnish the chicken with the orange segments and pour the sauce over them.

SUGGESTED ACCOMPANIMENT: *steamed snow peas.*

Saffron Chicken Stew

Serves 4
Working time: about 20 minutes
Total time: about 1 hour and 10 minutes

Calories **594**
Protein **37g.**
Cholesterol **90mg.**
Total fat **17g.**
Saturated fat **3g.**
Sodium **687mg.**

4 chicken legs, skinned, cut into thighs and drumsticks
1 garlic clove, halved
¼ tsp. freshly ground black pepper
½ tsp. salt
2 tbsp. safflower oil
1 medium-size eggplant (about ¾ lb.), cut into 1-inch cubes
1 medium-size yellow summer squash (about ½ lb.), cut into 2-inch cubes
6 scallions
3 celery stalks, trimmed and cut into ½-inch pieces
¼ lb. baby carrots
1 large ripe tomato, peeled, seeded and coarsely chopped
½ tsp. fennel seeds
⅛ tsp. saffron threads, crumbled
1 bay leaf
1 tsp. fresh thyme, or ¼ tsp. dried thyme leaves
1 cup dry vermouth
8 small red potatoes (about 1½ lbs.), with a band peeled from the middle of each
¼ cup coarsely chopped parsley
8 slices French bread, toasted

Rub the chicken pieces with the garlic and reserve it; sprinkle the chicken with the pepper and ¼ teaspoon of the salt. Heat 1 tablespoon of the oil in a 6-quart saucepan over medium heat. Brown the pieces in the oil for about three minutes on each side. Remove the chicken and set it on paper towels to drain.

Add the remaining tablespoon of oil to the pan. Add the garlic, eggplant, squash and the remaining ¼ teaspoon of salt, and sauté lightly over high heat for about one minute. Pour in 1½ quarts of water. Return the chicken pieces to the pan. Add the scallions, celery, carrots, tomato, fennel seeds, saffron, bay leaf, thyme and vermouth, and bring the mixture to a boil. Reduce the heat and simmer gently for about 30 minutes, skimming off the fat from time to time. Add the potatoes and simmer for 15 minutes more. The vegetables should be tender but not soft. Remove the bay leaf and garlic. Add the parsley a few minutes before serving.

Serve the stew in soup bowls, accompanied by the slices of toasted French bread — sprinkled, if you like, with freshly grated Swiss or Parmesan cheese, dusted with paprika and browned under the broiler.

Orange-Glazed Chicken

Serves 4
Working time: about 20 minutes
Total time: about 1 hour

Calories **457**
Protein **40g.**
Cholesterol **124mg.**
Total fat **23g.**
Saturated fat **6g.**
Sodium **421mg.**

one 3 lb. chicken, quartered
½ tsp. salt
freshly ground black pepper
1 tbsp. safflower oil
1 garlic clove, crushed
1 cup unsalted chicken stock
1 tsp. cornstarch, mixed with 1 tbsp. water
1 navel orange, peeled and segmented, the zest grated
Orange glaze
¼ cup orange juice
¼ cup brown sugar
2 tbsp. cider vinegar
1 tsp. Dijon mustard

Sprinkle the chicken with the salt and pepper. Heat the oil in a large, heavy-bottomed skillet over medium-high heat. Add the chicken pieces and brown them lightly — about four minutes on each side. Push the chicken to one side of the skillet, add the garlic, and sauté for 15 seconds. Stir in the stock and allow it to come to a simmer. Redistribute the chicken pieces in the pan. Reduce the heat to low and braise until the juices run clear when a thigh is pierced with the tip of a sharp knife — about 25 minutes.

Meanwhile, make the glaze. In a small saucepan over medium-low heat, combine the orange juice, brown sugar, vinegar and mustard. Bring the mixture to a simmer and cook it for three minutes.

When the chicken is cooked, transfer it to a broiling pan. Skim off and discard the fat from the braising liquid in the skillet. Bring the liquid to a simmer, stir in

44

and fasten each roll lengthwise with a small skewer.

Heat the oil in a heavy-bottomed skillet over medium heat and gently sauté the rolls, turning them, until golden — about four minutes. Remove the chicken and pour the sauce into the skillet, stirring, being sure to scrape up any brown bits from the bottom. Return the chicken to the skillet, cover loosely, and simmer for eight minutes, turning once.

Transfer the chicken to a heated platter, remove the skewers, and cut the rolls into ⅓-inch slices. Pour the sauce over the rolls and serve immediately.

SUGGESTED ACCOMPANIMENT: *steamed rice tossed with green peas and sautéed mushrooms.*

Poached Chicken with Black-Bean Onion Sauce

THE FERMENTED BLACK BEANS CALLED FOR IN THIS RECIPE ARE AVAILABLE AT STORES WHERE ASIAN FOODS ARE SOLD.

Serves 4
Working time: about 30 minutes
Total time: about 1 hour and 30 minutes

Calories **486**
Protein **45g.**
Cholesterol **126mg.**
Total fat **18g.**
Saturated fat **4g.**
Sodium **235mg.**

one 3-lb. chicken, trussed
2 tbsp. safflower oil
3 onions, sliced
1 tbsp. flour
2 tsp. fermented black beans, rinsed well
2 garlic cloves, finely chopped
1 cup dry white wine
3 to 4 cups unsalted beef stock
2 tbsp. brandy
1 small potato, peeled and cut into chunks
freshly ground black pepper
1 tbsp. unsalted butter, cut into pieces (optional)

Red-Pepper and Chicken Spirals

Serves 4
Working time: about 30 minutes
Total time: about 45 minutes

Calories **251**
Protein **28g.**
Cholesterol **72mg.**
Total fat **11g.**
Saturated fat **2g.**
Sodium **533mg.**

4 chicken breast halves, skinned, boned, the long triangular fillets removed and reserved for another use, lightly pounded to ¼-inch thickness
¼ tsp. salt
½ tsp. crushed Sichuan peppercorns, or ¼ tsp. crushed black peppercorns
3 scallions, blanched for 30 seconds, drained, cooled, patted dry, and halved lengthwise
1 cucumber, peeled, halved lengthwise, seeded, cut into ¼-inch-wide strips, blanched for 30 seconds, drained, cooled and patted dry
1 sweet red pepper, seeded, deribbed, cut into ½-inch strips, blanched for 2 minutes, drained and patted dry
2 tbsp. safflower oil
Mirin sauce
3 tbsp. low-sodium soy sauce
1 tbsp. sugar
2 tbsp. mirin, or 2 tbsp. dry sherry
2 tsp. rice vinegar
½ tsp. crushed Sichuan peppercorns, or ¼ tsp. crushed black peppercorns

To prepare the sauce, combine the soy sauce, sugar, *mirin* or sherry, vinegar, crushed peppercorns and 3 tablespoons of water in a small bowl. Set aside.

Sprinkle the chicken with the salt and crushed peppercorns. Cut the scallions, cucumber strips and pepper strips to fit inside the breast halves. Arrange some scallions, 2 or 3 cucumber strips, and 2 or 3 pepper strips across the grain of the meat at the wide edge of each cutlet. Roll the chicken around the vegetables

Pour the oil into a deep, heavy-bottomed casserole set over medium-low heat, and stir in the onions. Cover the casserole and cook, stirring occasionally, until the onions are greatly reduced in bulk and quite limp — about 30 minutes.

Uncover the casserole and stir in the flour, black beans and garlic. Cook, stirring, for one minute. Add the wine, 3 cups of the stock, the brandy, potato and some pepper. Lower the chicken into the pot. If necessary, pour in enough additional stock or water to almost cover the bird.

Place a sheet of aluminum foil over the chicken and cover the casserole. Poach gently over medium-low heat, turning the bird several times, until the juices run clear when a thigh is pierced with the tip of a sharp knife — about 45 minutes. Transfer the chicken to a carving board and cover it with the foil to keep it warm.

To prepare the sauce, first skim the fat off the cooking liquid. Set a sieve or colander over a bowl and pour the liquid through it. Reserve ¼ cup of the onions. Transfer the drained potato pieces and the remaining onions to a food processor or blender, add ½ cup of the strained cooking liquid, and purée the mixture until smooth. Pour in an additional cup of the cooking liquid and purée again until smooth.

Pour the sauce into a small pan and warm it over low heat. Remove the sauce from the heat and, if desired, swirl in the butter. (The butter lends richness and gloss to the sauce.)

Carve the chicken into serving pieces. Spoon some sauce over the pieces and scatter the reserved onions over them. Pass the remaining sauce separately.

SUGGESTED ACCOMPANIMENTS: *polenta; green beans.*

Cranberried Chicken

Serves 4
Working time: about 20 minutes
Total time: about 3 hours

Calories **610**
Protein **42g.**
Cholesterol **133mg.**
Total fat **13g.**
Saturated fat **5g.**
Sodium **133mg.**

one 3 lb. chicken, cut into serving pieces and skinned
5 to 7 cups cranberry juice
½ cup loosely packed basil, lightly crushed to bruise the leaves, or 1½ tbsp. dried basil
1 onion, sliced
½ lb. cranberries
½ cup sugar
2 tbsp. raspberry vinegar
1 tsp. cornstarch, mixed with 2 tbsp. water
1 tbsp. unsalted butter, cut into pieces

In a large, nonreactive pot, simmer 5 cups of the cranberry juice with the basil and onion for 10 minutes. Let the liquid cool, then add the chicken pieces. Marinate for two hours at room temperature or overnight in the refrigerator, turning the pieces occasionally.

If needed, pour in enough water to cover the chicken pieces. Bring the liquid to a simmer and reduce the heat. Partially cover the pot. Poach the chicken gently, skimming the foam from the surface, until the juices run clear when a thigh is pierced with the tip of a sharp knife — 15 to 20 minutes.

Simmer the cranberries in 2 cups of juice with the sugar until they almost burst — about seven minutes. Drain the cranberries and discard the liquid.

Transfer the chicken to a heated serving platter and cover it to keep it warm. Strain the poaching liquid and return it to the pot. Add the vinegar and bring the liquid to a boil. Cook over medium-high heat until the

liquid is reduced to about 1½ cups — 15 to 25 minutes. Stir in the cornstarch mixture and the cooked cranberries, and simmer until the sauce has thickened slightly — two or three minutes. Remove the pot from the heat and swirl in the butter. Spoon some of the sauce over the chicken and pass the rest separately.

SUGGESTED ACCOMPANIMENT: *wild rice; braised fennel.*

Poached Chicken with Fennel

Serves 6
Working time: about 30 minutes
Total time: about 1 hour

Calories **338**
Protein **29g.**
Cholesterol **96mg.**
Total fat **11g.**
Saturated fat **4g.**
Sodium **515mg.**

6 chicken legs, skinned
1 tsp. black peppercorns
2 garlic cloves, peeled
1 cup anis or other licorice-flavored liqueur
3 cups unsalted chicken stock
1 onion, thinly sliced
½ tsp. fennel seed
1 tsp. salt
2 large fennel bulbs, the tough outer layer and feathery green tops trimmed and reserved, the bulbs cut lengthwise into 6 pieces
1 celery stalk, trimmed, cut into ¼-inch-wide strips about 3 inches long
1 bay leaf
2 large lettuce leaves, preferably romaine
½ lb. baby carrots, tops removed, peeled
1 tbsp. unsalted butter
freshly ground black pepper

Crush the peppercorns and the garlic with a mortar and pestle and mash them into a paste. Spread the paste over each chicken leg.

Bring the liqueur to a boil in a large, heavy-bottomed casserole. Add the chicken legs and turn them to coat them with the liqueur. Add the stock, onion, fennel seed and salt; if necessary, pour in enough water or additional stock to just cover the chicken. Return the liquid to a boil. Reduce the heat to medium low and simmer for 15 minutes.

Meanwhile, make a bouquet garni: Wrap the tough outer layer and trimmings from the fennel, the celery strips and the bay leaf in the lettuce leaves, and tie the bundle with butcher's twine. Submerge the bouquet garni in the poaching liquid.

At the end of the 15 minutes, add the fennel pieces, pressing them into the liquid. Cover the skillet and simmer for five minutes more. Add the carrots and continue cooking, uncovered, until the juices run clear when a thigh is pierced with the tip of a sharp knife — seven to 10 minutes. Transfer the chicken and vegetables to a warmed serving platter.

To make the sauce, reduce the poaching liquid over high heat to about 1¼ cups. Remove and discard the bouquet garni. Whisk the butter and some pepper into

the sauce and pour it over the legs and vegetables; garnish them, if you like, with the feathery fennel tops.

SUGGESTED ACCOMPANIMENT: *sautéed onions and potatoes.*

Poached Chicken Strips in Gingered Orange Sauce

Serves 6
Working time: about 45 minutes
Total time: 1 hour and 30 minutes

Calories **180**
Protein **20g.**
Cholesterol **54mg.**
Total fat **5g.**
Saturated fat **2g.**
Sodium **185mg.**

4 chicken breast halves, skinned and boned (about 1 lb.), cut into ½-inch-wide strips
¼ tsp. salt
freshly ground black pepper
1 cup fresh orange juice
3 cups unsalted chicken stock
1½ to 2-inch piece fresh ginger (¾ to 1 oz.), peeled and cut into chunks
2 navel oranges, the zest julienned and the flesh segmented
¼ tsp. aromatic bitters
1 tsp. bourbon
2 tbsp. cream cheese
1 tbsp. cornstarch

Put the chicken strips in a shallow dish and sprinkle them with ⅛ teaspoon of the salt and some pepper. Pour in the orange juice. Turn the pieces to coat them with the juice. Cover the dish with plastic wrap and refrigerate for one hour.

Lift the chicken strips out of the marinade and set them aside. To make the poaching liquid, pour the marinade into a large saucepan or skillet. Add 2 cups of the stock, the remaining ⅛ teaspoon of salt and some pepper. Squeeze each ginger chunk through a garlic press into the pan, scraping the paste from the outside bottom of the press into the pot and then turning the press over to add the juices. Bring the liquid to a boil, reduce the heat, cover, and simmer for four minutes. Remove the pan from the heat and let the ginger steep in the poaching liquid for 15 minutes.

While the ginger is steeping, put the julienned zest in a small saucepan. Cover the zest with ½ cup of the stock, the bitters and the bourbon. Cook briskly over medium-high heat until almost all the liquid has evaporated, and set the pan aside. In another small saucepan, pour the remaining ½ cup of stock over the orange segments; cover and set aside.

Return the poaching liquid to a boil. Add the chicken strips and reduce the heat to medium. Simmer the

liquid until the chicken feels firm but springy to the touch — about one minute. Remove the chicken with a slotted spoon and set it in the center of a warmed serving platter.

In a small bowl, soften the cream cheese with the back of a spoon. Stir in the cornstarch. Pour about ½ cup of the hot poaching liquid into the bowl and whisk well. Add another cup of the poaching liquid, then pour the contents of the bowl back into the poaching liquid and cook over medium heat, whisking, until the sauce thickens slightly — two or three minutes.

Heat the orange segments in the chicken stock. Spoon some sauce over the chicken strips and garnish them with the julienned zest. Lift the orange segments out of the stock and arrange them around the chicken. Pass the remaining sauce separately.

SUGGESTED ACCOMPANIMENT: *kasha cooked in chicken stock with sliced mushrooms.*

Chicken, Eggplant and Tomato Sauté

Serves 4
Working time: about 45 minutes
Total time: about 1 hour

Calories **370**
Protein **30g.**
Cholesterol **75mg.**
Total fat **19g.**
Saturated fat **4g.**
Sodium **207mg.**

4 chicken breast halves, skinned and boned (about 1 lb.)
2 small eggplants, sliced in ⅜-inch-thick rounds
1 tsp. unsalted butter
4 tbsp. virgin olive oil
freshly ground black pepper
¼ tsp. salt
¼ cup dry sherry
2 tbsp. fresh lemon juice
1 tsp. fresh thyme, or ¼ tsp. dried thyme leaves
1 oz. dried mushrooms, rinsed and soaked for one hour in 1 cup warm water, the remaining water strained through doubled cheesecloth to remove grit and reserved
3 large ripe tomatoes, peeled, sliced in ¾-inch-thick rounds, and placed on paper towels to drain
1 tbsp. red wine vinegar
2 garlic cloves, finely chopped
2 scallions, trimmed and finely chopped

In a large saucepan, bring 2 quarts of water to a boil. Blanch the eggplant slices a few at a time in the boiling water for 30 seconds. Remove them with a slotted spoon and drain them on paper towels.

Heat the butter and 1 tablespoon of the oil in a heavy-bottomed skillet over medium-high heat. Sauté the chicken breasts on one side until they brown — about four minutes. Turn them over and sprinkle them with the pepper and ⅛ teaspoon of the salt. Reduce

the heat to low and cook for two minutes. Then add the sherry, lemon juice, thyme and ¼ cup of the water in which the mushrooms soaked. Simmer, covered, until the pieces feel firm but springy to the touch — about five minutes. Remove the pan from the heat and set it aside.

Preheat the oven to 200° F. Heat 1 tablespoon of the remaining oil in a large skillet over medium-high heat. Sauté one third of the eggplant slices in a single layer until golden brown, turning them once. Repeat the process twice more with the remaining eggplant, adding ½ tablespoon of the oil to the skillet before each batch. Cover the bottom of an ovenproof serving dish with the slices.

Heat the remaining tablespoon of oil in the skillet over medium-high heat. Sprinkle the tomato slices with the remaining ⅛ teaspoon of salt and sauté them until softened — about two minutes on the first side and one to two minutes on the second, depending on the ripeness of the tomatoes.

Arrange the tomatoes on top of the eggplant. Remove the chicken pieces from their liquid and layer them on top. Put the dish in the oven to keep warm while you make the sauce.

Bring the liquid in the heavy-bottomed skillet to a simmer over medium heat, then add the mushrooms and the remaining mushroom liquid along with the vinegar, garlic and half of the chopped scallions. Simmer the mixture over low heat until it is reduced by half — about 10 minutes. Spoon this sauce over the chicken, then sprinkle with the remaining chopped scallions and serve at once.

SUGGESTED ACCOMPANIMENT: *Bibb lettuce salad.*

Chicken Paprika with Yogurt

Serves 4
Working time: about 45 minutes
Total time: about 1 hour

Calories **473**
Protein **46g.**
Cholesterol **143mg.**
Total fat **26g.**
Saturated fat **9g.**
Sodium **328mg.**

one 3 lb. chicken, cut into serving pieces, the legs and breast halves skinned
2 tbsp. safflower oil
¼ tsp. salt
1½ cups finely chopped onions
1 garlic clove, finely chopped
1 cup unsalted chicken stock
2 tbsp. paprika, preferably Hungarian
¾ cup plain low-fat yogurt
¾ cup sour cream

In a large, heavy-bottomed skillet, heat the oil over medium-high heat. Add as many chicken pieces as will fit without crowding, and sauté them on one side until brown — about four minutes. Turn the pieces, sprinkle them with the salt, and sauté until the second sides brown — three to four minutes more. Transfer the chicken to a plate. Repeat with the remaining pieces.

Reduce the heat to medium low and add the onions and garlic to the oil remaining in the skillet. Cook, stirring occasionally, until the onions turn translucent — about 10 minutes. Stir in the chicken stock and the paprika, and bring the liquid to a simmer.

Return all of the chicken pieces to the pan, reduce the heat to low, and cover. Simmer until the juices run clear when a thigh is pierced with the tip of a sharp knife — about 25 minutes. Transfer the chicken to a heated platter and cover with foil to keep warm.

Skim any fat from the liquid in the skillet. Bring the liquid to a boil over medium-high heat and reduce the stock to about ½ cup — three to four minutes. In a small bowl, whisk together the yogurt and sour cream. Stir in a little of the cooking liquid, then reduce the heat to low and whisk the yogurt mixture into the pan. Cook for one minute, then pour the sauce over the chicken and serve immediately.

SUGGESTED ACCOMPANIMENTS: *egg noodles; green peas.*

Braised Chicken with Plums and Lemons

Serves 4
Working time: about 20 minutes
Total time: about 45 minutes

Calories **261**
Protein **28g.**
Cholesterol **88mg.**
Total fat **11g.**
Saturated fat **5g.**
Sodium **171mg.**

4 chicken breast halves, skinned and boned (about 1 lb.)
2 cups unsalted chicken stock
4 red plums, blanched in the stock for one minute, peeled (skins reserved), cut in half and pits removed
2 tsp. sugar
2 tbsp. unsalted butter
⅛ tsp. salt
freshly ground black pepper
2 tbsp. chopped shallots
8 paper-thin lemon slices

In a saucepan over medium heat, cook the plum skins in the chicken stock until the liquid is reduced to ½ cup. Strain the stock and return it to the pan. Reduce the heat to low, and add the plum halves and sugar. Sim-mer the mixture for one minute, then remove it from the stove and set aside. Preheat the oven to 375° F.

In a heavy-bottomed ovenproof skillet over medium heat, melt the butter. Lay the breasts in the skillet and sauté them lightly on one side for about two minutes. Turn them over, salt and pepper the cooked side, and add the shallots. Place the plum halves cut side down between the breasts. Pour the stock into the skillet and arrange two lemon slices on each breast.

Put the uncovered skillet in the oven. Cook until the chicken feels firm but springy to the touch — about 10 minutes. Remove the skillet from the oven and lift out the plums and breasts with a slotted spoon. Place them on a warmed platter and return the lemon slices to the sauce. Cover the chicken and plums with foil to keep them warm. Simmer the sauce over medium-high heat until it is reduced to about ¼ cup — five to seven min-utes. Put the lemon slices back on top of the breasts and arrange the plums around them. Pour the sauce over all and serve.

SUGGESTED ACCOMPANIMENT: *mashed rutabaga and potatoes.*

Chicken with Orange and Onion

Serves 8
Working time: about 30 minutes
Total time: about 1 hour and 15 minutes

Calories **368**
Protein **42g.**
Cholesterol **125mg.**
Total fat **14g.**
Saturated fat **3g.**
Sodium **257mg.**

two 3 lb. chickens, wings removed, quartered and skinned
2 tbsp. flour
½ tsp. salt
freshly ground black pepper
2 tbsp. safflower oil
zest of 1 orange, julienned
3 onions, thinly sliced
2 tsp. fresh thyme, or ½ tsp. dried thyme leaves
juice of 4 oranges (about 1¾ cup)
2 tbsp. fresh lemon juice
1 tbsp. honey
¾ cup dry white wine

Dust the chicken pieces with the flour. Sprinkle them with ¼ teaspoon of the salt and some of the pepper.

In a large, heavy-bottomed skillet, heat the oil over medium-high heat and sauté the chicken in several batches until golden brown — about five minutes on each side. Transfer the pieces to a 9-by-13-inch baking dish and scatter the orange zest over them.

Preheat the oven to 350° F. Over medium-low heat, cook the onions in the oil in the pan, stirring occasionally, until they are translucent — about 10 minutes. Stir in the thyme and the remaining ¼ teaspoon of salt and spread the mixture over the chicken pieces.

Pour the orange and lemon juice, honey and wine into the skillet. Bring the liquid to a boil and reduce it to about 1 cup. Pour the liquid over the chicken. Cook the pieces uncovered in the oven, basting once with the liquid, until the juices run clear when a thigh is pierced with the tip of a sharp knife — about 35 minutes.

SUGGESTED ACCOMPANIMENTS: *new potatoes cooked in their jackets; steamed celery.*

Chicken Legs Stewed with Prunes

Serves 4
Working time: about 40 minutes
Total time: about 3 hours and 45 minutes

Calories **500**
Protein **30g.**
Cholesterol **98mg.**
Total fat **12g.**
Saturated fat **4g.**
Sodium **263mg.**

4 large chicken legs, skinned
1 cup brandy
20 pitted prunes (about ⅓ lb.)
1 tbsp. unsalted butter
¼ tsp. salt
freshly ground black pepper
1 large onion, cut in half and thinly sliced
1 large carrot, cut diagonally into ¼-inch slices
4 garlic cloves, finely chopped
1 tsp. dry mustard
1 tsp. fresh thyme, or ¼ tsp. dried thyme leaves
1¾ cup unsalted chicken stock
10 parsley stems, tied in a bunch with butcher's twine
3 tbsp. fresh lemon juice
1 tbsp. chopped fresh parsley

Pour the brandy over the prunes and marinate them for at least two hours at room temperature or overnight in the refrigerator.

Heat the butter in a large, heavy-bottomed skillet over medium-high heat. Lightly brown the chicken legs for about five minutes on each side. Sprinkle the salt and pepper over the legs and transfer them to a large, heavy-bottomed casserole, and set them aside. In the skillet used to brown the legs, combine the onion, carrot, garlic, mustard and thyme, and reduce the heat to medium. Sauté, stirring frequently, until the onion is translucent — five to seven minutes.

Preheat the oven to 325° F.

Add the prunes, brandy and stock to the onion-and-carrot mixture. Let the liquid come to a simmer and continue cooking for three minutes, then empty the skillet into the casserole; the mixture should nearly cover the legs. Drop in the bunch of parsley stems.

Cover the casserole and cook in the oven for one hour. Reduce the oven temperature to 200° F. Transfer the legs to a serving platter and cover them with foil. Open the oven door to partially vent the heat, and put the platter inside. Add the lemon juice to the sauce, remove the bunch of parsley and reduce the liquid by half over medium heat — 15 to 20 minutes. Pour the sauce over the chicken legs and serve immediately, garnished with the chopped parsley.

SUGGESTED ACCOMPANIMENT: *steamed cauliflower.*

Lemon-Mustard Chicken with Root Vegetables

Serves 6
Working time: about 20 minutes
Total time: about 45 minutes

Calories **263**
Protein **29g.**
Cholesterol **80mg.**
Total fat **9g.**
Saturated fat **3g.**
Sodium **261mg.**

6 large chicken breast halves, skinned, fat removed
1 tbsp. safflower oil
2 tbsp. unsalted butter
1 onion, cut into 12 pieces
1 garlic clove, finely chopped
½ cup dry sherry
¼ tsp. salt
freshly ground black pepper
2 tbsp. fresh lemon juice
2 tbsp. Dijon mustard
2 cups unsalted chicken stock
2 carrots, cut into ½-inch rounds
2 parsnips, cut into ½-inch rounds
1 small rutabaga, or 2 medium white turnips, peeled and cut into ½-inch cubes
zest of 1 lemon, grated
¼ cup chopped parsley

Heat the oil and butter in a large, heavy-bottomed skillet or casserole over medium-high heat. Sauté the chicken, bone side up, until the pieces turn golden — about four minutes. Remove the chicken and set it aside. Add the onion pieces to the pan, and sauté for two minutes. Add the garlic and sauté for about 15 seconds. Pour off the fat. Add the sherry to deglaze the pan, and stir. Lower the heat and simmer until the liquid is reduced by half — about four minutes.

Return the chicken breasts, bone side down, to the simmering mixture and sprinkle them with the salt and pepper. Stir in the lemon juice, mustard and stock; then add the carrots, parsnips and rutabaga or turnips. Bring the sauce to a boil, stirring. Reduce the heat to low, partially cover the pan, and simmer until the vegetables are tender — about 20 minutes. Arrange the chicken and vegetables in a serving dish. Pour the sauce over the chicken, and garnish with the lemon zest and parsley before serving.

SUGGESTED ACCOMPANIMENTS: *curly endive salad; pumpernickel bread.*

Sauté them in the olive oil in a large heavy-bottomed skillet over medium-high heat until they are nicely browned — about five minutes on each side. Remove the pieces and arrange them on top of the chick-peas and almonds.

In the same skillet, cook the onion over medium-low heat until translucent — about 10 minutes. Add the garlic, ginger, turmeric, cinnamon, cumin and currants, and mix well. Cook another two to three minutes. Spoon the mixture onto the chicken.

Add 1 cup of the stock and the lemon juice and bring to a simmer on top of the stove, then cover the casserole and place it in the oven. Cook until the chicken juices run clear when a thigh is pierced with the tip of a sharp knife — about 45 minutes.

Shortly before the chicken is done, bring the remaining 1½ cups of chicken stock to a boil in a saucepan and slowly pour in the couscous, stirring continuously. Remove from the heat and allow to stand five minutes, then fluff with a fork.

Spoon the couscous onto a serving platter and arrange the chicken pieces, chick-peas and almonds on top. Pour the juices over all.

SUGGESTED ACCOMPANIMENTS: *yogurt; steamed Swiss chard.*

Braised Chicken, Almonds and Chick-Peas

IN THE MOROCCAN ORIGINAL, THE SKIN IS LEFT ON. IN THIS SKINLESS VERSION, WHOLE-WHEAT FLOUR ADDS COLOR AND FLAVOR TO THE CHICKEN.

Serves 4
Working time: about 20 minutes
Total time: about 1 day

Calories **681**
Protein **51g.**
Cholesterol **105mg.**
Total fat **25g.**
Saturated fat **4g.**
Sodium **617mg.**

one 2½ lb. chicken, skinned and cut into quarters
1 cup dried chick-peas, soaked overnight in water and drained
½ cup whole toasted almonds, coarsely chopped
1 tsp. whole-wheat flour
¼ tsp. salt
¼ tsp. freshly ground black pepper
2 tbsp. virgin olive oil
1 large onion, chopped
4 garlic cloves, finely chopped
½ tsp. powdered ginger
⅛ tsp. turmeric
⅛ tsp. cinnamon
⅛ tsp. ground cumin
2 tbsp. dried currants
2½ cups unsalted chicken stock
2 tbsp. fresh lemon juice
1⅔ cups precooked couscous

Put the soaked chick-peas in a large saucepan, covering with cold water to a level 1 inch above them. Bring to a boil, then lower the heat and simmer for 60 minutes. Drain the chick-peas and place them in an oven-proof casserole with the almonds.

Preheat the oven to 350° F. Mix the flour with the salt and pepper, and dust the chicken pieces all over.

Chicken Casserole with Dried Fruits and Caramelized Onions

Serves 4
Working time: about 30 minutes
Total time: about 1 hour and 45 minutes

Calories **587**
Protein **34g.**
Cholesterol **108mg.**
Total fat **20g.**
Saturated fat **6g.**
Sodium **468mg.**

8 chicken thighs, skinned
1 tbsp. safflower oil
1 tbsp. plus ½ tsp. unsalted butter
½ tsp. salt
freshly ground black pepper
1 cup brown rice
1 small onion, chopped
2½ cups unsalted chicken stock
1 bouquet garni, made by tying together 2 sprigs fresh thyme, several parsley stems and 1 bay leaf (if fresh thyme is unavailable, tie up ½ tsp. of dried thyme leaves in a piece of cheesecloth with the other herbs)
⅓ cup dried apricots, cut in half
¼ cup golden raisins
¼ cup dried currants
1 tbsp. grainy mustard
¼ tsp. grated orange zest (optional)
1 cup pearl onions, blanched for 30 seconds and peeled, or 1 cup frozen pearl onions without sauce
⅛ tsp. sugar

In a 4-quart heavy-bottomed casserole, heat the oil and the tablespoon of the butter over medium-high heat. Cook four of the chicken thighs on one side until lightly browned — about four minutes. Turn the thighs and sprinkle them with ⅛ teaspoon of the salt and some pepper. Sauté them on the second side for three minutes more. Remove the thighs from the casserole and set them aside. Repeat the process with the remaining thighs and set them aside.

Reduce the heat to medium. Add the rice and chopped onion to the casserole and cook until the grains of rice are translucent — about five minutes. Add 1½ cups of the stock, the remaining ¼ teaspoon of salt and the bouquet garni. Bring the liquid to a boil. Lower the heat, cover the pot, and simmer for 20 minutes. Preheat the oven to 350° F.

Stir the apricots, raisins, currants, mustard and orange zest, if using, into the casserole. Return the chick-en pieces to the casserole, pressing them down into the rice. Pour the remaining cup of stock over the top. Cover and bake in the oven for 35 minutes.

Meanwhile, to caramelize the pearl onions, put them in a small skillet with the sugar and the ½ teaspoon of butter. Pour in just enough water to cover the onions. Boil rapidly until no water remains — 10 to 15 minutes. Watching the onions carefully lest they burn, shake the pan until they are evenly browned all over.

Add the caramelized onions to the casserole and bake until the rice is tender — about 15 minutes more. Remove the bouquet garni and serve the chicken from the casserole accompanied by the rice, fruit and onion.

SUGGESTED ACCOMPANIMENT: *Belgian endive salad.*

Chicken Stew with Zucchini and Tomatoes

Serves 4
Working time: about 35 minutes
Total time: about one hour

Calories **325**
Protein **32g.**
Cholesterol **66mg.**
Total fat **6g.**
Saturated fat **1g.**
Sodium **420mg.**

2½ lb. ripe tomatoes, peeled, seeded and chopped, or 28 oz. canned unsalted tomatoes, coarsely chopped, with their juice
1½ cups unsalted chicken stock
1 tsp. sugar
2 garlic cloves, finely chopped
1 tsp. dried basil
½ to ¾ tsp. chili powder
½ tsp. salt
freshly ground black pepper
2 chicken breast halves, skinned
3 oz. wide egg noodles (about 1½ cups)
2 zucchini (about 8 oz.), trimmed and cut into ½-inch-thick rounds

Put the tomatoes, stock, sugar, garlic, basil, chili powder, salt and some pepper into a large, heavy-bottomed pot over medium heat. Bring the liquid to a simmer and cook the mixture for 10 minutes.

Add the chicken breasts to the pot and poach them for 12 minutes. With a slotted spoon, remove the breasts — they will still be slightly undercooked — and set them aside.

Cook the noodles in 6 cups of boiling water with ¾ teaspoon of salt for three minutes. Drain the noodles well, then add them to the stew along with the zucchini rounds. When the chicken breasts are cool enough to handle, remove the meat from the bones. Cut the meat into ½-inch pieces and return it to the pot. Continue cooking the stew until the zucchini are tender — about five minutes more. Serve immediately.

Chicken Gumbo

Serves 6
Working time: about 35 minutes
Total time: about 1 hour and 10 minutes

Calories **295**
Protein **29g.**
Cholesterol **81mg.**
Total fat **12g.**
Saturated fat **3g.**
Sodium **315mg.**

1 tbsp. finely chopped garlic
1 tbsp. chopped fresh thyme, or ¾ tsp. dried thyme leaves
1 tsp. dry mustard
½ tsp. salt
½ tsp. paprika, preferably Hungarian
½ tsp. cracked black peppercorns
12 oz. chicken breast meat, cut crosswise into ½-inch-wide strips
12 oz. chicken thigh meat, cut into ½-inch-wide strips
juice of 1 lemon
1 tbsp. unsalted butter
1 large onion, sliced
5 celery stalks, cut lengthwise into ¼-inch strips, each strip cut into 1-inch-long bâtonnets
1½ tbsp. flour
2½ lb. ripe tomatoes, peeled, seeded and chopped, or 28 oz. canned unsalted tomatoes, drained and chopped
2 bay leaves
1 tbsp. olive oil
8 oz. okra, trimmed and cut into 1-inch lengths
2 cups unsalted chicken stock
1 sweet red pepper, seeded, deribbed and cut lengthwise into ¼-inch-wide strips
1 green pepper, seeded, deribbed and cut lengthwise into ¼-inch-wide strips

Mix the garlic with the thyme, mustard, salt, paprika and pepper. Toss the chicken strips with one third of the spice mixture and the lemon juice. Set the chicken aside to marinate at room temperature while you prepare the vegetables.

Melt the butter in a large, heavy-bottomed pot over medium high heat. Add the onion and the celery bâtonnets, and sauté them, stirring frequently, until the onions are translucent — about eight minutes. Stir in the flour and the remaining two thirds of the spice mixture; continue cooking for two minutes more. Add the tomatoes and bay leaves. Reduce the heat and simmer the mixture for 15 minutes.

Meanwhile, heat the olive oil in a large, heavy-bottomed skillet over medium-high heat. Add the okra and sauté it, stirring frequently, until the pieces are well browned — about five minutes. Set the okra aside.

Add the marinated chicken strips, the stock and peppers to the tomato mixture. Simmer the stew for 20 minutes more, stirring several times.

Before serving, stir the okra into the stew and allow it to heat through.

EDITOR'S NOTE: *Rice pilaf makes an excellent foil for gumbo.*

Cajun Chicken Wings

Serves 4
Working time: about 20 minutes
Total time: about 1 hour

Calories **334**
Protein **28g.**
Cholesterol **87g.**
Total fat **21g.**
Saturated fat **6g.**
Sodium **353mg.**

12 chicken wings, tips removed
5 bay leaves, crumbled into small bits
¾ tsp. caraway seeds
½ to ¾ tsp. cayenne pepper
¾ tsp. ground coriander
¾ tsp. ground cumin
4 garlic cloves, finely chopped
1 ½ tsp. dry mustard
2 tsp. paprika, preferably Hungarian
¾ tsp. dried thyme leaves
½ tsp. salt
2 tbsp. brandy
2 tbsp. fresh lemon or lime juice

Defat the chicken wings by cooking them in boiling water for 10 minutes. Drain, and set aside to cool. Preheat the oven to 375° F.

Using a large mortar and pestle, grind together the bay-leaf bits, caraway seeds, cayenne pepper, coriander, cumin, garlic, mustard, paprika, thyme and salt for about 10 minutes. Add the brandy and lemon or lime juice to the pulverized herbs, and stir into a thick paste.

With a pastry brush, cover both sides of each wing with the herb paste. When no more paste remains in the mortar, squeeze the last few drops from the brush. Arrange the chicken wings on a baking sheet.

Bake until the skin turns a deep brown and is quite crisp — 30 to 35 minutes.

SUGGESTED ACCOMPANIMENTS: *baked butternut squash; sautéed mushrooms.*

Chicken Wrapped in Crisp Phyllo

Serves 6
Working time: about 1 hour
Total time: about 1 day

Calories **500**
Protein **37g.**
Cholesterol **94mg.**
Total fat **27g.**
Saturated fat **7g.**
Sodium **547mg.**

6 chicken breast halves, skinned and boned (about 1½ lb.)
one 8-oz. box of phyllo dough
¾ tsp. salt
¾ tsp. freshly ground black pepper
4 tbsp. safflower oil
1 garlic clove, finely chopped
1 shallot, finely chopped
¾ lb. fresh spinach, washed and stemmed
¼ cup dry white wine
1 cup unsalted chicken stock
1 tbsp. heavy cream
2 oz. pistachio nuts, shelled, peeled and coarsely chopped (about ⅓ cup)
1 cup low-fat ricotta cheese

Defrost the frozen phyllo dough, unopened, in the refrigerator overnight; then leave it at room temperature for two hours before unwrapping it.

Slice each breast diagonally into three medallions. Sprinkle the pieces with ½ teaspoon each of the salt and pepper. Heat 1 tablespoon of the oil in a heavy-bottomed skillet over medium-high heat. Sear the chicken pieces for about 30 seconds on each side in several batches, adding as much as 2 additional tablespoons of oil as necessary between batches. Set the chicken aside on a plate.

Immediately add the garlic and shallot, and sauté them for about 30 seconds, stirring. Add the spinach, reduce the heat to low, and cover. Cook until the spinach is wilted — about two minutes. Remove the pan from the heat and take out half of the spinach mixture. Chop this finely and reserve it for the filling.

Heat the pan again over medium heat. Pour in the wine and stock, and stir to deglaze the pan. Stir in the remaining salt and pepper and the cream, and cook until the liquid is reduced by half. Purée the sauce in a blender. Pour it into a small saucepan and set it aside.

Preheat the oven to 325° F. To make the filling, combine the pistachios, ricotta and chopped spinach mixture. Gently blot the chicken medallions with paper towels to remove any excess juice. Unwrap the dough. Peel off a stack of three sheets and place them on a dry work surface. Cover the remaining sheets with a ▶

damp — not wet — paper towel to prevent them from drying out as you work.

Center a piece of chicken near an edge of the dough. Spread a thin layer of filling over the chicken, then top it with another medallion, a second layer of filling and a third chicken slice. Fold the sides of the dough over the chicken and roll it up. Place the roll seam side down in an oiled baking dish. Repeat with the remaining chicken pieces and phyllo sheets to make six rolls in all. Brush the rolls with the remaining tablespoon of oil.

Bake the rolls for 45 minutes. If additional baking is required to brown the phyllo, raise the temperature to 450° F. and keep the rolls in the oven a few minutes more. Warm the sauce and serve the rolls on top of it, as shown here, or pass it separately.

SUGGESTED ACCOMPANIMENT: *sautéed mushrooms and snow peas.*

Chicken-and-Cheese-Filled Calzones

THIS RECIPE WAS INSPIRED BY THE ITALIAN *CALZONE*, A KIND OF PIE MADE WITH PIZZA DOUGH.

Serves 4
Working time: about 1 hour
Total time: about 3 hours

Calories **626**
Protein **37g.**
Cholesterol **71mg.**
Total fat **22g.**
Saturated fat **6g.**
Sodium **589mg.**

two 6 oz. chicken breast halves, skinned, boned and cut in half vertically
1 tbsp. virgin olive oil
1 tbsp. cornmeal
Dough
2 packages active dry yeast or rapid-rise dry yeast
¼ tsp. sugar
2½ to 2¾ cups bread flour
½ tsp. salt
¼ tsp. fennel seeds, crushed
3 tbsp. virgin olive oil
Tomato and red pepper sauce
3 ripe tomatoes, peeled, seeded and chopped
1 red pepper, seeded, deribbed and chopped
1 onion, chopped
2 garlic cloves, finely chopped
¼ tsp. fennel seeds, crushed
1 tsp. fresh thyme, or ¼ tsp. dried thyme leaves
¾ tsp. chopped fresh oregano, or ¼ tsp. dried oregano
¼ tsp. salt
freshly ground black pepper
Cheese filling
¾ cup low-fat ricotta cheese
3 tbsp. freshly grated Parmesan cheese

To make the dough, pour ¼ cup of lukewarm water into a small bowl and sprinkle the yeast and sugar into it. Let stand for two to three minutes, then stir the mixture until the yeast and sugar are completely dissolved. Allow the mixture to sit in a warm place until the yeast bubbles up and the mixture has doubled in volume — three to five minutes.

Sift 2½ cups of the flour and the salt into a large bowl. Stir in the fennel seeds. Make a well in the center and pour in the yeast mixture, ¾ cup of lukewarm water and the oil. Mix the dough by hand; as soon as it can be gathered into a ball, place it on a floured board and add as much as needed of the additional ¼ cup flour if the dough is too soft and sticky. Knead until smooth and elastic — about 10 minutes.

To make the dough in a food processor, put the flour, salt and fennel seeds into the bowl of the processor and pulse twice to mix. Combine the yeast mixture with ¾ cup of lukewarm water and the oil. With the motor running, pour in the mixture as fast as the flour will absorb it; process until a ball of dough forms. Then process until the dough comes away from the sides of the bowl — about 40 seconds more.

Put the dough in a clean bowl and cover it with a towel. Set the bowl in a warm, draft-free place until the dough has doubled in size — about 1½ hours, or 45 minutes if you are using rapid-rise yeast.

To make the sauce, place the tomatoes, red pepper, onion, garlic, fennel seeds, thyme, oregano, salt and pepper in a large, heavy-bottomed saucepan. Simmer the mixture over medium heat, stirring frequently, until the liquid is absorbed — about 30 minutes. Remove from the heat and set aside.

Meanwhile, in a small bowl, mix the ricotta and Parmesan cheeses. Set aside. Preheat the oven to 475° F.

In a large, heavy-bottomed skillet, heat the oil over medium-high heat. Place the breasts in the skillet and sauté them for about two minutes on one side; turn and cook them on the other side — about two minutes more. (The meat should not be cooked through.) Remove the chicken from the heat and set aside.

Punch down the dough. Cut it into four equal pieces. Flatten each piece with the palm of the hand to produce a circle about 1 inch thick. Carefully stretch the dough by holding each round by its edge and rotating it with the fingers to obtain circles 6 inches in diameter. Alternatively, the dough can be stretched by patting it into a circle with the fingertips.

To assemble the calzones, place a chicken piece on each round of dough, a little off-center. Spread one quarter of the sauce on each breast and top with one quarter of the cheese filling. Moisten the inside edges of the dough with water and bring them up over the cheese to form a seal, and overlap the dough by ½ inch. Crimp the dough to close the calzones.

Place a baking sheet in the preheated oven for two minutes. Remove the pan from the oven and sprinkle the cornmeal on the areas on which the calzones will bake. Place the calzones on the cornmeal and brush the dough with the excess oil from the skillet. Bake until golden — 15 to 20 minutes.

SUGGESTED ACCOMPANIMENT: *spinach salad.*

Chicken on a Bed of Savoy Cabbage

Serves 8
Working time: about 45 minutes
Total time: about 1 hour

Calories **397**
Protein **46g.**
Cholesterol **128mg.**
Total fat **16g.**
Saturated fat **4g.**
Sodium **366mg.**

two 3 lb. chickens, cut into serving pieces, all but the wings skinned
1 head Savoy cabbage (3 to 4 lb.)
⅓ cup whole-wheat flour
¼ tsp. cinnamon
1½ tbsp. safflower oil
½ tsp. salt
1 tbsp. virgin olive oil
3 ripe tomatoes, peeled, seeded and chopped
1 garlic clove, finely chopped
Curry sauce
2 carrots, thinly sliced
1½ cups plain low-fat yogurt
1 to 3 tsp. curry powder
1 tbsp. virgin olive oil
½ tsp. cinnamon
1 tbsp. honey
¼ tsp. salt

In order for its flavors to meld, make the sauce first. Cook the carrots in 1 cup of water in a small covered saucepan over medium heat until they are soft — about eight minutes. Drain the carrots and transfer them to a food processor or blender. Add 2 or 3 tablespoons of the yogurt and purée the mixture, scraping the sides down once. Add the remaining yogurt, 1 teaspoon of the curry powder, the olive oil, cinnamon, honey and salt, and purée again. Taste the sauce and blend in up to 2 teaspoons additional curry if desired. Transfer the sauce to a serving vessel and set it aside where it will stay lukewarm.

Discard any brown or wilted outer leaves of the cabbage. Slice the head into quarters, then cut out the core. Cut each quarter crosswise into three pieces, then separate the leaves and set them aside.

Preheat the oven to 400° F. Mix the flour with the cinnamon and coat the chicken pieces with this mixture. Heat 1 tablespoon of the safflower oil in a large, heavy-bottomed skillet over medium-high heat. Sauté half of the pieces on one side until brown — four to five minutes. Turn the pieces over and sprinkle them with ⅛ teaspoon of the salt. Sauté the chicken on the second side until brown — about four minutes more. Transfer the pieces to an ovenproof serving dish with their smooth sides facing up. Add the remaining ½ tablespoon of safflower oil to the skillet and sauté the remaining chicken pieces the same way. Arrange the pieces smooth sides up in the dish. Reserve the skillet for the tomatoes and cabbage.

Bake the chicken pieces until the juices run clear when a thigh is pierced with the tip of a sharp knife — 25 to 30 minutes.

While the chicken is baking, cook the cabbage. Pour enough water into a large pot to cover the bottom by about ½ inch. Set a vegetable steamer in the pot and put the cabbage in the steamer. Cover the pot tightly and bring the water to a boil. Steam the cabbage, uncovering it once to stir it, until it is wilted — five to seven minutes. Drain the cabbage well.

Heat the olive oil in the skillet over medium heat. Add the tomatoes and garlic, and cook for one minute. Stir in the cabbage and the remaining ¼ teaspoon of salt; toss well to heat the vegetables through. Set the skillet aside.

When the chicken is cooked, remove the pieces, leaving the juices in the serving dish. Arrange the cabbage and tomatoes in the bottom of the dish, then place the chicken on top. Serve the sauce separately.

SUGGESTED ACCOMPANIMENT: *steamed red potatoes with freshly cut chives.*

Lime-and-Mint Chicken

Serves 6
Working time: about 15 minutes
Total time: about 4 hours and 15 minutes

Calories **248**
Protein **27g.**
Cholesterol **98mg.**
Total fat **12g.**
Saturated fat **3g.**
Sodium **183mg.**

12 chicken thighs, skinned
½ tsp. sugar
Lime marinade
1 cup fresh lime juice
⅓ cup dry white wine
¾ cup chopped fresh mint leaves, plus 6 whole mint sprigs reserved for garnish
1½ tsp. cumin seeds, crushed, or ¾ tsp. ground cumin
3 scallions, thinly sliced
1 large dried red chili, seeded and thinly sliced (see caution, page 125), or ½ to ¾ tsp. crushed red pepper
¼ tsp. salt

Combine the marinade ingredients in a shallow bowl or dish large enough to hold the chicken thighs. Put the thighs in the bowl and coat them with the marinade. Cover the bowl with a lid or plastic wrap and refrigerate it for four to six hours.

Preheat the broiler. Remove the chicken from the marinade and arrange the pieces in a broiler pan. Strain the marinade into a small bowl and reserve both the strained liquid and the drained mint mixture. Broil the chicken 4 to 6 inches below the heat source until it is browned — six to eight minutes. Remove the pan from the oven and turn the pieces over. Spoon some of the mint mixture over each thigh. Broil the thighs until the juices run clear when a piece is pierced with the tip of a sharp knife — six to eight minutes more.

While the chicken is broiling on the second side, stir the sugar into the strained marinade. Put the liquid in a small saucepan and boil it over high heat for two minutes, stirring frequently, to produce a light sauce.

To serve, spoon some of the sauce over each thigh and garnish with the mint sprigs.

SUGGESTED ACCOMPANIMENTS: *baked sweet potatoes; steamed cauliflower.*

Greek-Style Chicken and Rice Casserole

Serves 8
Working time: about 30 minutes
Total time: about 1 hour

Calories **276**
Protein **17g.**
Cholesterol **52mg.**
Total fat **11g.**
Saturated fat **3g.**
Sodium **244mg.**

2 tbsp. safflower oil
8 chicken thighs, skinned
1 cup rice
1 onion, chopped
4 garlic cloves, finely chopped
1 cup unsalted chicken stock
28 oz. canned unsalted whole tomatoes
3 tbsp. chopped fresh oregano, or 2 tsp. dried oregano
1 tbsp. fresh thyme, or 1 tsp. dried thyme leaves
12 oil-cured olives, pitted and quartered, or 12 pitted black olives, coarsely chopped
1 oz. feta cheese, rinsed and crumbled (about ¼ cup)

Heat the oil in a large, heavy-bottomed casserole over medium-high heat. Add four of the thighs and cook them until they are lightly browned — about four minutes on each side. Remove the first four thighs and brown the other four. Set all the thighs aside.

Reduce the heat to medium and add the rice, onion, garlic and ¼ cup of the stock. Cook the mixture, stirring constantly, until the onion is translucent — about four minutes. Add the remaining ¾ cup of stock, the tomatoes, the oregano and the thyme. Push the thighs down into the rice mixture. Bring the liquid to a boil, reduce the heat, and simmer the chicken, tightly covered, until the rice is tender — 20 to 30 minutes.

Stir the olives into the chicken and rice, and serve the casserole with the feta cheese on top.

Roast Capon with Sage Corn Bread Stuffing

Serves 8
Working time: about 45 minutes
Total time: about 2 hours and 15 minutes

Calories **444**
Protein **42g.**
Cholesterol **110mg.**
Total fat **21g.**
Saturated fat **5g.**
Sodium **345mg.**

one 9 to 10 lb. capon, rinsed and patted dry
1 tbsp. unsalted butter
4 large onions, thinly sliced
1 tbsp. safflower oil
½ tsp. salt
1½ oz. boiled ham, cut into small cubes
½ cup unsalted chicken stock
Sage corn bread
1 cup yellow cornmeal
1 cup flour
1 tbsp. baking powder
¼ tsp. salt
¼ tsp. freshly ground black pepper
1 cup buttermilk
1 egg, beaten
2 tbsp. safflower oil
2 tbsp. chopped fresh sage, or 1½ tsp. dried sage

Preheat the oven to 425° F.

To prepare the corn bread, combine the cornmeal, flour, baking powder, salt and pepper. Stir in the buttermilk, egg, oil and sage. Pour the batter into a lightly oiled 8-by-8-inch baking pan and bake until golden brown — 20 to 25 minutes. Reduce the oven temperature to 375° F.

Meanwhile, melt the butter in a heavy-bottomed saucepan over medium-low heat. Add the onions and cook for 20 minutes, stirring occasionally. Add the tablespoon of oil and cook until the onions are caramelized — about 40 minutes more. Scrape the bottom often to avoid sticking and burning.

While the onions are cooking, truss the capon. Place a metal steamer or rack in the bottom of a large stockpot, and pour in enough water to cover the bottom of the pot to a depth of about 1 inch. Bring the water to a boil, then place the capon in the pot and cover it tightly. Steam for 20 minutes over high heat. Remove the capon, sprinkle its skin immediately with ¼ teaspoon of the salt, and allow the bird to stand while you prepare the stuffing.

Crumble the corn bread into a bowl and stir in the caramelized onions, ham and chicken stock. Pour off any juices from the cavity of the bird and sprinkle the inside with the remaining ¼ teaspoon of salt. Fill the capon loosely with the stuffing, and cover the opening with a small piece of aluminum foil. Place any excess stuffing in a small ovenproof dish, moisten it with a little chicken stock, cover with foil and bake along with the capon during the last 20 minutes of roasting time. Put the bird breast side up on a rack in a roasting pan. Roast the capon until the skin is crisp and golden and the juices run clear when a thigh is pierced with the tip of a sharp knife — about one hour and 10 minutes.

SUGGESTED ACCOMPANIMENTS: *sautéed apples; mashed rutabaga.*

EDITOR'S NOTE: *The process of steaming followed by roasting helps to defat the capon considerably, resulting in a crisp skin and fewer calories.*

Roast Chicken with Apples, Turnips and Garlic

Serves 4
Working time: about 30 minutes
Total time: about 1 hour and 30 minutes

Calories **378**
Protein **39g.**
Cholesterol **103mg.**
Total fat **17g.**
Saturated fat **5g.**
Sodium **197mg.**

one 3 lb. chicken
1 tbsp. paprika, preferably Hungarian
½ tsp. freshly ground black pepper
⅛ tsp. salt
1 tsp. unsalted butter
2 or 3 Golden Delicious apples, peeled, cored and cut into eighths
3 small white turnips, peeled, quartered and thinly sliced
6 garlic cloves, peeled
juice of half a lemon

Preheat the oven to 325° F. Mix the paprika, pepper and salt, and rub the chicken inside and out with them.

Butter a roasting pan and put the chicken in it. Arrange the apples, turnips and garlic around the bird. Trickle the lemon juice over the top of the apples and turnips. Roast the chicken until it is golden brown all over and a leg moves easily when wiggled up and down — 65 to 75 minutes. Baste the bird with the pan juices two or three times during the cooking.

When the chicken is done, skim the fat from the pan and mash the apples, turnips and garlic together with the pan juices. Serve in a separate bowl.

SUGGESTED ACCOMPANIMENT: *sugar-snap peas.*

Spatchcocked Chicken with Basil-Yogurt Sauce

THE WORD "SPATCHCOCK" COMES FROM THE IRISH TERM "DISPATCH COCK," A DISH FOR A SUDDEN OCCASION. HERE IT REFERS TO A WHOLE CHICKEN THAT IS SPLIT OPEN AND FLATTENED FOR EVEN COOKING.

Serves 4
Working time: about 25 minutes
Total time: about 1 hour and 15 minutes

Calories **392**
Protein **45g.**
Cholesterol **91mg.**
Total fat **20g.**
Saturated fat **6g.**
Sodium **367mg.**

one 3 lb. chicken, rinsed and patted dry
1 cup plain low-fat yogurt
1 cup fresh basil leaves, chopped, or 2 cups fresh spinach leaves, lightly steamed and squeezed dry
3 scallions, chopped
2 garlic cloves, finely chopped
1 tbsp. virgin olive oil
⅓ cup freshly grated Parmesan or Romano cheese
⅛ tsp. salt
freshly ground black pepper

Prepare the bird for roasting as demonstrated in the steps below. Preheat the oven to 400° F. Cover the bottom of a large pot with 1 inch of water. Set a steamer or rack in the pot, and bring the water to a boil. Place the chicken skin side up on the steamer. Cover tightly and steam the chicken for 15 minutes over high heat.

While the chicken is steaming, make the sauce. Combine the yogurt, basil or spinach, scallions, garlic, oil and half of the Parmesan or Romano cheese in a food processor or blender. Process until smooth, then transfer the sauce to a sauceboat and set it aside at room temperature.

Set the steamed chicken on a rack in a roasting pan.

Sprinkle it with the salt and some pepper. Roast until the skin is a crispy, light brown — about 25 minutes.

Remove the bird from the oven and sprinkle the remaining cheese over it. Return the chicken to the oven and roast until the cheese is golden brown — eight to 10 minutes more.

Allow the chicken to stand 10 minutes, then carve it into serving pieces. Pass the sauce separately.

SUGGESTED ACCOMPANIMENTS: *stewed tomatoes; brown rice.*

EDITOR'S NOTE: *The process of steaming followed by roasting helps to defat the chicken considerably, resulting in a crisp skin and fewer calories.*

Spatchcocking a Chicken

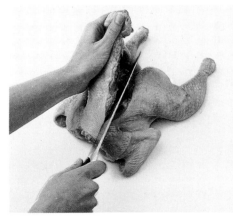

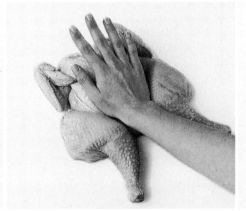

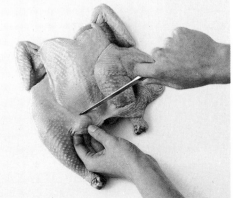

1 *REMOVING THE BACKBONE. Place a whole chicken breast side down on a work surface. With a heavy chef's knife, cut down along one side of the backbone from the tail toward the neck, using a sawing motion to cut through the rib cage. Repeat this process on the other side and pull the backbone free.*

2 *FLATTENING THE BIRD. Turn the bird breast side up, with its drumsticks pointed toward you. Then, with one forceful motion, press the heel of your hand down on the breastbone to flatten out the breast. Tuck the wing tips behind the chicken's shoulders.*

3 *SECURING THE DRUMSTICKS. To keep the drumsticks from spreading out as the bird cooks, tuck them into a flap of skin: First pull the skin around the tail cavity taut, then cut a slit about ¾ inch long between a thigh and the tapered end of the breast. Thread the end of the drumstick through the slit. Repeat the procedure to secure the second leg.*

Oven-Fried Cinnamon Chicken

Serves 4
Working time: about 15 minutes
Total time: about 1 hour

Calories **424**
Protein **47g.**
Cholesterol **125mg.**
Total fat **17g.**
Saturated fat **3g.**
Sodium **563mg.**

one 3 lb. chicken, cut into four serving pieces and skinned
½ tsp. salt
½ tsp. freshly ground white pepper
¼ cup flour
¼ tsp. turmeric
1 tsp. cinnamon
3 egg whites
1 cup fresh bread crumbs
2 tbsp. safflower oil

Preheat the oven to 325° F. Mix the salt, pepper and flour, and spread on a plate. In a small bowl, whisk the turmeric and cinnamon into the egg whites. Dredge the chicken pieces in the flour, then dip them in the egg whites and coat them with the bread crumbs.

In a heavy-bottomed ovenproof skillet large enough to hold the chicken pieces in a single layer, heat the oil over medium heat. Lay the pieces bone side up in the skillet and brown them lightly on one side — about two minutes. Turn the pieces over, put the skillet in the oven, and bake for 30 minutes.

Remove the skillet and increase the oven temperature to 450° F. Wait about five minutes, then place the skillet in the oven and allow the coating to crisp for four or five minutes, taking care not to burn it.

SUGGESTED ACCOMPANIMENTS: *sautéed cherry tomatoes; green beans with tarragon.*

Dry-Martini Cornish Hens

Serves 4
Working time: about 30 minutes
Total time: 1 to 2 days

Calories **299**
Protein **28g.**
Cholesterol **88mg.**
Total fat **14g.**
Saturated fat **4g.**
Sodium **360mg.**

four 1 lb. Cornish hens, giblets reserved for another use, cavities washed and patted dry
2 tbsp. juniper berries, crushed
zest of 2 lemons, cut into ¼-inch-wide strips
2 cups unsalted chicken stock
¾ cup gin
¼ cup dry vermouth
½ tsp. salt
freshly ground black pepper

To make the marinade, combine the juniper berries, lemon zest, 1½ cups of the stock, ½ cup of the gin, the vermouth, salt and pepper in a small bowl. Place the hens in a deep dish that holds them snugly, and pour the marinade over them. Swirl some of the marinade into the cavity of each bird. Cover the dish with a lid or plastic wrap, and refrigerate it for 24 to 48 hours. Turn the hens from time to time as they marinate.

Preheat the oven to 375° F. Remove the birds from the marinade and put 1 tablespoon of the marinade liquid, a few of the crushed juniper berries and some of the lemon zest in the cavity of each bird. Discard the remaining marinade. Tie each pair of legs together with butcher's twine. Arrange the hens breast side up on the rack of a roasting pan so that they do not touch. Roast them until they are golden brown — 40 to 45 minutes. Pour the juices, juniper berries and lemon zest from the cavity of each hen into the roasting pan, and set the birds on a warmed serving platter.

To make the sauce, remove the rack and place the roasting pan over medium-high heat. Add the remaining ½ cup of stock and the remaining ¼ cup of gin. Cook the sauce, stirring with a wooden spoon to dislodge any brown bits, until the liquid is reduced by about half and has thickened — seven to 10 minutes. Strain the sauce and serve it with the hens. Garnish the birds, if you like, with twists of freshly cut lemon peel.

SUGGESTED ACCOMPANIMENTS: *steamed baby carrots; red potatoes.*

Cornish Hens with Pineapple and Mint

Serves 4
Working time: about 1 hour
Total time: about 1 hour and 30 minutes

Calories **424**
Protein **27g.**
Cholesterol **52mg.**
Total fat **11g.**
Saturated fat **4g.**
Sodium **331mg.**

two 1½ lb. Cornish hens, neck, gizzard and heart reserved
1 cup bulgur, rinsed and drained
1 pineapple, peeled and cored
2 navel oranges, the zest of one grated and reserved for the stuffing
2 scallions, sliced into thin rounds
½ cup chopped fresh mint, a few whole sprigs reserved for garnish
½ tsp. salt
freshly ground black pepper
1 tbsp. unsalted butter
8 garlic cloves, unpeeled
¼ cup dry white wine

Put the bulgur in a small bowl and add enough boiling water to cover. Let the bulgur soak for 10 minutes. Empty the bowl into a sieve to drain the bulgur. Cut a few slices from the pineapple and reserve them for use as a garnish. Coarsely chop the rest of the pineapple in a food processor or by hand. Cook the chopped pineapple in a skillet over medium-low heat until the juices have evaporated — 20 to 25 minutes.

Meanwhile, prepare each hen: Starting at the neck, use your fingers to separate the skin from either side of the breast. Then, with a knife, cut through the membrane attaching the skin to the breast, taking care not to puncture the skin. Remove and discard any bits of fat. Preheat the oven to 450° F.

To prepare the stuffing, first segment one of the oranges: Cut away the peel with a knife, cutting deep enough to remove the bitter white pith and expose the flesh. Then hold the orange over a bowl to catch its juice as you slice down to the core on either side of each segment. Dislodge the segments and let them fall into the bowl as you proceed. Cut the second orange in half and squeeze its juice into the bowl. Remove the orange segments from the juice and cut them into small pieces; reserve the juice for the sauce. Combine the orange pieces, the bulgur and the chopped pineapple in a mixing bowl. Mix in the scallions, mint, salt, some pepper and the orange zest.

Gently push about ½ cup of the stuffing under the skin of each bird, molding the skin into a smooth, round shape. Tuck the neck flap under each bird. Reserve the extra stuffing in a small ovenproof bowl or baking dish, and cover it with foil.

Melt the butter in a small pan over medium-low heat. Place the hens on an oiled rack in a roasting pan.

Distribute the neck, gizzard, heart and garlic cloves in the bottom of the pan. Brush the birds with some of the butter and roast them in the upper third of the oven for 15 minutes. Baste them with the remaining butter and any accumulated pan juices, and return them to the oven along with the reserved stuffing. Roast until the hens are golden brown and the juices run clear when a thigh is pierced with the tip of a sharp knife — 20 to 25 minutes more.

Remove the birds from the oven and turn it off, leaving the stuffing inside while you prepare the sauce. Remove the rack, garlic and giblets from the pan, and skim off the fat. Reserve the giblets for later use in the stockpot. Set the pan over medium heat and stir in the orange juice and wine to deglaze it. Squeeze the garlic cloves from their skins and add them to the sauce. Simmer and stir for one minute. Pour the sauce through a sieve set over a small bowl. Press the soft garlic through the sieve with a wooden spoon and stir the sauce well.

Cut each bird in half lengthwise, and set the halves on a platter or on individual plates. Arrange the warm stuffing around each bird and spoon the sauce over the top. Garnish with the whole mint sprigs and raw pineapple, and serve hot.

SUGGESTED ACCOMPANIMENT: *steamed kale.*

Roast Breast of Turkey with Fruit Stuffing

Serves 8
Working time: about 30 minutes
Total time: about 1 hour

Calories **255**
Protein **23g.**
Cholesterol **59mg.**
Total fat **7g.**
Saturated fat **3g.**
Sodium **92mg.**

1¾ to 2 lb. boneless turkey breast half, with skin
⅛ tsp. salt
1 tbsp. safflower oil
chopped fresh sage or parsley for garnish
Fruit stuffing
2 tbsp. unsalted butter
⅓ cup finely chopped onion
1 large tart green apple, peeled, cored and diced
1 tsp. sugar
1 tsp. chopped fresh sage, or ¼ tsp. dried sage
¼ tsp. ground cloves
4 oz. dried apricots, cut into small pieces

⅓ cup seedless raisins
3 tbsp. unsalted turkey or chicken stock
¼ cup apple cider
Cider sauce
1 tbsp. finely chopped onion
2 tbsp. dry white wine
1 cup apple cider
½ cup unsalted turkey or chicken stock
1 tsp. red wine vinegar

To make the stuffing, melt the butter in a heavy-bottomed saucepan over medium heat. Sauté the onion until it is translucent — about 10 minutes. Add the apple and sugar and continue cooking, stirring occasionally, until the apple is tender but not mushy — about five minutes. Stir in the sage, cloves, apricots, raisins, stock and apple cider. Reduce the heat and cover the pan tightly. Cook until all of the liquid is absorbed — about five minutes — stirring once. Trans-

fer to a bowl and allow to cool. (The stuffing can be prepared a day ahead and refrigerated.)

Preheat the oven to 350° F. Put the turkey, skin side down, on a flat surface. Using a sharp knife, cut a flap in the breast by slicing from the long, thin side toward the thicker side, being careful not to cut all the way through. Open the flap and place the turkey between two pieces of plastic wrap. Pound lightly to flatten to an even thickness of about ½ inch. Sprinkle the turkey with the salt and mound the stuffing in the center. Wrap the flap around the stuffing and roll the breast snugly to form a cylinder with the skin on the outside. Tuck in the ends and tie securely with butcher's twine.

Heat the oil in a roasting pan and brown the skin side of the roll for three to four minutes. Turn the turkey skin side up and put the pan in the oven. Roast for 20 to 25 minutes, or until the juices run clear when the meat is pierced with the tip of a sharp knife. Remove the turkey from the pan and keep warm.

To make the sauce, pour off any fat in the pan and discard. Add the onion and wine and cook over medium-high heat, stirring to deglaze the pan. Add the cider, stock and vinegar and continue cooking until the sauce is reduced by a quarter — about 10 minutes.

To serve, remove the butcher's twine and cut the turkey into ¾-inch slices. Arrange on a heated serving platter and garnish with fresh sage leaves or parsley. Pass the sauce separately.

SUGGESTED ACCOMPANIMENT: *green peas and pearl onions.*

Roast Gingered Turkey Breast

Serves 6
Working time: about 10 minutes
Total time: about 1 day

Calories **162**	
Protein **26g.**	
Cholesterol **59mg.**	
Total fat **5g.**	
Saturated fat **1g.**	
Sodium **164mg.**	

1 turkey breast half (about 1½ lb.), skinned and boned
2 tsp. safflower oil
Ginger marinade
3 garlic cloves, finely chopped
¾ tsp. ground cinnamon
2 tbsp. peeled and grated fresh ginger
¼ cup unsalted turkey or chicken stock
1 tsp. dark sesame oil
1 tbsp. low-sodium soy sauce

To make the marinade, combine the garlic, cinnamon, ginger, stock, sesame oil and soy sauce in a shallow bowl just large enough to hold the turkey breast. Using a knife with a sharp point, poke several ½-inch-deep slits in the thick part of the meat to allow the marinade to penetrate. Put the turkey in the bowl with the marinade and turn it to coat it. Cover and refrigerate for eight to 24 hours, turning occasionally.

Preheat the oven to 350° F. Remove the turkey from the marinade, scraping any clinging garlic and ginger back into the bowl. Reserve the marinade and allow the turkey to come to room temperature. Heat the safflower oil in a heavy-bottomed ovenproof skillet over medium-high heat. Sauté the turkey until golden on one side — about four minutes — and turn. Use a pastry brush to baste with the accumulated juices and continue cooking for one minute. Put the skillet in the oven and roast the turkey until it feels firm but springy to the touch — 15 to 20 minutes — basting once with the reserved marinade. Let the turkey rest for at least five minutes before slicing. Serve hot or cold.

SUGGESTED ACCOMPANIMENTS: *rice salad with currants and toasted pine nuts; sautéed carrots.*

Turkey Cutlets with Citrus

Serves 4
Working time: about 30 minutes
Total time: about 30 minutes

Calories **264**
Protein **27g.**
Cholesterol **66mg.**
Total fat **11g.**
Saturated fat **3g.**
Sodium **127mg.**

eight ¼-inch-thick turkey cutlets (about 1 lb.), pounded to ⅛-inch thickness
1 large navel orange
1 lime
flour for dredging
1½ tbsp. virgin olive oil
¼ cup dry white wine
¼ cup unsalted turkey or chicken stock
1 tbsp. finely chopped shallots, or 2 scallions, chopped
1 tsp. finely chopped fresh thyme, or ¼ tsp. dried thyme leaves
1 tsp. finely chopped fresh sage, or ¼ tsp. dried sage
½ tsp. sugar
⅛ tsp. salt
freshly ground black pepper
1 tbsp. unsalted butter
2 tbsp. coarsely chopped parsley

Use a knife to cut the peel from the orange and lime, taking care to remove all of the bitter white pith. Cut the fruit into ¼-inch cubes and set aside.

Make ⅛-inch slits along the cutlets' edges at 1- to 2-inch intervals to prevent the turkey from curling while cooking. Dredge the cutlets in the flour and shake off the excess. Heat a large heavy-bottomed skillet over medium-high heat and add 1 tablespoon of the oil. Put four cutlets in the pan and sauté for 45 seconds. Turn them over and sauté until the pink around the edges has turned white — about 30 seconds more. Transfer the cooked cutlets to a heated serving plate and keep warm. Add the remaining ½ tablespoon of oil to the pan, sauté the rest of the cutlets, and keep warm.

To prepare the sauce, add the wine, stock and shallots to the skillet and bring to a boil over medium-high heat. Reduce the liquid by half, to about ¼ cup, stirring frequently. Lower the heat to medium and stir in the fruit, thyme, sage, sugar, salt and pepper. Whisk in the butter and simmer, stirring occasionally, for five minutes. Add the parsley at the last minute. Pour the sauce over the cutlets and serve immediately.

SUGGESTED ACCOMPANIMENT: *bulgur; green peas.*

Minced Turkey with Lime and Cilantro

Serves 8
Working time: about 30 minutes
Total time: about 30 minutes

Calories **160**
Protein **16g.**
Cholesterol **31mg.**
Total fat **6g.**
Saturated fat **1g.**
Sodium **201mg.**

¾ lb. cooked turkey breast meat, finely chopped
Yogurt sauce
1 cup plain low-fat yogurt
1 tsp. finely chopped cilantro
1 tsp. sugar
2 tbsp. fresh lime juice
⅛ tsp. salt
⅛ tsp. cayenne pepper
Turkey morsels
½ cup fresh bread crumbs
⅓ cup finely sliced scallion greens
zest of 1 lime, grated
2 tsp. finely chopped cilantro
¼ tsp. chili powder
¼ tsp. salt
1 egg white
¼ cup flour
2 tbsp. safflower oil

To prepare the sauce, pour the yogurt into a small bowl and whisk in the cilantro, sugar, lime juice, salt and cayenne. Let stand 15 minutes.

Place the turkey in a bowl with the bread crumbs, scallions, zest, cilantro, chili powder and salt. Add the egg white and knead by hand or mix with a spoon.

With dampened hands, gently form the meat mixture into balls the size of large marbles and lightly dust with flour. Heat the oil in a heavy-bottomed skillet over medium heat and fry as many balls as possible without crowding until brown all over — for five or six minutes. Drain on paper towels and transfer to a warm platter. Serve with the sauce.

Honey-Glazed Roast Turkey

Serves 12
Working time: about 1 hour
Total time: about 5 hours

Calories **480**
Protein **50g.**
Cholesterol **151mg.**
Total fat **15g.**
Saturated fat **6g.**
Sodium **368mg.**

one 12 lb. fresh or thawed turkey, the neck, gizzard and heart reserved for gravy
¾ tsp. salt
freshly ground black pepper
2 tbsp. honey

Orange-and-sweet-potato stuffing

zest of 1 lemon, cut into fine strips
4 navel oranges, the zest of 2 cut into fine strips
6 medium sweet potatoes, peeled and cut into ½-inch cubes
6 tbsp. unsalted butter
3 large onions, chopped
¼ cup fresh lemon juice
½ cup unsalted turkey or chicken stock
⅛ tsp. salt
freshly ground black pepper
½ tsp. ground cloves
¾ tsp. dry mustard
6 slices cracked-wheat bread, cut into cubes and lightly toasted
2 tbsp. brandy

Port-and-orange gravy

the turkey neck, gizzard and heart
1 tbsp. safflower oil
1 carrot, chopped
1 celery stalk, coarsely chopped
2 medium onions, coarsely chopped
1 garlic clove, coarsely chopped
1 cup white wine
1 bay leaf
1 tsp. fresh thyme, or ¼ tsp. dried thyme leaves
the roasting juices from the turkey (about 1 cup), degreased
the juice and grated zest of one orange
1 tbsp. red wine vinegar
2 tbsp. cornstarch
⅓ cup port
½ tsp. salt
freshly ground black pepper

To prepare the stuffing, blanch the lemon and orange zest in 1 cup of boiling water for one minute. Drain and set aside. Using a sharp knife, peel the oranges and divide them into sections. Cut each section in half and reserve.

In a large saucepan, bring 2 quarts of water to a boil. Drop in the sweet-potato cubes and blanch them for three minutes. Drain and set aside.

In a large, heavy-bottomed casserole, melt 4 tablespoons of the butter over medium-low heat. Add the onion and cook it until translucent, stirring occasionally — about 10 minutes. Add the lemon and orange zest, oranges, sweet potatoes, lemon juice, stock, salt and pepper. Cook until the sweet potato cubes are tender — seven to 10 minutes. Remove from the heat and add the cloves, mustard, the remaining 2 tablespoons of butter, the bread cubes and the brandy. Mix thoroughly. Allow to cool before using.

To make a stock for the gravy, chop the turkey neck into pieces. Heat the oil in a heavy-bottomed saucepan over medium-high heat. Add the neck, gizzard, heart, carrot, celery, onions and garlic. Sauté, stirring, until the vegetables begin to brown — about five minutes. Add the white wine, bay leaf, thyme and 3 cups of water. Reduce the heat to low and simmer for one hour, skimming off impurities as necessary. Strain the stock, pushing down on the contents to extract all the liquid; there should be 2 to 2½ cups. Set it aside.

Preheat the oven to 350° F. Rinse the turkey inside and out under cold running water and dry it thoroughly with paper towels. Rub the salt and pepper inside the body and neck cavities and outside the bird.

To stuff the turkey, loosely fill both cavities. Tie the drumsticks together with butcher's twine and tuck the wing tips under the bird. Put the turkey on a rack in a shallow roasting pan. Add 1 cup of water to the pan.

To keep the turkey moist and prevent it from overbrowning, make a tent of aluminum foil. Use an extrawide sheet of foil (or two sheets of regular foil crimped together) that measure 1½ feet longer than the pan. Lay the foil shiny side down over the turkey, and tuck it loosely around the inside edges of the pan. Roast the turkey in the oven for two and one half hours.

Take the turkey from the oven and carefully remove the foil tent. Brush the turkey all over with the honey. Turn the heat down to 325° F., then return the turkey to the oven, and roast it uncovered for one hour. The bird is done when a meat thermometer inserted in the thickest part of the thigh reads 180° F. There should be about 1 cup of roasting juices in the pan.

Let the turkey stand for at least 20 minutes before carving it. In the meantime, remove the stuffing from the cavities and set it aside in a bowl loosely covered with foil to keep it warm.

To make the gravy, combine the stock, reserved roasting juices, orange juice and zest, and vinegar in a saucepan. Bring the mixture to a boil. Mix the cornstarch and the port and whisk them into the saucepan; return the gravy to a boil. Reduce the heat to low and simmer for five minutes. Add the salt and pepper and serve piping hot with the carved bird and the stuffing.

EDITOR'S NOTE: *To roast a larger turkey, increase the cooking time by 20 to 25 minutes per pound, and leave the foil tent on until one hour of cooking time remains. To cook the turkey* *unstuffed, rub orange peel and ¼ teaspoon of cloves inside the cavity for extra flavor, and subtract five minutes per pound from the total cooking time.*

If you wish to cook the stuffing separately as a dressing, put it in a baking dish with an additional ¼ cup of stock. Cover the dish with aluminum foil and bake the dressing in a preheated 325° F. oven for 45 minutes. Uncover the dish and return it to the oven for another 45 minutes.

Duck with Mushrooms and Snow Peas

Serves 4
Working time: about 1 hour
Total time: about 3 hours

Calories **459**
Protein **30g.**
Cholesterol **69mg.**
Total fat **25g.**
Saturated fat **8g.**
Sodium **288mg.**

one 5 lb. duck, cut into four serving pieces
1 cup chopped onion
1 carrot, finely chopped
2 tbsp. flour
3 garlic cloves, finely chopped
¼ tsp. salt
freshly ground black pepper
3 cups unsalted chicken stock
1 cup dry white wine
3 or 4 fresh parsley sprigs
1 small bay leaf
½ tsp. fresh thyme, or ¼ tsp. dried thyme leaves
½ tsp. grated lemon zest
¼ lb. mushrooms, halved, or quartered if large
½ lb. snow peas, strings removed, blanched a few seconds in boiling water, refreshed in cold water and drained

Preheat the oven to 450° F.

Heat a heavy-bottomed skillet over medium heat and put in the duck pieces skin side down, without overlapping any of them. Sauté until the skin turns golden brown — two to three minutes. Turn the pieces and brown them on the other side — one to two minutes more. Transfer the duck pieces to a large, heavy-bottomed ovenproof casserole.

Place the casserole in the oven and bake it for 10 minutes; this renders the fat from the duck. Remove the casserole, spoon off the fat, and turn the pieces. Bake for another 10 minutes.

Remove the duck pieces from the casserole and pour off all but 1 tablespoon of fat. Add the onion and carrot to the casserole and stir well to scrape up any bits of meat that have baked onto the bottom. Cook the vegetables over medium heat for three minutes.

Return the duck pieces to the casserole and sprinkle them on one side with 1 tablespoon of the flour. Turn the pieces and sprinkle them on the second side with the remaining tablespoon of flour. Bake the casserole in the oven for an additional five minutes.

Reduce the oven temperature to 400° F. Stir the garlic into the meat and vegetables and sprinkle in the salt and pepper. Add the stock, wine, parsley, bay leaf, thyme and lemon zest, and bring the mixture to a simmer over medium-high heat. Place aluminum foil directly over the casserole contents, then cover with a lid and bake for 20 minutes.

Remove the duck pieces from the casserole. Pour the sauce into a small saucepan. Return the duck pieces to

the casserole and allow them to cool. Cover and refrigerate both the duck and the sauce until the sauce jells — two hours or overnight.

Spoon off the layer of congealed fat from the top of the sauce and discard it. Bring the sauce to a boil over medium-high heat, then cook it until it is reduced to about 2½ cups — 10 to 15 minutes. Pour the sauce over the duck in the casserole and reheat it over medium heat. Once the sauce is bubbling, add the mushrooms and cook for five minutes. Finally, stir in the snow peas, cover, and cook for one minute more. Serve very hot.

Roast Duck Stuffed with Pears and Garlic

Serves 4
Working time: about 30 minutes
Total time: about 2 hours and 15 minutes

Calories **407**
Protein **25g.**
Cholesterol **77mg.**
Total fat **27g.**
Saturated fat **10g.**
Sodium **212mg.**

one 5 lb. duck, rinsed and patted dry
1 tbsp. unsalted butter
15 to 20 garlic cloves, peeled, the large ones cut in half
1 lb. Seckel or Bosc pears, slightly underripe, cut into ¾-inch cubes and tossed with 1 tbsp. fresh lime juice
1 tbsp. fresh rosemary, or 1 tsp. dried rosemary
1 tsp. sugar
¼ tsp. salt
1 bunch watercress for garnish

Trim any excess skin and fat from around the neck of the duck. Remove any fat from the cavity. Cover the bottom of a large pot with 1 inch of water and set a metal rack or steamer in the pot. Bring the water to a boil on top of the stove. To help release fat while steaming, lightly prick the duck all over with a wooden pick or a skewer, taking care not to pierce the flesh below the layer of fat. Place the duck breast side down in the pot. Cover tightly and steam the duck for 30 minutes.

Preheat the oven to 350° F.

While the duck is steaming, melt the butter in a heavy-bottomed skillet over medium heat. Cook the garlic cloves in the butter, stirring frequently, until they begin to soften and brown — about 12 minutes. Stir in the pears, rosemary and sugar, and cook until the pears are soft — about eight minutes more. Set the stuffing aside.

When the duck has finished steaming, sprinkle it inside and out with the salt. Place the duck on a rack in a roasting pan, breast side down, and roast it for 15 minutes. Remove the duck and reduce the oven temperature to 325° F. Turn the duck breast side up on the rack. Prick the breast and legs of the duck. Fill the cavity with the pear-garlic mixture. Return the bird to the oven and roast it until the skin turns a deep golden brown — about one hour and 30 minutes. Cut the duck into quarters and garnish with the watercress.

SUGGESTED ACCOMPANIMENTS: *barley; broiled tomatoes.*

EDITOR'S NOTE: *The process of steaming followed by roasting helps to defat the duck considerably, resulting in a crisp skin and fewer calories.*

3 *Chilled to preserve their savor, such rich-fleshed fish as bluefish, shad, pompano, butterfish, and Chinook salmon tempt with plump goodness.*

Fish and Shellfish

Repeat these steps with the remaining fillets. Drizzle any remaining garlic butter over the top.

Bake the fish until it feels firm to the touch and the coating is golden brown — 10 to 12 minutes. Serve immediately.

SUGGESTED ACCOMPANIMENTS: *tomato salad; green beans.*

Crisp Baked Porgies with Tomato and Mint

Serves 4
Working time: about 25 minutes
Total time: about 40 minutes

Calories **280**
Protein **22g.**
Cholesterol **58mg.**
Total fat **15g.**
Saturated fat **3g.**
Sodium **210mg.**

4 porgies (or croaker or perch), about ½ lb. each, dressed
½ cup skim milk
1 egg white, beaten
⅓ cup cornmeal
¼ cup sliced blanched almonds, chopped
½ cup chopped fresh mint
1 scallion, trimmed and thinly sliced
freshly ground black pepper
1 tbsp. safflower oil
1 tbsp. unsalted butter
¼ tsp. salt
2 large ripe tomatoes, peeled, seeded and finely chopped
1 tbsp. fresh lime or lemon juice
1 tbsp. red wine vinegar

Rinse the dressed porgies under cold running water and pat them dry. Mix the milk and egg white in a shallow bowl. Soak the fish in this mixture for 15 minutes, turning them twice. Preheat the oven to 350° F.

While the porgies are soaking, combine the cornmeal, almonds, ¼ cup of the mint, the scallion and a generous grinding of pepper in a shallow dish. At the end of the soaking time, dredge each porgy in the cornmeal mixture to coat it evenly.

Heat the oil and butter in a large ovenproof skillet (preferably one with a nonstick surface) over medium heat. Add the porgies and cook them on the first side for four minutes. Sprinkle the fish with ⅛ teaspoon of the salt and turn them over; sprinkle them with the remaining ⅛ teaspoon of salt and cook them on the second side for two minutes. Put the skillet in the oven for 15 minutes to finish cooking the porgies.

While the fish are baking, make the sauce: Combine the tomatoes, the remaining ¼ cup of mint, the lime or lemon juice, the vinegar and some pepper in a bowl.

When the porgies are done, transfer them to a serving platter; pass the sauce separately.

SUGGESTED ACCOMPANIMENTS: *corn on the cob.*

Black Sea Bass Fillets with Cracked Anise and Mustard Seeds

Serves 4
Working time: about 15 minutes
Total time: about 25 minutes

Calories **190**
Protein **22g.**
Cholesterol **62mg.**
Total fat **9g.**
Saturated fat **4g.**
Sodium **230mg.**

two skinned black sea bass fillets (or rockfish), about ½ lb. each, cut in half on the diagonal
1 shallot, finely chopped
2 tsp. anise or fennel seeds
1 tbsp. mustard seeds
⅓ cup dry bread crumbs
2 tsp. fresh thyme, or ½ tsp. dried thyme leaves
freshly ground black pepper
2 tbsp. unsalted butter
1 garlic clove, very finely chopped
juice of ½ lemon
¼ tsp. salt

Preheat the oven to 500° F. Lightly butter the bottom of a heavy, shallow baking dish. Sprinkle the chopped shallot into the dish.

Crack the anise or fennel seeds and the mustard seeds with a mortar and pestle, or on a cutting board with the flat of a heavy knife. Transfer the seeds to a wide, shallow bowl or pan, and combine them with the bread crumbs, thyme and some pepper. Put the butter and garlic into a saucepan and melt the butter.

Rinse the fillets under cold running water and pat them dry with paper towels. Rub the fillets with the lemon juice and sprinkle them with the salt and some pepper. Brush a fillet on both sides with some of the garlic butter, then coat it well with the bread-crumb mixture and lay it on the shallot in the baking dish.

Salmon Steaks in Three-Pepper Stew

Serves 4
Working time: about 30 minutes
Total time: about 45 minutes

Calories **310**
Protein **25g.**
Cholesterol **90mg.**
Total fat **18g.**
Saturated fat **4g.**
Sodium **155mg.**

4 salmon steaks, about 5 oz. each
2 lb. ripe tomatoes, peeled, seeded and chopped
2 red peppers, seeded, deribbed and cut into ¼-inch-wide strips
2 green peppers, seeded, deribbed and cut into ¼-inch-wide strips
2 jalapeño peppers, finely chopped (caution, page 125)
2 garlic cloves, finely chopped
1 tbsp. chopped fresh marjoram, or 1 tsp. dried marjoram
⅛ tsp. salt
freshly ground black pepper
1 tbsp. virgin olive oil
juice of 1 lime

Put the chopped tomatoes in a fine sieve and set them aside to drain for at least 30 minutes.

While the tomatoes are draining, remove the skin from the salmon steaks with a small, sharp knife. Divide each steak into two boneless pieces by cutting down each side of the backbone and around the ribs. Reassemble each steak as shown in the photograph, with the skinned sides facing out, the thicker parts interlocking, and the tapered flaps wrapped around the whole. Put the steaks in a baking dish, cover it tightly with heavy-duty plastic wrap and set it aside.

In a second baking dish, combine the red, green and jalapeño peppers with the garlic, marjoram, salt, some black pepper and 1 teaspoon of the oil. Cover the dish tightly and microwave the contents on high for four minutes, stirring once midway through the cooking time. Remove the pepper stew from the oven and let it stand while you cook the fish.

Microwave the fish on high, rotating the dish half a turn after two minutes, until the fish is slightly translucent — about four minutes in all. Let the fish stand while you prepare the tomato sauce. Put the drained tomatoes in a small bowl with the lime juice and the remaining 2 teaspoons of oil, and stir the mixture well.

Serve the salmon steaks surrounded by the pepper stew with the fresh tomato sauce on the side.

SUGGESTED ACCOMPANIMENT: *French bread.*

Pike with Onions, Cabbage and Apple

Serves 6
Working time: about 25 minutes
Total time: about 1 hour

Calories **200**
Protein **18g.**
Cholesterol **52mg.**
Total fat **6g.**
Saturated fat **2g.**
Sodium **145mg.**

one 3-lb. pike (or walleye)
1 tbsp. safflower oil
3 onions, thinly sliced
2 cups thinly sliced cabbage (about ½ lb.)
1 cup dry white wine
1 tbsp. cider vinegar
¼ tsp. caraway seeds
¼ tsp. salt
freshly ground black pepper
1 red apple, cored and cut into thin wedges
1½ tbsp. unsalted butter
1 tbsp. finely cut chives

To loosen the scales of the pike, scald the fish: Put it in the sink or a large basin and pour a kettle of boiling water over it. Scale and clean the fish. Cut off and discard the head.

Preheat the oven to 450° F. Heat the oil in a large, heavy-bottomed skillet over medium-high heat. Add the onions and sauté them until they are translucent — about four minutes. Add the cabbage, wine, vinegar, caraway seeds, salt and some pepper, and stir well. Bring the liquid to a boil, then reduce the heat to medium and simmer the mixture for 10 minutes.

Transfer the vegetable mixture to a baking dish large enough to accommodate the pike. Set the pike on top of the vegetables and arrange the apple wedges around it. Bake the fish until the flesh is opaque and feels firm to the touch — about 20 minutes.

Transfer the pike and the apples to a heated serving platter and cover them with aluminum foil; set the platter aside while you finish cooking the cabbage and onions. Return the cabbage-and-onion mixture to the skillet and cook it over high heat until only about ¼ cup of liquid remains — approximately 10 minutes. Add the butter and stir until it melts. Place the vegetables around the fish on the serving platter, sprinkle the chives over the fish and serve immediately.

SUGGESTED ACCOMPANIMENTS: *wild-rice pilaf; lima beans.*

Almond-Sprinkled Mahimahi Stuffed with Chilies and Tomatoes

THE COLORFUL DOLPHIN CALLED MAHIMAHI — A FISH, NOT A
MAMMAL — IS CAUGHT IN SEMITROPICAL WATERS ON BOTH
COASTS OF NORTH AMERICA.

Serves 6
Working time: about 40 minutes
Total time: about 1 hour

Calories **260**
Protein **25g.**
Cholesterol **103mg.**
Total fat **14g.**
Saturated fat **3g.**
Sodium **300mg.**

1½ lb. mahimahi fillet (or sea trout)
2 tbsp. virgin olive oil
3 garlic cloves, thinly sliced
1 or 2 small chili peppers, seeded and finely chopped (caution, page 125)
1 red onion, thinly sliced
1 lb. ripe tomatoes, peeled, seeded and chopped
2 lemons
½ tsp. salt
¾ cup coarsely chopped fresh parsley
1 tbsp. unsalted butter
½ cup sliced almonds

Rinse the fillet under cold running water and pat it dry
with paper towels. With a sharp, thin-bladed knife, cut
a large flap on one side of the center line of the fillet:
Holding the knife parallel to the center line at a flat
angle, use short slicing strokes to cut from the middle
toward the edge of the fillet. (Take care not to cut all
the way through to the edge nor down to the bottom
of the fillet.) Repeat the process to cut a flap on the
other side of the center line. Set the fish aside.

Preheat the oven to 475° F.

To prepare the stuffing, first pour the oil into a large,
heavy-bottomed skillet over medium-high heat. Add
the garlic and chili peppers and cook them for 30 seconds. Stir in the onion and cook for two minutes more.
Add the tomatoes, the juice of one of the lemons and
¼ teaspoon of the salt. Cook the mixture, stirring often, until the tomatoes are very soft and almost all the
liquid has evaporated — about 10 minutes.

While the stuffing mixture is cooking, cut six paper-
thin slices from the remaining lemon and set them
aside. Rub the juice from the remainder of the lemon
over the outside of the fish and inside the flaps as well.
Put the fish in a lightly oiled baking dish.

Stir the parsley into the tomato stuffing. Open the
flaps on the fillet and fill the pocket with the stuffing.
Close over the flaps and arrange the lemon slices in
a decorative pattern on top of the stuffing. Bake the
fish until it is opaque and feels firm to the touch —
20 to 25 minutes.

Just before the fish is done, melt the butter in a small
skillet over medium heat. Add the almonds and the
remaining ¼ teaspoon of salt; toast the almonds, stirring constantly, until they are lightly browned — two to

three minutes. Remove the pan from the heat. Carefully transfer the baked fish to a serving platter and scatter the almonds over the top. Serve immediately.

SUGGESTED ACCOMPANIMENT: *steamed rice.*

Oven-Steamed Rockfish

Serves 6
Working time: about 10 minutes
Total time: about 50 minutes

Calories **120**
Protein **21g.**
Cholesterol **42mg.**
Total fat **2g.**
Saturated fat **0g.**
Sodium **335mg.**

one 3-lb. whole rockfish (or black sea bass or ocean perch), cleaned and scaled
2 tbsp. dry sherry
2 tsp. cornstarch
⅛ tsp. salt
one 2-inch piece of fresh ginger, peeled and julienned
4 scallions, trimmed and cut into 2-inch-long pieces
¼ cup loosely packed cilantro leaves
2 tbsp. low-sodium soy sauce
1 tbsp. Chinese black vinegar or balsamic vinegar
¼ tsp. sugar

Combine the sherry, cornstarch and salt in a small bowl. Rinse the fish under cold running water and pat it dry with paper towels. Cut four or five diagonal slashes on each side of the fish. Rub the sherry marinade over the fish, inside and out, working some of it into the slashes. Place the fish on the shiny side of a large piece of aluminum foil and let it marinate for at least 15 minutes.

Preheat the oven to 450° F. Insert a strip of ginger and a piece of scallion into each of the slashes on the fish. Place the remaining ginger and scallions in the body cavity. Lay a few cilantro leaves on the outside of the fish; put the remaining leaves in the cavity.

Combine the soy sauce, vinegar and sugar, and pour the mixture over the fish. Fold the foil over the fish and crimp the edges to seal the package tightly.

Set the foil package on a baking sheet and bake the fish until its flesh is opaque and feels firm to the touch — about 25 minutes. Carefully transfer the fish to a warmed serving platter. Pour over the fish any liquid that has collected in the foil during baking, and serve immediately.

SUGGESTED ACCOMPANIMENTS: *stir-fried broccoli and water chestnuts; steamed rice.*

Catfish Gratin

Serves 6
Working time: about 40 minutes
Total time: about 1 hour and 10 minutes

Calories **300**
Protein **19g.**
Cholesterol **47mg.**
Total fat **9g.**
Saturated fat **3g.**
Sodium **170mg.**

1 lb. skinned catfish fillets
juice of 1 lemon
freshly ground black pepper
2 lb. boiling potatoes, scrubbed
2½ lb. ripe tomatoes, quartered, or 28 oz. canned unsalted whole tomatoes, chopped, the juice reserved
1 jalapeño pepper, seeded and chopped (caution, page 125)
2 garlic cloves, finely chopped
1 tsp. chopped fresh oregano, or ½ tsp. dried oregano
¼ tsp. ground cumin
¼ tsp. cayenne pepper
¼ tsp. salt
1 tbsp. virgin olive oil
2 onions, thinly sliced
Herbed topping
½ cup dry bread crumbs
2 tbsp. chopped fresh parsley
¼ tsp. chopped fresh oregano, or ⅛ tsp. dried oregano
⅛ tsp. ground cumin
1½ tbsp. unsalted butter

Rinse the catfish fillets under cold running water and pat them dry with paper towels. Put them on a plate and drizzle the lemon juice over them. Season the fillets with a liberal grinding of black pepper and set them aside while you prepare the potatoes.

Put the potatoes in a saucepan, pour in enough water to cover them by about 1 inch and bring the water to a boil. Reduce the heat to medium and cook the potatoes until they are tender when pierced with a fork — about 20 minutes.

While the potatoes are cooking, prepare the sauce. Put the fresh tomatoes in a large skillet with ½ cup of water. (If you are using canned tomatoes, add their juice but no water.) Cook the tomatoes over medium heat, stirring frequently, until they are very soft and most of the liquid has evaporated — about 20 minutes. Purée the tomatoes in a food mill or work them through a sieve. Combine the tomato purée with the jalapeño pepper, garlic, oregano, cumin, cayenne pepper and salt.

Heat the oil in a large, heavy-bottomed skillet over medium-high heat. Add the onions and cook them, stirring constantly, until they are golden brown and quite soft — about seven minutes. Add ½ cup of water to the onions to deglaze the pan; stir well and set the pan aside.

Preheat the oven to 450° F. When the potatoes are cool enough to handle, peel them and cut them into chunks. In a large baking dish, mix the potatoes with the tomato sauce and the onions. Carefully place the fillets on top of the potato mixture.

To prepare the topping, combine the bread crumbs, parsley, oregano and cumin. Sprinkle the topping over the fillets, covering them completely. Cut the butter into small pieces and scatter them over the topping. Bake the dish until the fish feels firm to the touch — 15 to 20 minutes, depending on the fillets' thickness.

SUGGESTED ACCOMPANIMENT: *spinach salad.*

Skate with Red Pepper and Green Beans

Serves 4
Working (and total) time: about 40 minutes

Calories **325**
Protein **31g.**
Cholesterol **61mg.**
Total fat **10g.**
Saturated fat **1g.**
Sodium **275mg.**

2 lb. skate wings (or ray), skinned
2 cups dry white wine
1 cup fish stock or water
1 shallot, thinly sliced
2 fresh thyme sprigs, or ¾ tsp. dried thyme leaves
8 whole cloves
4 scallions, trimmed and thinly sliced, the white parts kept separate from the green
¼ cup red wine vinegar
2 tbsp. virgin olive oil
1 tbsp. fresh lemon juice
1 red pepper, seeded, deribbed and thinly sliced
¼ tsp. salt
freshly ground black pepper
5 oz. green beans, trimmed, halved lengthwise diagonally

Rinse the skate well under cold running water. In a large, nonreactive skillet, combine the wine, the stock or water, the shallot, thyme and cloves. Bring the mixture to a boil, then reduce the heat to medium low and put the skate in the liquid. Poach the fish until it is opaque — about 12 minutes.

While the skate is cooking, prepare the vinaigrette: Combine the white scallion parts, the vinegar, oil and lemon juice in a large bowl. Set the vinaigrette aside.

When the skate is cooked, transfer it to a plate. Strain the poaching liquid into a bowl, then pour the strained liquid back into the skillet. Add the pepper strips, the salt and some pepper, and cook over medium-low heat for five minutes. Add the beans to the skillet; cook the vegetables for five minutes more.

With a slotted spoon, transfer the vegetables to the bowl containing the vinaigrette. Stir the green scallion parts into the vegetable mixture. Increase the heat under the skillet to high and cook the liquid rapidly until it is syrupy — two to three minutes. Pour the liquid into the vegetable mixture.

With your fingers, lift the skate meat from the cartilage. Put the meat on a serving platter and arrange the vegetables around it, spooning some of the vinaigrette over the top. Serve warm or cold.

EDITOR'S NOTE: *If the skate wings have not been skinned beforehand, slip a sharp, thin-bladed knife between the skin and the flesh. Pressing the knife against the flesh and working toward the edge of the wing, cut away the skin with short slicing strokes. Turn the wing over and repeat the process to remove the skin from the other side.*

Red Snapper in Saffron Sauce

Serves 4
Working (and total) time: about 30 minutes

Calories **240**
Protein **24g.**
Cholesterol **63mg.**
Total fat **7g.**
Saturated fat **4g.**
Sodium **270mg.**

1 lb. skinned red snapper fillets (or grouper)
¼ tsp. salt
1 cup dry white wine
1 shallot, chopped
1 garlic clove, crushed
1 fresh thyme sprig, or ½ tsp. dried thyme leaves
1 tsp. fennel seeds, crushed
10 black peppercorns, cracked
1 tbsp. unsalted butter
20 saffron threads, steeped in ¼ cup hot water for 10 minutes
1 tsp. Dijon mustard
¼ cup light cream, mixed with ½ tsp. cornstarch

Gently rinse the fillets under cold running water and pat them dry with paper towels. Sprinkle the fish with the salt and set it aside.

In a large, heavy-bottomed skillet, combine the wine, shallot, garlic, thyme, fennel seeds, peppercorns and butter. Bring the mixture to a boil, then reduce the heat to medium and simmer for three minutes. Put the fillets in the liquid and reduce the heat to low. Cover the pan and poach the fish until it is opaque and feels firm to the touch — about six minutes. Carefully transfer the fish to a warmed serving dish and cover the fish with aluminum foil to keep it warm.

Increase the heat under the skillet to medium high and reduce the poaching liquid to approximately ½ cup — about five minutes. Strain the liquid into a small saucepan. Pour into the saucepan any juices that have collected on the serving dish, then stir in the saffron mixture and the mustard. Simmer the sauce for two minutes. Whisk in the cream-and-cornstarch mixture, and cook the sauce until it thickens slightly — about one minute more. Pour the sauce around the fillets and serve at once.

SUGGESTED ACCOMPANIMENT: *boiled red potatoes*.

Petrale Sole with Curried Tomato Sauce

PETRALE SOLE, A LARGE PACIFIC FLOUNDER, IS PRIZED FOR THE FIRM TEXTURE OF ITS FLESH.

Serves 4
Working time: about 20 minutes
Total time: about 50 minutes

Calories **195**
Protein **23g.**
Cholesterol **57mg.**
Total fat **6g.**
Saturated fat **1g.**
Sodium **215mg.**

1 lb. petrale or gray sole fillets, rinsed and patted dry
1 shallot, finely chopped
1 garlic clove, finely chopped
⅛ tsp. salt
freshly ground black pepper
1 tbsp. dry white wine
⅓ cup fish stock or water
parsley sprigs
Curried tomato sauce
1 tbsp. virgin olive oil
2 garlic cloves, finely chopped
2 tsp. curry powder
2½ lb. ripe tomatoes, peeled, seeded and finely chopped
⅛ tsp. salt
freshly ground black pepper
2 tsp. tomato paste
1 tbsp. chopped fresh parsley

To make the sauce, heat the oil in a large, heavy-bottomed saucepan over low heat. Add the garlic and stir until it is soft but not browned — about 30 seconds. Sprinkle in the curry powder and cook for 30 seconds more, stirring constantly. Stir in the tomatoes, salt and some pepper, and simmer until the tomatoes are very soft — about 30 minutes. Add the tomato paste, then purée the sauce, return it to the pan, and set it aside.

Preheat the oven to 425° F. Lightly oil the bottom of a heavy, shallow baking dish. Cut a piece of parchment paper or aluminum foil to the dimensions of the dish, and lightly oil one side of it. Set it aside.

Sprinkle the chopped shallot and garlic into the baking dish. Fold the fillets in half, arrange them in the dish and sprinkle them with the salt and some pepper. Pour the wine and the stock or water over the fish. Lay the parchment paper or foil, oiled side down, over the fish. Bake the fillets until their flesh is opaque — approximately nine minutes.

Remove the parchment paper or foil and set it aside. With two slotted spatulas, carefully transfer the fillets to a warmed serving platter. Re-cover the fillets with the parchment paper or foil and keep them warm. Strain the cooking liquid through a fine sieve into the reserved tomato sauce. Bring the sauce to a boil and cook it, stirring, until it thickens — about two minutes. Stir in the chopped parsley.

Spoon the sauce around the fish fillets and garnish them with the parsley sprigs. Serve immediately, with the remaining sauce on the side.

SUGGESTED ACCOMPANIMENT: *julienned zucchini.*

Baked Whitefish with Garlic and Glazed Carrots

Serves 4
Working time: about 15 minutes
Total time: about 1 hour

Calories **265**
Protein **23g.**
Cholesterol **54mg.**
Total fat **14g.**
Saturated fat **2g.**
Sodium **270mg.**

1 whole whitefish (about 2 lb.), scaled and dressed
1 lb. carrots, peeled and sliced diagonally into about 1-inch-long pieces
1 tbsp. fresh lemon juice
freshly ground black pepper
6 garlic cloves, finely chopped
¼ tsp. salt
1 tbsp. virgin olive oil

Preheat the oven to 400° F. Put the carrots in a baking dish that is large enough to accommodate the fish. Add the lemon juice, a generous grinding of pepper and one third of the chopped garlic. Pour ¾ cup of water into the dish and toss the ingredients well.

Sprinkle the fish inside and out with the salt and some pepper, and rub the remaining garlic all over it. Push the carrots to the sides of the dish and lay the fish on the bottom. Drizzle the oil over the fish. Bake, stirring the carrots every 15 minutes, until the fish is golden and the carrots are tender — about 45 minutes.

SUGGESTED ACCOMPANIMENT: *Brussels sprouts.*

Grilled Sablefish Coated with Cracked Black Pepper

Serves 6
Working time: about 35 minutes
Total time: about 4 hours and 30 minutes

Calories **290**
Protein **16g.**
Cholesterol **71mg.**
Total fat **22g.**
Saturated fat **7g.**
Sodium **200mg.**

1½ lb. sablefish (or whitefish) fillets, skinned
⅓ cup fresh lemon juice
½ cup red wine vinegar
3 garlic cloves, crushed
1½ tbsp. sugar
¼ tsp. salt
3 tbsp. black peppercorns, cracked
¾ cup fish stock or vegetable stock
2 tsp. fresh thyme, or ½ tsp. dried thyme leaves
2 tbsp. cold unsalted butter, cut into small pieces
2 thyme sprigs for garnish

In a shallow bowl just large enough to hold the fillets in a single layer, stir together the lemon juice, vinegar, garlic, sugar and salt. Lay the fillets in the liquid, cover the bowl and let the fish marinate in the refrigerator for at least four hours; halfway through the marinating time, turn the fillets over.

Preheat the grill or broiler. Remove the fillets from the marinade and pat them dry with paper towels. Sprinkle half of the cracked pepper over the fillets and press the pepper firmly into the flesh with your fingertips. Turn the fillets over and coat them with the remaining black pepper in the same manner.

If you are grilling the fillets, place them approximately 4 inches above the heat source and cook them on the first side for six minutes. Gently turn the fillets over and cook them on the second side until their flesh just flakes — about six minutes more.

If you are broiling the fillets, cook them about 4 inches below the heat source for four to five minutes on each side.

While the fish is cooking, strain the marinade into a small nonreactive saucepan over medium heat and add the stock and thyme. Cook the mixture until it is reduced to about ½ cup — approximately five minutes. When the fillets are cooked, transfer them to a heated serving platter. Whisk the butter into the sauce, pour the sauce over the fillets, garnish with the thyme sprigs, and serve at once.

SUGGESTED ACCOMPANIMENT: *tomato salad sprinkled with chopped scallions.*

Southwest Gumbo

Serves 8
Working time: about 40 minutes
Total time: about 1 hour

Calories **290**
Protein **32g.**
Cholesterol **109mg.**
Total fat **8g.**
Saturated fat **1g.**
Sodium **390mg.**

3 tbsp. olive oil
8 oz. fresh okra, trimmed and cut into 1-inch lengths
1 large onion, coarsely chopped
1 cup very finely chopped celery
1 large garlic clove, finely chopped
1 large shallot, finely chopped
3 tbsp. masa harina
1 tsp. filé powder
1 tsp. salt
1 tsp. sugar
1 tsp. freshly ground black pepper
1 tsp. ground cumin
4 cups fish stock
1 green pepper, seeded, deribbed and coarsely chopped
1 sweet red pepper, seeded, deribbed and coarsely chopped
1 lb. tomatillos, husked, cored and cut into thin wedges
⅓ cup chopped fresh parsley
2 tbsp. finely chopped cilantro
8 drops hot red-pepper sauce
1 lb. halibut steaks (or sea bass), rinsed, skinned and cut into 1-inch cubes
1 lb. orange roughy fillets (or grouper), rinsed and cut into 1-inch pieces
1 lb. medium shrimp, peeled, deveined if necessary

Heat 1 tablespoon of the olive oil in a large, heavy-bottomed, nonreactive pot over medium-high heat. Add the okra and sauté it, turning frequently, until it is evenly browned — about five minutes. Remove the okra and set it aside.

Reduce the heat to medium and pour the remaining 2 tablespoons of oil into the pot. Add the onion and celery and cook them, covered, until the onion is translucent — about five minutes. Add the garlic and shallot and cook the mixture, stirring constantly, for two minutes more. Sprinkle in the masa harina, filé powder, salt, sugar, black pepper and cumin. Whisk in the stock and bring the liquid to a boil. Add the okra, the green pepper and red pepper, and the tomatillos. Partially cover the pot, then reduce the heat to maintain a simmer and cook the gumbo, stirring occasionally, for eight to 10 minutes.

Stir in the parsley, cilantro and red-pepper sauce. Add the halibut, orange roughy and shrimp, and gently stir the gumbo to incorporate the fish and shrimp. Cover the pot, reduce the heat to low and cook the gumbo for five minutes more. Serve immediately.

EDITOR'S NOTE: *Masa harina — finely ground white or yellow hominy — may be obtained at large supermarkets. If it is unavailable, substitute flour. Filé powder, used to flavor and thicken Creole soups and stews, is made from dried young sassafras leaves.*

Cod Stewed with Onions, Potatoes, Corn and Tomatoes

Serves 6
Working time: about 15 minutes
Total time: about 1 hour

Calories **310**
Protein **19g.**
Cholesterol **32mg.**
Total fat **4g.**
Saturated fat **1g.**
Sodium **305mg.**

1 tbsp. virgin olive oil
3 onions (about 1 lb.), thinly sliced
5 boiling potatoes (about 2 lb.), peeled and thinly sliced
2 cups fresh or frozen corn kernels
½ green pepper, seeded, deribbed and diced
hot red-pepper sauce
1 lb. cod (or haddock or pollock), skinned, rinsed under cold running water, and cut into chunks
2½ lb. ripe tomatoes, peeled, seeded and chopped, or 28 oz. canned unsalted whole tomatoes, drained and chopped
¼ tsp. salt
freshly ground black pepper
cilantro leaves for garnish (optional)

In a large, heavy-bottomed pot, heat the oil over medium heat. Add a layer of onions and a layer of potatoes. Sprinkle some of the corn and green pepper on top. Dribble a few drops of red-pepper sauce over the vegetables. Add a layer of fish and tomatoes and season with a little of the salt and some pepper. Repeat the process, building up successive layers, until the remaining vegetables and fish are used. Cover the pot and cook over medium-low heat until the potatoes are done — about 45 minutes. Garnish the stew with the cilantro leaves if you are using them. Serve at once.

Mussels in White Wine

Serves 8
Working (and total) time: about 30 minutes

Calories **120**
Protein **13g.**
Cholesterol **30mg.**
Total fat **5g.**
Saturated fat **3g.**
Sodium **195mg.**

4 to 5 lbs. mussels, scrubbed and debearded
1 onion, chopped
3 garlic cloves, crushed
2 bay leaves
1 cup finely chopped parsley
3 sprigs thyme
2 tbsp. unsalted butter
freshly ground black pepper
1 cup white wine

Put the mussels into a large, heavy-bottomed saucepan with the onion, garlic, bay leaves, parsley, and thyme. Add the butter and some pepper, and pour in the white wine. Cover the pan and cook the mussels over high heat, lifting and shaking the pan several times, until the shells have opened—three to five minutes, depending on the size and number of mussels.

With a slotted spoon, transfer the mussels to individual soup plates, discarding the bay leaves and any mussels that remain closed. Pour the cooking liquid through a strainer into the soup plates, and serve the mussels hot in their broth.

SUGGESTED ACCOMPANIMENT: *crusty bread.*

Steamed Clams with Spinach

Serves 4
Working (and total) time: about 20 minutes

Calories **115**
Protein **9g.**
Cholesterol **20mg.**
Total fat **4g.**
Saturated fat **2g.**
Sodium **100mg.**

1 tbsp. unsalted butter
1 onion, finely chopped
1 garlic clove, finely chopped
½ cup white wine
1 tbsp. chopped parsley
freshly ground black pepper
1½ lb. small clams in their shells, scrubbed
½ lb. fresh spinach, washed, stalks removed, leaves shredded
1 lemon, quartered

Melt the butter in a deep, nonreactive saucepan, add the onion and garlic, and cook, stirring continuously,

until the onion is soft but not colored—about five minutes. Stir in the wine, parsley, and some pepper, and bring the mixture to a boil. Add the clams and cook, covered, until their shells begin to open—about five minutes. With a slotted spoon, remove the clams from the pan; discard the loose top half of each shell. Place the clams in a warmed dish and cover them with a tea towel while cooking the spinach.

Add the spinach to the wine and onion mixture, and simmer it for two minutes over moderate heat. When the spinach is cooked, drain it thoroughly in a colander set over a bowl. Press the spinach to drain off any excess liquid. Return the liquid to the saucepan. Divide the spinach among four individual serving plates, and place an equal number of steamed clams on top of each portion of spinach.

Bring the reserved liquid to a boil and cook over high heat for one minute to reduce it. Spoon the liquid over the clams and spinach, and serve them garnished with the lemon wedges.

Ragout of Scallops and Red Peppers

Serves 4
Working (and total) time: about 45 minutes

Calories **225**
Protein **21g.**
Cholesterol **41mg.**
Total fat **8g.**
Saturated fat **1g.**
Sodium **250mg.**

1 lb. sea scallops, the bright white connective tissue removed
2 red peppers
freshly ground black pepper
1 tbsp. fresh lime juice
2 tbsp. red wine vinegar
2 tsp. fresh thyme, or ½ tsp. dried thyme leaves
2 tbsp. virgin olive oil
½ lb. mushrooms, wiped clean and quartered
¼ tsp. salt
½ cup dry white wine
1 bunch scallions, trimmed and cut into 1-inch-long pieces
2 Belgian endives (about ⅓ lb.), cut into 1-inch pieces, the pieces separated

Roast the peppers about 3 inches below a preheated broiler, turning them occasionally until they are blackened all over — about 15 minutes.

Meanwhile, rinse the scallops under cold running water. Cut the larger scallops in half. Put all the scallops in a bowl and sprinkle them with some black pepper. Stir in the lime juice and set the bowl aside.

Put the broiled peppers in a bowl and cover it with plastic wrap for one or two minutes (the trapped steam will loosen their skins). Working over the bowl to catch their juices, peel the peppers from top to bottom, then seed them. Coarsely chop the peppers and put them in a food processor or blender along with their reserved juices, the vinegar, thyme and some pepper; purée the mixture.

Pour the oil into a large, heavy-bottomed skillet over medium-high heat. When the oil is hot, add the mushrooms and sauté them for three minutes, stirring once. Sprinkle the mushrooms with ⅛ teaspoon of the salt, then pour in the wine. Continue cooking the mixture, stirring occasionally, until almost all of the liquid has evaporated — three to five minutes.

Pour the red-pepper purée into the skillet. Place the scallops on top and sprinkle them with some more black pepper and the remaining ⅛ teaspoon of salt. Cook the mixture for one minute, stirring frequently. Add the scallions and endives and continue cooking, stirring frequently, until the scallops are firm — two to three minutes more. Serve immediately.

SUGGESTED ACCOMPANIMENT: *steamed rice.*

Grilled Shrimp with Tomato-Ginger Sauce

Serves 4
Working time: about 40 minutes
Total time: about 1 hour and 15 minutes

Calories **215**
Protein **17g.**
Cholesterol **130mg.**
Total fat **8g.**
Saturated fat **1g.**
Sodium **70mg.**

24 medium shrimp (about 1 lb.), peeled and deveined
1 onion, chopped
½ cup dry white wine
2 tbsp. fresh lemon juice
1 tbsp. virgin olive oil
Tomato-ginger sauce
1 tbsp. virgin olive oil
3 scallions, trimmed and chopped
6 garlic cloves, chopped
1 tbsp. finely chopped fresh ginger
2 jalapeño peppers, seeded and chopped (caution, page 125)
¼ tsp. ground coriander
¼ tsp. ground cumin
¼ tsp. dry mustard
3 ripe tomatoes, peeled, seeded and chopped
1 tsp. brown sugar
1 tbsp. red wine vinegar

In a bowl, combine the onion, wine, lemon juice and oil. Add the shrimp and let them marinate in the refrigerator for one hour.

Meanwhile, make the sauce. Pour the oil into a large, heavy-bottomed skillet over medium-high heat. When the oil is hot, add the scallions, garlic, ginger and jalapeño peppers; cook for two minutes, stirring constantly. Stir in the coriander, cumin and mustard, and cook the mixture for one minute more. Add the tomatoes and cook them, stirring constantly, for one minute. Remove the skillet from the heat and stir in the brown sugar and vinegar. Transfer the sauce to a serving bowl and let it cool.

Near the end of the marinating time, preheat the broiler. Thread the shrimp in interlocking pairs onto four skewers. Brush the shrimp with any remaining marinade and broil them about 2 inches below the heat source until they are opaque — approximately three minutes.

Serve the shrimp on their skewers atop a bed of rice, with the sauce presented alongside.

SUGGESTED ACCOMPANIMENTS: *steamed rice; chicory salad.*

Shrimp and Green Bean Salad

Serves 4
Working time: about 30 minutes
Total time: about 1 hour

Calories **185**
Protein **20g.**
Cholesterol **133mg.**
Total fat **6g.**
Saturated fat **1g.**
Sodium **235mg.**

1 lb. medium shrimp, the shells left on
1½ lb. green beans, trimmed and cut in half
1½ tbsp. tarragon vinegar
1 tbsp. safflower oil
2 tbsp. chopped fresh tarragon, or 2 tsp. dried tarragon
2 tbsp. finely cut chives
¼ tsp. salt
freshly ground black pepper
½ cup plain low fat yogurt
1 tbsp. sour cream
1½ tsp. Dijon mustard
1 tsp. tomato paste
1 tbsp. chopped fresh parsley

Bring 8 cups of water to a boil in a large saucepan. Add the beans and boil them until they are just tender — about six minutes. Drain the beans and refresh them under cold running water. Pat the beans dry and transfer them to a bowl. Set the bowl aside.

Bring 4 cups of water to a simmer in the saucepan. Add the shrimp, cover the pan, and simmer the shrimp until they are opaque — two to three minutes. Drain the shrimp; when they are cool enough to handle, peel them (and, if you like, devein them). Add the shrimp to the beans.

In a small bowl, whisk together the vinegar, oil, half of the tarragon, 1 tablespoon of the chives, ⅛ teaspoon of the salt and some pepper. Arrange the shrimp and beans on a serving platter and spoon the vinegar-and-oil marinade over it. Let the dish marinate at room temperature for 30 minutes.

Near the end of the marinating time, prepare the dressing: Whisk together the yogurt, sour cream, mustard and tomato paste. Stir in the parsley, the other half of the tarragon and the remaining tablespoon of chives, the remaining ⅛ teaspoon of salt and some pepper. Pour the dressing into a small serving bowl and serve it alongside the salad.

SUGGESTED ACCOMPANIMENT: *whole-wheat pita bread.*

Sautéed Shrimp with Sherry and Chilies

Serves 4
Working time: about 20 minutes
Total time: about 1 hour

Calories **140**
Protein **16g.**
Cholesterol **138mg.**
Total fat **4g.**
Saturated fat **1g.**
Sodium **55mg.**

1 lb. shrimp, peeled and deveined if necessary, the shells reserved
1 whole garlic bulb, the cloves separated and peeled
4 dried red chili peppers (caution, page 125)
1 tsp. fresh rosemary, or ½ tsp. dried rosemary
½ tsp. fennel seeds
⅓ cup dry sherry
1 red pepper, seeded, deribbed and julienned
1 scallion, trimmed and julienned
1 tbsp. unsalted butter

Put the shrimp shells in a saucepan with the garlic, chili peppers, rosemary, fennel seeds and 1 quart of water. Bring the water to a boil, then reduce the heat to medium low and simmer the mixture for 30 minutes.

Strain the poaching liquid, discard the solids and return the liquid to the saucepan. Boil the liquid rapidly until only about 1½ cups remain — five to 10 minutes. Pour in the sherry and bring the liquid to a simmer. Poach the shrimp until they are opaque — approximately one minute. Remove the shrimp with a slotted spoon and set them aside.

Boil the remaining poaching liquid until only 2 or 3 tablespoons remain — about five minutes. Add the ju-

lienned red pepper, reduce the heat to medium, and cook the pepper for two minutes. Return the shrimp to the saucepan. Add the scallion and butter, and stir until the butter has melted and the shrimp are warm. Serve immediately.

SUGGESTED ACCOMPANIMENT: *steamed rice.*
EDITOR'S NOTE: *Served cold, this dish makes an ideal prelude to summer meals; olive oil or safflower oil should be used in place of the butter.*

4 *Asian inspired, this beef stew with water chestnuts and butternut squash takes its character from the tangerine juice and peel it includes (recipe, page 119).*

Beef, Veal, Lamb, and Pork

Rump Roast with Root Vegetables

Serves 8
Working time: about 20 minutes
Total time: about 2 hours

Calories **205**
Protein **24g.**
Cholesterol **60mg.**
Total fat **7g.**
Saturated fat **2g.**
Sodium **165mg.**

one 2¼-lb. rump roast, trimmed of fat
1 tsp. safflower oil
¼ tsp. salt
½ tsp. cracked black peppercorns
1 garlic clove, finely chopped
2 large carrots, peeled and sliced into ¾-inch-thick rounds
2 large turnips, peeled and cut into ½-inch-thick wedges
1 rutabaga, peeled and cut into ¾-inch cubes
½ lb. small white onions
½ tbsp. fresh thyme, or ¾ tsp. dried thyme leaves
4 tsp. cornstarch
¼ cup low-fat milk
2 tsp. grainy mustard

Preheat the oven to 325° F.

Heat a large, nonstick skillet over medium-high heat. Add the oil, tilting the pan to coat the bottom. Sear the roast in the pan — approximately one minute on each side.

Transfer the meat to a roasting pan, sprinkle the meat with the salt, peppercorns and garlic, and roast the beef until it is medium rare and registers 140° F. on a meat thermometer — about one hour and 15 minutes. Remove the roast from the pan and set it aside. Skim and discard any fat from the juices in the pan; set the pan with its juices aside.

Toss the carrots, turnips, rutabaga and onions with the thyme. Pour enough water into a large pot to fill it 1 inch deep. Place a vegetable steamer in the pot and bring the water to a boil. Put the vegetables into the steamer, cover the pot, and cook the vegetables until they are tender — about 10 minutes. Remove the vegetables from the steamer and keep them warm.

Pour about 1 cup of the steaming liquid into the roasting pan. Simmer the liquid over medium-high heat, stirring constantly to dissolve any caramelized roasting juices on the bottom of the pan. Mix the cornstarch and milk in a small bowl, then whisk this mixture into the simmering liquid. Stir the liquid until the sauce thickens, then whisk in the mustard. Remove the pan from the heat and keep it warm.

Slice the roast and arrange the slices on a platter. Toss the vegetables with some of the sauce and place them around the meat. Serve the roast with the remaining sauce passed separately.

SUGGESTED ACCOMPANIMENT: *steamed kale or spinach.*

Beef Tenderloin Filled with Basil and Sun-Dried Tomatoes

Serves 4
Working time: about 35 minutes
Total time: about 2 hours

Calories **340**
Protein **28g.**
Cholesterol **74mg.**
Total fat **17g.**
Saturated fat **4g.**
Sodium **415mg.**

one 1¼-lb. beef tenderloin roast, trimmed of fat
1 cup loosely packed basil leaves, thinly sliced
¼ cup sun-dried tomatoes packed in oil, drained and finely chopped
1 tsp. safflower oil

Stuffed cherry tomatoes

2 whole garlic bulbs, the cloves separated but not peeled
1 cup loosely packed fresh basil leaves
⅛ tsp. salt
freshly ground black pepper
1 tsp. fresh lemon juice
¼ cup plain low-fat yogurt
24 cherry tomatoes

Preheat the oven to 325° F.

Using a well-scrubbed sharpening steel or some other thick, pointed tool, pierce the tenderloin through the center; rotate the sharpening steel to create a ½-inch-wide hole.

Combine the thinly sliced basil leaves with the sun-dried tomatoes. Using your fingers, fill the tenderloin with the basil-tomato mixture.

Heat the oil in a heavy-bottomed, ovenproof skillet

over high heat. When the oil is hot, sear the roast until it is well browned on all sides — three to five minutes. Transfer the skillet to the oven. For medium-rare meat, roast the tenderloin for 25 to 30 minutes or until a thermometer inserted in the meat registers 140° F. Remove the tenderloin from the oven and let it rest until it is cool — about 45 minutes.

Meanwhile, prepare the filling for the cherry tomatoes. Put the garlic cloves into a small saucepan and pour in just enough water to cover them. Bring the water to a boil, then reduce the heat, and simmer the cloves until they are very soft — 30 to 45 minutes. Drain the garlic; when the cloves are cool enough to handle, squeeze the pulp from the skins into a blender or a food processor. Add the unsliced basil leaves, the salt, some pepper, the lemon juice and the yogurt, and purée the mixture. Set the purée aside.

Cut the tops off the cherry tomatoes. With a melon baller or a small spoon, scoop out the seeds. Using a piping bag or a spoon, fill the tomatoes with the purée.

Carve the tenderloin into ¼-inch-thick slices and transfer them to plates or a platter. Arrange the filled tomatoes around the slices of tenderloin and serve the meat at room temperature.

SUGGESTED ACCOMPANIMENT: *whole-wheat dinner rolls.*

Roast Beef with Cloves and Red Peppers

Serves 12
Working time: about 30 minutes
Total time: about 2 hours

Calories **180**
Protein **23g.**
Cholesterol **63mg.**
Total fat **7g.**
Saturated fat **2g.**
Sodium **155mg.**

one 3½-lb. tip roast, trimmed of fat
4 sweet red peppers
1 tsp. ground cloves
1 tbsp. safflower oil
½ tsp. salt
freshly ground black pepper
1 cup unsalted brown stock or unsalted chicken stock
2 white onions (about 1 lb.)
½ cup dry white wine

Roast the peppers about 2 inches below a preheated broiler, turning them as they blister, until they are blackened on all sides — about 15 minutes in all. Transfer the peppers to a bowl and cover it with plastic wrap; the trapped steam will loosen their skins. Set the bowl aside.

Preheat the oven to 275° F. Sprinkle the meat all over with ½ teaspoon of the cloves.

Heat the oil in a large, heavy-bottomed skillet over high heat. When it is hot, add the beef and sear it until it is well browned on all sides — about five minutes. Transfer the beef to a shallow, flameproof casserole and sprinkle it with ¼ teaspoon of the salt and a generous grinding of pepper.

Roast the beef for one hour. If the meat juices begin to blacken in the bottom of the casserole, pour in a few tablespoons of the stock.

While the roast is cooking, peel the peppers, working over a bowl to catch the juice. Strain the juice and set it aside. Slice the peppers into strips about 1 inch long and ½ inch wide. Cut the onions in half from top to bottom, then slice them with the grain into strips roughly the same size as the pepper strips.

When the roast has cooked for one hour, add to the casserole the peppers and their juice, the onions, the stock, the wine, the remaining ½ teaspoon of cloves and the remaining ¼ teaspoon of salt. For medium-rare meat, roast the beef for 30 minutes longer, or until a meat thermometer inserted into the center registers 140°F.

Remove the casserole from the oven and set the roast aside while you finish the dish.

With a slotted spoon, transfer the vegetables to a bowl. Boil the liquid remaining in the casserole until it is reduced to about ½ cup. Cut the meat into very thin slices and arrange them on a platter with the vegetables surrounding them. Drizzle the sauce over the beef and serve immediately.

SUGGESTED ACCOMPANIMENT: *roasted sweet potatoes.*

Mushroom-Stuffed Top Loin Roast

Serves 8
Working time: about 45 minutes
Total time: about 2 hours

Calories **190**
Protein **26g.**
Cholesterol **65mg.**
Total fat **7g.**
Saturated fat **3g.**
Sodium **200mg.**

one 2½-lb. top loin roast, trimmed of fat
½ lb. fresh shiitake mushrooms, wiped clean, caps finely chopped, stems reserved
½ lb. mushrooms, wiped clean, caps finely chopped, stems reserved

2½ cups dry white wine
½ cup Madeira or port
8 scallions, white parts finely chopped, green parts reserved
grated zest of 3 lemons
½ tsp. salt
freshly ground black pepper
¼ cup toasted bread crumbs

Preheat the oven to 400° F.

Combine the mushrooms, 2 cups of the white wine, and the Madeira or port in a large, nonreactive skillet. Bring the liquid to a boil over medium-high heat, then continue cooking it until all the liquid has evaporated — about 15 minutes. Transfer the mushrooms to a bowl and mix in the chopped scallions, lemon zest, salt and some pepper. Set the mixture aside.

Using the techniques shown below, cut the roast and stuff it. Put the roast into a roasting pan and cover the exposed mushroom mixture with the bread crumbs. Scatter the reserved mushroom stems and scallions around the meat and roast it for 30 minutes.

Pour the remaining ½ cup of white wine over the roast and continue roasting the beef for 15 minutes for medium-rare meat. (The internal temperature should be 140° F.) Transfer the roast to a cutting board and allow it to rest for 15 minutes.

Heat the juices in the roasting pan over medium heat, scraping up any caramelized juices with a wooden spoon to dissolve them. Skim off the fat, strain the juices and keep them warm.

Carve the roast into eight slices and serve them with the juices spooned on top.

SUGGESTED ACCOMPANIMENT: *steamed spinach.*
EDITOR'S NOTE: *If fresh shiitake mushrooms are unavailable in your market, regular mushrooms may be substituted.*

Stuffing a Top Loin Roast

1 *TRIMMING THE FAT IN STRIPS. With a small, thin-bladed knife (here, a boning knife), cut into the fatty layer of the loin roast to form a tab. Pull the tab taut, and insert the knife under it. Carefully slide the knife toward you to remove a strip of fat. Continue cutting off strips until the entire layer of fat is removed.*

2 *MAKING THE FIRST SLICE. Steadying the roast with one hand, place a slicing knife along the meat's edge, about one third of the way down from the surface. With a smooth sawing motion, cut across the meat, stopping just short of the edge so that the flaps remain attached.*

3 *MAKING THE SECOND SLICE. Rotate the meat on the work surface and unfold the thinner flap from the thicker one. Now cut through the inside edge of the thicker flap, again leaving a small hinge of meat to keep the pieces connected.*

4 *STUFFING THE LOIN. Unfold the newly formed flap. You will have three joined squares of meat. Spread one third of the stuffing onto the middle square and fold the left flap over it. Spread half of the remaining stuffing on top (above). Fold the right flap over the stuffing and cover the flap with the rest of the stuffing.*

Top Round Steak with Mushrooms and Red Onions

Serves 8
Working time: about 1 hour
Total time: about 3 hours (includes marinating time)

Calories **245**
Protein **29g.**
Cholesterol **72mg.**
Total fat **8g.**
Saturated fat **3g.**
Sodium **70mg.**

one 2½-lb. top round steak, trimmed of fat
2 red onions, cut into ½-inch-thick slices
1½ cups red wine
¼ cup raspberry vinegar or distilled white vinegar
¼ cup fresh lime juice
20 juniper berries
1 lb. fresh mushrooms, wiped clean
¾ cup unsalted brown stock or unsalted chicken stock
2 tbsp. cornstarch
freshly ground black pepper
¼ cup finely chopped fresh parsley

Spread the onion slices in the bottom of a shallow baking dish. Set the steak on the onions; pour the wine, vinegar and lime juice over the steak, then scatter the juniper berries over all. Let the steak marinate at room temperature for two hours or put it into the refrigerator overnight.

Remove the steak and onions from the marinade, and pat them dry with paper towels. Strain the marinade into a bowl and set it aside. Discard the berries.

Heat a large, nonstick skillet over high heat. Add the onion slices and sauté them until they are tender — about four minutes on each side. Remove them from the skillet and keep them warm. Cook the steak in the skillet over medium-high heat for four minutes on each side for medium-rare meat. Remove the steak from the skillet and let it rest while you prepare the mushrooms.

Sauté the mushrooms in the skillet over high heat, stirring occasionally, until most of the juices have evaporated — about five minutes. Remove the mushrooms with a slotted spoon and set them aside. Pour the steak marinade into the skillet and boil it until it has reduced by half — about 10 minutes. Mix the stock and the cornstarch together and whisk them into the reduced marinade. Bring the liquid to a boil and continue cooking until it thickens slightly — about one minute. Season the mushrooms with some black pepper and stir them, along with the parsley, into the sauce.

Slice the steak and arrange it on a serving platter with the onions. Spoon the mushrooms around the steak just before serving.

SUGGESTED ACCOMPANIMENT: *French bread.*

Sautéed Beef Tossed with Red Cabbage and Apples

Serves 8
Working time: about 30 minutes
Total time: about 45 minutes

Calories **220**
Protein **19g.**
Cholesterol **50mg.**
Total fat **7g.**
Saturated fat **2g.**
Sodium **145mg.**

1¾ lb. sirloin steak, trimmed of fat and cut into thin strips about 1½ inches long
¼ cup chopped shallots
¼ tsp. salt
1 cup unsalted brown stock or unsalted chicken stock
2 cups red wine
2 tsp. caraway seeds
1 small red cabbage (about 2½ lb.), cored, quartered and sliced
2 tart green apples, cored, quartered and cut into strips 2 inches long and ¼ inch wide
1 tbsp. honey
¼ cup fresh lemon juice
1 tsp. freshly ground black pepper
1½ tbsp. safflower oil
2 scallions, trimmed and sliced

Combine the shallots, salt, stock, wine and 1 teaspoon of the caraway seeds in a nonreactive saucepan over medium heat. Simmer the liquid until it is reduced to ½ cup — about 40 minutes.

Meanwhile, place the cabbage in a large bowl with the apples and the remaining teaspoon of caraway seeds. Mix the honey and lemon juice, and pour it over the cabbage mixture. Toss the mixture well and set it aside.

Place the meat in a bowl and sprinkle it with the pepper. Pour the reduced liquid over the meat and stir the mixture well.

Heat 1 tablespoon of the oil in a large, heavy-bottomed skillet set over high heat. Add the beef and scallions and sauté them, stirring, until the meat is browned — about one and a half minutes. Transfer the mixture to a bowl.

Heat the remaining ½ tablespoon of oil in the skillet over medium-high heat. Add the cabbage-and-apple mixture and cook it, stirring frequently, until the cabbage has wilted slightly — three to four minutes. Return the beef to the skillet, toss the mixture well, and serve it at once.

SUGGESTED ACCOMPANIMENT: *broad egg noodles.*

Stir-Fried Ginger Beef with Watercress

Serves 4
Working time: about 20 minutes
Total time: about 1 hour and 10 minutes

Calories **195**
Protein **21g.**
Cholesterol **54mg.**
Total fat **7g.**
Saturated fat **2g.**
Sodium **440mg.**

1 lb. top round steak, trimmed of fat and sliced into thin strips 3 inches long
½ tbsp. peanut oil
1 bunch watercress, trimmed, washed and dried
Ginger marinade
one 2-inch piece fresh ginger, peeled and finely chopped
1 tbsp. chili paste, or 1 tsp. hot red-pepper flakes
¼ cup dry sherry
¼ cup unsalted chicken stock
cornstarch
1 tsp. sugar
Cucumber salad
2 cucumbers, seeded and cut into thick strips
¼ tsp. salt
¼ cup rice vinegar or distilled white vinegar
1 tsp. dark sesame oil

Combine all of the marinade ingredients in a bowl. Add the beef and toss it well; cover the bowl and marinate the meat for one hour at room temperature.

Combine the cucumbers, salt, vinegar and sesame oil in a bowl. Refrigerate the salad.

When the marinating time is up, drain the beef, reserving the marinade. Heat the oil in a large, nonstick skillet or a well-seasoned wok over high heat. Add the beef and stir fry it until it is well browned — about two minutes. Add the reserved marinade; stir constantly until the sauce thickens — about one minute. Add the watercress and toss the mixture quickly. Serve the stir-fried beef and watercress immediately, accompanied by the chilled cucumber salad.

SUGGESTED ACCOMPANIMENT: *rice with sweet red peppers.*

Beef Braised in Beer

Serves 8
Working time: about 30 minutes
Total time: about 3 hours

Calories **290**
Protein **31g.**
Cholesterol **85mg.**
Total fat **8g.**
Saturated fat **3g.**
Sodium **240mg.**

one 2½-lb. arm pot roast, trimmed of fat
½ tsp. safflower oil
8 large onions (about 4 lb.), sliced
2 cups unsalted brown stock or unsalted chicken stock
2 tbsp. flour
12 oz. dark beer
4 garlic cloves, chopped
2 tbsp. julienned fresh ginger
1 bay leaf
4 fresh thyme sprigs, or 1 tsp. dried thyme leaves
1 strip of lemon zest
2 tbsp. dark molasses
½ tsp. salt
freshly ground black pepper

Preheat the oven to 325° F. Heat the oil in a large, nonstick skillet over high heat. Add the pot roast and sear it until it is well browned on both sides — about five minutes in all. Transfer the roast to an ovenproof casserole or Dutch oven.

Reduce the heat under the skillet to medium. Add the onions to the skillet and cook them, stirring frequently, until they begin to soften — about 10 minutes. Deglaze the pan with two tablespoons of the stock. Continue cooking the onions, adding another two tablespoons of stock whenever the liquid in the skillet has evaporated, until the onions are very soft and their juices have caramelized — 15 to 20 minutes more. Sprinkle the flour over the onions; cook the mixture, stirring constantly, for one minute.

Pour 1 cup of the remaining stock into the skillet and stir well to incorporate the flour. Increase the heat to medium high and boil the mixture until it is quite thick — three to four minutes. Pour in the rest of the stock and the beer. Bring the liquid to a simmer, then transfer the contents of the skillet to the casserole or Dutch oven. Add the garlic, ginger, bay leaf, thyme, lemon zest, molasses, salt and some pepper to the casserole. Cover the pan and braise the roast in the oven until it is very tender — about two hours.

Transfer the roast to a cutting board, slice it, and arrange the slices on a serving platter. Remove the bay leaf, the thyme sprigs if you used them, and the lemon zest from the sauce, and pour it over the meat.

SUGGESTED ACCOMPANIMENTS: *noodles tossed with fresh parsley; steamed parsnips.*

Lemon-Cardamom Braised Beef

Serves 8
Working time: about 1 hour
Total time: about 3 hours

Calories **240**
Protein **29g.**
Cholesterol **78mg.**
Total fat **8g.**
Saturated fat **3g.**
Sodium **290mg.**

one 3-lb. tip roast, trimmed of fat
2 tsp. safflower oil
2 onions, cut into eighths
2 celery stalks, coarsely chopped
2 garlic cloves, chopped
3 cups unsalted brown stock or unsalted chicken stock,
½ cup dry white wine
zest of 1 lemon, cut into strips
½ tsp. ground cardamom or ground ginger
½ tsp. salt
2½ tbsp. fresh lemon juice
1 tbsp. Dijon mustard
freshly ground black pepper
1 lb. carrots
1 lb. zucchini, halved lengthwise, the halves sliced on the diagonal into ½-inch-wide pieces

Heat the oil in a Dutch oven or a large, deep skillet over high heat. Sear the beef until it is browned on all sides — 10 to 15 minutes. Tuck the onions, celery and garlic around the beef, and add the stock, wine, lemon zest, ¼ teaspoon of the cardamom or ginger, and ¼ teaspoon of the salt. Bring the liquid to a boil, then lower the heat to maintain a slow simmer. Cover the skillet, leaving the lid slightly ajar, and braise the beef for one hour. Turn the beef over and continue cooking it until it is tender — one hour and 30 minutes to two hours. Transfer the beef to a cutting board and cover it loosely with aluminum foil.

Strain the cooking liquid through a fine sieve into a saucepan. Whisk in 1½ tablespoons of the lemon juice, the mustard, a generous grinding of pepper, the remaining ¼ teaspoon of cardamom or ginger, and the remaining ¼ teaspoon of salt. Simmer the sauce over medium heat until it is reduced to 1¼ cups.

While the sauce is reducing, peel the carrots and cut them with a roll cut. Using a chef's knife, slice off the tip of a carrot on the diagonal. Roll the carrot a half turn and slice off another piece — it will have nonparallel ends. Continue rolling and slicing until you reach the stem end. Repeat the procedure to prepare the remaining carrots.

Pour enough water into a saucepan to fill it 1 inch deep. Set a vegetable steamer in the pan and bring the water to a boil. Add the carrots and cover the pan ▶

tightly. Steam the carrots until they begin to soften — five to seven minutes. Transfer them to a large skillet over medium-high heat. Add the zucchini, the remaining 1 tablespoon of lemon juice, ½ cup of the sauce and a liberal grinding of pepper. Cook the vegetables, stirring frequently, until almost all of the liquid has evaporated and the vegetables are glazed —

seven to 10 minutes.

Cut the beef into thin slices and arrange them on a warmed serving platter along with the vegetables. Briefly reheat the remaining sauce and pour it over the beef. Serve immediately.

SUGGESTED ACCOMPANIMENT: *whole-grain muffins.*

Beef Braised with Fennel

Serves 4
Working time: about 15 minutes
Total time: about 1 hour and 15 minutes

Calories **245**
Protein **27g.**
Cholesterol **76mg.**
Total fat **10g.**
Saturated fat **3g.**
Sodium **250mg.**

one 1¼-lb. boneless sirloin steak, trimmed of fat and cut into 4 pieces
¼ tsp. salt
freshly ground black pepper
1 tbsp. safflower oil
1 large fennel bulb, thinly sliced
1 cup unsalted brown stock or unsalted chicken stock
¼ cup dry white wine
1 large carrot, peeled and grated
1 tbsp. cornstarch, mixed with 2 tablespoons of water

With a meat mallet or the flat of a heavy knife, pound the steak pieces to a thickness of ½ inch. Season the

meat with the salt and some pepper. Heat 1 teaspoon of the oil in a large, nonstick skillet over medium-high heat and sear the meat on both sides. Transfer the meat to a plate and set it aside.

Heat the remaining 2 teaspoons of oil in the skillet and add the fennel. Cook the fennel, stirring occasionally, until it begins to brown — 10 to 12 minutes. Return the meat to the skillet. Pour in the stock and white wine and, if necessary, enough water to raise the liquid level two thirds up the side of the meat. Bring the liquid to a simmer, cover the skillet, and braise the meat for 25 minutes. Turn the pieces and continue cooking them for 20 minutes.

Stir the carrot into the skillet and cook it for 10 minutes. Whisk the cornstarch mixture into the simmering liquid; stir constantly until the sauce thickens slightly. Serve the beef and fennel immediately.

SUGGESTED ACCOMPANIMENT: *lettuce and tomato salad.*

Roulades in Tomato Sauce

Serves 8
Working time: about 1 hour and 30 minutes
Total time: about 4 hours

Calories **235**	one 2-lb. top round roast, trimmed of fat
Protein **25g.**	and cut on the diagonal into 16 scallopini
Cholesterol **57mg.**	1 tsp. safflower oil
Total fat **8g.**	3 onions, finely chopped
Saturated fat **3g.**	4 garlic cloves, finely chopped
Sodium **165mg.**	2 carrots, finely chopped
	56 oz. canned unsalted whole tomatoes, with their juice
	2 bay leaves
	3 tbsp. chopped parsley
	2 tbsp. chopped fresh oregano, or 2 tsp. dried oregano
	½ cup dry bread crumbs
	¼ cup freshly grated Parmesan cheese
	2 tbsp. finely chopped prosciutto or boiled ham
	¼ cup dry white wine

Mix the oil, onions, garlic and carrots in a large, heavy-bottomed saucepan. Cover the pan and cook the mix-ture over low heat until the onions are translucent — about 15 minutes.

Purée the tomatoes in a food processor or a blender. Add the purée and bay leaves to the onion-and-carrot mixture. Increase the heat to medium and simmer the vegetables, uncovered, until they become a thick sauce — about two hours.

While the sauce is simmering, make the roulades. In a bowl, combine the parsley, oregano, bread crumbs, cheese, prosciutto or ham, and the wine. Spread the scallopini flat on the work surface and spread some of the stuffing mixture on each one. Roll up each slice and tie it with two short pieces of string to secure it.

Add the roulades to the thickened sauce and sim-mer them until the meat is tender — about one hour. Lift the roulades from the sauce and remove the string. Spoon the sauce over the roulades and serve them immediately.

SUGGESTED ACCOMPANIMENT: *fettuccine.*

Beef Curry

Serves 8
Working time: about 25 minutes
Total time: about 2 hours

Calories **265**
Protein **22g.**
Cholesterol **54mg.**
Total fat **8g.**
Saturated fat **2g.**
Sodium **140mg.**

2 lb. top round, trimmed of fat and cut into ½-inch pieces
2 cups unsalted brown stock or unsalted chicken stock
1 cup dry white wine
1 onion, chopped
1 carrot, thinly sliced on the diagonal
¾ cup chopped, pitted prunes
1 pear, peeled, quartered, cored and thinly sliced
1 tbsp. honey
2 tsp. curry powder
¼ tsp. salt
1 tbsp. safflower oil
2 plantains or bananas, cut into ¼-inch rounds
1½ tbsp. fresh lemon juice

Combine the stock, wine and 1½ cups of water in a large, heavy-bottomed, nonreactive pot and bring the liquid to a boil. Add the beef and reduce the heat to medium low; cook the meat with the lid slightly ajar for 30 minutes, skimming the surface of the liquid from time to time.

Add the onion, carrot, prunes, pear, honey, curry powder and salt, and continue cooking slowly until the meat is very tender and the sauce has thickened — about one hour.

Ten minutes before serving, heat the oil in a large, heavy-bottomed or nonstick skillet over medium-high heat. Add the plantains or bananas and cook them, turning them occasionally, until they begin to brown. Sprinkle the fruit with the lemon juice; continue cooking the fruit until it has browned — about 10 minutes for plantains, five minutes for bananas.

To serve, mound the curry in the center of a warmed serving platter and surround it with the plantains or bananas. Serve at once.

SUGGESTED ACCOMPANIMENT: *brown rice tossed with peas and grated lemon zest.*

Tangerine Beef Stew

Serves 4
Working time: about 40 minutes
Total time: about 2 hours and 30 minutes

Calories **595**
Protein **29g.**
Cholesterol **69mg.**
Total fat **17g.**
Saturated fat **4g.**
Sodium **380mg.**

3 tbsp. safflower oil
1 lb. boneless beef shin (sold as cross-cut shank) or other stew beef, trimmed of all fat and cut into 1-inch cubes
½ tbsp. Chinese five-spice powder
1 tbsp. flour
1 garlic clove, finely chopped
2 tsp. finely chopped fresh ginger
2 leeks, trimmed, the green tops discarded, the white parts split, washed thoroughly to remove all grit, and thinly sliced (about 1 ½ cups)
1 cup red wine
2 cups unsalted brown stock
3 strips tangerine zest, each about 2 inches long and 1 inch wide, pinned together with 1 whole clove
¼ cup fresh tangerine juice
1 cup fresh water chestnuts, peeled and sliced, or 1 cup canned water chestnuts, drained, rinsed and sliced
1 lb. butternut squash, peeled, seeded and cut into rectangles about 1 ½ inches long, ¾-inch wide and ¼-inch thick
½ tsp. salt
1 cup rice
2 tbsp. julienned tangerine zest (optional), blanched

Pour 2 tablespoons of the oil into a heavy-bottomed pot over medium-high heat. Sprinkle the beef cubes with the five-spice powder and the flour and toss them to coat them evenly. Add as many beef cubes to the oil as will fit in a single layer without touching. Brown the meat well on one side, then turn the pieces and continue cooking them, turning as necessary, until they are browned on all sides. Use a slotted spoon to transfer the beef to a plate, then cook any remaining cubes.

Pour off any oil remaining in the pot and clean the pot. Reduce the heat to low and pour in the last tablespoon of oil. Add the garlic, ginger and leeks, and cook them, stirring often, for five minutes. Return the beef cubes to the pot. Add the wine, stock, tangerine-zest strips and tangerine juice. Cover the pot and gently simmer the stew for one and one half hours.

Add the water chestnuts, squash and salt, and continue simmering the stew until the squash is tender — about 20 minutes. While the water chestnuts and squash are cooking, cook the rice. Spoon the stew over the rice; garnish it, if you like, with the julienned zest.

EDITOR'S NOTE: *This recipe works equally well when lamb shanks or veal shanks are used in place of the beef. A root vegetable such as carrot, sweet potato or turnip may be substituted for the squash. A variation of Chinese five-spice powder may be made at home by chopping in a blender equal parts Sichuan peppercorns, fennel seeds, ground cloves and ground cinnamon.*

Mexican Meat Loaf

Serves 6
Working time: about 1 hour
Total time: about 2 hours and 45 minutes
(includes rising)

Calories **430**
Protein **28g.**
Cholesterol **57mg.**
Total fat **11g.**
Saturated fat **4g.**
Sodium **275mg.**

1¼ lb. beef round, trimmed of fat and ground
2 ancho chili peppers, or 1 sweet red pepper, seeded, deribbed and finely chopped (caution, page 125)
1 tbsp. safflower oil
1 large onion, finely chopped
1 green pepper, seeded, deribbed and finely chopped
2 garlic cloves, finely chopped
⅛ tsp. salt
¼ tsp. ground cumin
cayenne pepper
freshly ground black pepper
1 cup fresh bread crumbs
2 oz. grated Cheddar cheese (about ½ cup)
2 tbsp. light brown sugar
1 tbsp. cornmeal
Spiced Dough
1 package active dry yeast
¼ tsp. sugar
2¾ cups bread flour
¼ tsp. salt
1 jalapeño pepper, seeded, deribbed and finely chopped
1 tsp. dried oregano

To make the dough, pour ¼ cup of lukewarm water into a bowl and sprinkle the yeast and sugar into it. After two minutes, stir the mixture until the yeast and sugar are dissolved.

Sift 2½ cups of the flour and the salt into a large bowl. Stir in the chopped jalapeño pepper and the oregano. Make a well in the center, pour the yeast mixture and ¾ cup of lukewarm water into it, and stir the ingredients together with a wooden spoon. Mix the dough by hand until it feels slightly sticky. If the mixture is too wet and clings to your hands, work in the remaining ¼ cup of flour, a tablespoon at a time, until the dough can be gathered into a ball. Place the dough on a floured surface and knead it until it has become smooth and elastic — about 10 minutes.

Put the dough into a lightly oiled bowl, turn the dough over once to coat it with the oil, and cover it with a damp cloth. Set the bowl in a warm, draft-free place until the dough has doubled in volume — approximately one hour and 30 minutes. Meanwhile, prepare the meat filling.

Remove and discard the stems and seeds from the ancho chilies if you are using them. Chop the chilies coarsely and soak them in 1 cup of boiling water for 10 minutes. Meanwhile, combine 2 teaspoons of the oil, the onion, the green pepper and the sweet red pepper, if you are using it, in a heavy-bottomed or nonstick skillet over medium heat. Cook the mixture, stirring occasionally, until the onion is lightly browned; add

Sirloin-Filled Pita Sandwiches

Serves 6
Working (and total) time: about 1 hour and 15 minutes

Calories **300**
Protein **22g.**
Cholesterol **38mg.**
Total fat **11g.**
Saturated fat **3g.**
Sodium **205mg.**

¾ lb. sirloin steak, trimmed of fat and thinly sliced
1 red onion, thickly sliced
6 whole-wheat pita breads
¼ lb. part-skim mozzarella, grated
3 garlic cloves, finely chopped
12 Kalamata olives or black olives, pitted and chopped
2 large ripe tomatoes, each cut into 6 slices
1 tbsp. safflower oil

Put the onion slices on the rack of a broiler pan and broil them until they are soft — about four minutes. Remove the onions from the rack and set them aside. Lay the slices of meat on the rack and broil them until they are browned — about two minutes.

Split a pita bread into two rounds. On the bottom half, layer one sixth of the onion, beef, cheese, garlic, olives and tomatoes. Set the top half in place. Repeat the process to make five more sandwiches.

Lightly brush the outside of the sandwiches with the oil. Toast the sandwiches in a waffle iron or in a skillet over medium heat until the bread is crisp and brown and the cheese has melted — about four minutes. Cut each sandwich in two before serving.

the garlic and cook for an additional minute. Transfer the onion mixture to a large bowl and set it aside.

Wipe out the skillet with a paper towel and pour in the remaining teaspoon of oil, tilting the skillet from side to side to distribute the oil. Add the beef and cook it over medium heat, crumbling it into small pieces with a wooden spoon. Cook the beef, stirring it constantly, until it loses its raw, red color. Sprinkle the beef with the salt, cumin, a pinch of cayenne pepper and some black pepper. Stir the mixture well and transfer it to the bowl containing the onion mixture; stir in the bread crumbs, cheese and brown sugar. If you are using the ancho chilies, purée them with ¾ cup of their soaking liquid in a food processor or a blender. Strain the purée through a sieve onto the onion-beef mixture, then stir it in. Set the mixture aside.

Preheat the oven to 425° F.

When the dough has doubled in volume, punch it down. Remove the dough from the bowl and roll it out on a lightly floured surface into a ¼-inch-thick rectangle measuring 10 inches by 16 inches. Transfer the dough to a baking sheet dusted with the cornmeal. Spoon the meat filling, slightly off center, in a straight line down the length of the rectangle, leaving a 2-inch border at either end. Brush the edges with a little water. Fold the wider side over the filling and securely seal the loaf by pressing its edges together. Tuck the ends under, and brush the surface of the dough with water to give it a hard crust. With a knife, lightly score the meat loaf's surface in a wide crisscross pattern. Bake the meat loaf for 10 minutes, then reduce the heat to 325° F., and bake the loaf for 30 minutes more. Transfer the meat loaf to a serving platter and allow it to rest for 10 to 15 minutes before slicing; then serve it.

SUGGESTED ACCOMPANIMENT: *mixed salad greens.*

Beef Tenderloin and Potato Roast

Serves 4
Working time: about 20 minutes
Total time: about 1 hour and 10 minutes

Calories **290**
Protein **27g.**
Cholesterol **73mg.**
Total fat **9g.**
Saturated fat **3g.**
Sodium **145mg.**

one 1¼-lb. beef tenderloin roast, trimmed of fat and cut into 8 slices
½ tsp. ground allspice
¼ cup chopped parsley
1 tbsp. red wine vinegar
⅛ tsp. salt
1 lb. baking potatoes, scrubbed and cut into ¼-inch-thick slices
2 onions, thinly sliced
½ cup unsalted brown stock or unsalted chicken stock

Preheat the oven to 350° F.

Mix the allspice, 2 tablespoons of the parsley, the vinegar and the salt in a small bowl. With your fingers, rub this mixture into the beef pieces and place them in a shallow dish. Let the meat marinate at room temperature while you make the potato gratin.

Combine the potatoes and onions in a flameproof baking dish. Pour in the stock and 1 cup of water. Bring the liquid to a boil over medium-high heat, then bake the potatoes in the oven until they are tender and have browned — about 45 minutes. (If you do not have a flameproof baking dish, bring the potatoes, onions, stock and water to a boil in a saucepan, then transfer the mixture to a baking dish, and proceed as above.)

When the potatoes are cooked, remove the dish from the oven and increase the temperature to 450° F.

Heat a nonstick skillet over medium-high heat. Pat the beef slices dry with a paper towel and sear them for 30 seconds on each side. Set the beef on top of the potatoes and return the dish to the oven. Bake the beef and potatoes for three minutes; turn the meat and bake it for three minutes more.

Sprinkle the remaining 2 tablespoons of parsley over the top before serving the roast.

SUGGESTED ACCOMPANIMENT: *steamed Brussels sprouts.*

Layered Meat Loaf

Serves 8
Working time: about 40 minutes
Total time: about 2 hours

Calories **220**
Protein **23g.**
Cholesterol **56mg.**
Total fat **8g.**
Saturated fat **3g.**
Sodium **230mg.**

1¾ lb. beef round, trimmed of fat and ground
2 large, ripe tomatoes (about 1 lb.), peeled, seeded and chopped
1 onion, chopped
3 garlic cloves, finely chopped
1½ tsp. chopped fresh oregano, or ½ tsp. dried oregano
½ cup port or Madeira
2 tbsp. red wine vinegar
1 tbsp. sugar
¼ tsp. salt
freshly ground black pepper
6 tbsp. freshly grated Parmesan cheese
⅔ cup dry bread crumbs
1 egg white
1 tbsp. safflower oil
2 bunches watercress, trimmed and washed
1 tbsp. fresh thyme, or 1 tsp. dried thyme leaves

Heat a large, heavy-bottomed skillet over medium-high heat. Put in the tomatoes, onion, garlic and oregano. Cook the vegetables, stirring occasionally, for five minutes. Add the port or Madeira, vinegar, sugar, ⅛ teaspoon of the salt and some pepper. Cook the mixture until almost all of the liquid has evaporated —

about 10 minutes. Purée the mixture and place all but ¼ cup of it in a large bowl. Preheat the oven to 400° F.

Add the beef, 4 tablespoons of the grated cheese, ⅓ cup of the bread crumbs, the remaining ⅛ teaspoon of salt, some pepper and the egg white to the tomato mixture in the bowl. Mix the ingredients well and set the meat aside while you prepare the watercress.

Heat the oil in a large, heavy-bottomed skillet over high heat. Add the watercress, thyme, and some pepper. Cook, stirring constantly, until the watercress has wilted and almost all of the liquid has evaporated — three to four minutes. Chop the watercress finely. Place it in a bowl and combine it with the remaining ⅓ cup of bread crumbs.

To layer the meat loaf, divide the beef mixture into three equal portions. Using a rolling pin or your hands, flatten each portion into a rectangle 5 inches wide, 8 inches long and ¾ inch thick.

Place one rectangle in a shallow baking pan. Top it with half of the watercress mixture, spreading the watercress evenly over the surface. Lay another rectangle on top and cover it with the remaining watercress. Finish with the final rectangle, then spread the reserved tomato sauce over the top and sides of the loaf. Sprinkle on the remaining 2 tablespoons of Parmesan cheese and bake the meat loaf for one hour and 10 minutes. Let the meat loaf stand for 10 minutes, then carefully transfer it to a platter, slice it and serve.

SUGGESTED ACCOMPANIMENT: *boiled new potatoes.*

Chunky Beef Chili

Serves 8
Working time: about 1 hour
Total time: about 4 hours

Calories **230**
Protein **27g.**
Cholesterol **75mg.**
Total fat **10g.**
Saturated fat **3g.**
Sodium **460mg.**

2 dried ancho chili peppers, stemmed, seeded and quartered
2 jalapeño peppers, stemmed, seeded and coarsely chopped (caution, page 125)
2 tbsp. safflower oil
2 lb. beef chuck, trimmed of fat and cut into ½-inch chunks
2 large onions, finely chopped
2 celery stalks, finely chopped
2 garlic cloves, finely chopped
2 tbsp. finely chopped fresh ginger
1 tbsp. ground cumin
1 tbsp. Mexican oregano
¼ tsp. cayenne pepper
¼ tsp. freshly ground black pepper
1 tbsp. flour
14 oz. canned unsalted tomatoes, coarsely chopped, with their juice
1 bay leaf
1 ½ tsp. salt
½ tsp. grated orange zest

Put the ancho chilies into a small saucepan; pour in 2 cups of water and boil the liquid for five minutes. Turn off the heat and let the chilies soften for five minutes.

Transfer the chilies to a blender or food processor with ½ cup of their soaking liquid; reserve the remaining liquid. Add the jalapeño peppers and purée the chilies until the mixture is very smooth. Strain the purée through a sieve into the reserved soaking liquid, rubbing the solids through with a spoon.

Heat ½ tablespoon of the oil in a large, nonstick or heavy-bottomed skillet over medium-high heat. Add about one fourth of the beef chunks and cook them, turning the pieces frequently, until they are browned all over — approximately eight minutes. Transfer the browned beef to a large, heavy-bottomed pot. Brown the rest of the meat the same way, using all but ½ tablespoon of the remaining oil in the process.

Add the last ½ tablespoon of oil to the skillet along with the onions, celery and garlic. Sauté the vegetables for five minutes, stirring frequently. Stir in the ginger, cumin, oregano, cayenne pepper and black pepper, and cook the mixture for one minute. Add the flour and cook for one minute more, stirring constantly. Transfer the mixture to the pot.

Pour the reserved chili mixture and 2 cups of water into the pot. Stir in the tomatoes and their juice along with the bay leaf, salt and orange zest. Cook the mixture, uncovered, over very low heat until the meat is tender — two and one half to three hours. (Do not allow the mixture to boil or the meat will toughen.) If the chili begins to get too thick, add water, ½ cup at a time, until it reaches the desired consistency.

EDITOR'S NOTE: *Black beans make an excellent accompaniment to this orange-scented chili.*

Chilies — A Cautionary Note

Both dried and fresh hot chilies should be handled with care. Their flesh and seeds contain volatile oils that can make skin tingle and cause eyes to burn. Rubber gloves offer protection — but the cook should still be careful not to touch the face, lips or eyes when working with chilies.

Soaking fresh chilies in cold, salted water for an hour will remove some of their fire. If canned chilies are substituted for fresh ones, they should be rinsed in cold water in order to eliminate as much of the brine used to preserve them as possible.

Lentil-Sausage Stew

Serves 6
Working time: about 15 minutes
Total time: about 1 hour

Calories **185**
Protein **12g.**
Cholesterol **12mg.**
Total fat **6g.**
Saturated fat **2g.**
Sodium **515mg.**

3 oz. chorizo sausage, skinned, sliced into very thin rounds, all but 8 of the rounds cut into thin strips
1 large onion, very finely chopped
1 ½ cups lentils, picked over
3 cups unsalted brown or chicken stock
1 large carrot, sliced into thin rounds
2 celery stalks, thinly sliced
1 tbsp. chopped fresh basil, or 2 tsp. dried basil
½ tsp. salt
freshly ground black pepper

Cook the chorizo rounds and strips in a large, heavy-bottomed pot over medium-low heat for three minutes. Remove the rounds and set them aside. Add the onion and continue cooking until the onion is translucent — about six minutes.

Rinse the lentils under cold running water and add them to the pot along with the stock and 3 cups of water. Bring the liquid to a simmer and cook the mixture, covered, until the lentils are soft — about 35 minutes. Add the carrot, celery, basil, salt and some pepper; simmer the stew, covered, until the carrot rounds are tender — seven to 10 minutes. Garnish the stew with the reserved chorizo rounds; serve at once.

Medallions of Veal with Rosemary and Red Wine

Serves 6
Working time: about 15 minutes
Total time: about 1 hour and 15 minutes
(includes marinating)

Calories **200**
Protein **21g.**
Cholesterol **95mg.**
Total fat **12g.**
Saturated fat **3g.**
Sodium **215mg.**

6 medallions of veal (about 4 oz. each), trimmed of fat	
12 or more sprigs rosemary	
2 tbsp. virgin olive oil	
1 garlic clove, crushed	
1 lemon, finely grated zest only	
1 tbsp. chopped fresh parsley	
1 tbsp. unsalted butter	
1 cup red wine	
⅔ cup unsalted veal stock or unsalted chicken stock	
¼ tsp. salt	
freshly ground black pepper	

Spear each medallion of veal with two or three small rosemary sprigs. Blend 1½ tablespoons of the oil with the garlic, lemon zest, and parsley in a shallow dish. Add the medallions to this marinade and turn them carefully until they are well coated. Cover and marinate at room temperature for at least one hour.

Heat the remaining oil with the butter in a nonstick skillet. Add the medallions and cook for two to three minutes on each side, until they are well browned but still slightly pink inside. Transfer the veal to a plate lined with paper towels. Cover and keep hot.

Pour off all the excess fat from the skillet, and stir in the wine and stock. Bring to a boil, stirring, then boil gently until the liquid is reduced by half. Season with the salt and some pepper.

Arrange the medallions on a hot serving plate, strain the sauce over them and, if desired, garnish with more rosemary sprigs. Serve immediately.

SUGGESTED ACCOMPANIMENT: *green beans or asparagus.*

Veal Cutlets with Gorgonzola and Fennel

Serves 4
Working (and total) time: about 40 minutes

Calories **240**
Protein **27g.**
Cholesterol **105mg.**
Total fat **12g.**
Saturated fat **2g.**
Sodium **380mg.**

one 1-lb. piece loin of veal, trimmed of fat, cut diagonally into ¼-inch-thick slices and slightly flattened
1 tbsp. virgin olive oil
2 tbsp. anise-flavored liqueur or unsalted veal stock or unsalted chicken stock
1 large fennel bulb, cut into slices, feathery tops reserved
3 oz. Gorgonzola cheese, mashed
2 tbsp. skim milk
2 tsp. chopped fresh sage, or ½ tsp. dried sage
2 tsp. chopped fresh thyme, or ½ tsp. dried thyme leaves
⅛ tsp. salt
freshly ground black pepper

Preheat the oven to 275° F. Heat the oil in a nonstick skillet over medium-high heat, add as many pieces of veal as the pan will comfortably hold, and cook them for three to five minutes until they are just tender, turning once and pressing the pieces of veal firmly with a spatula to keep them as flat as possible. Transfer the veal to a platter, cover, and keep it hot in the oven. Cook the remainder of the veal in the same way.

Add the anise-flavored liqueur or stock to the cooking juices in the pan, increase the heat, and stir briskly to deglaze. Add the fennel and toss over high heat for two to three minutes, then remove it with a slotted spoon and keep it hot with the veal.

Lower the heat, add the Gorgonzola and milk, and cook gently, stirring, until the cheese has melted and formed a sauce with the cooking juices and milk. Add the chopped sage, thyme, salt, and some pepper, and remove the pan from the heat.

To assemble the dish, arrange the meat and fennel on individual plates. Spoon the sauce over the meat and garnish with the reserved fennel tops. Serve the dish immediately.

EDITOR'S NOTE: *Adding anise-flavored liqueur to the cooking juices heightens the flavor of the fennel.*

Roast Five-Spice Leg of Lamb

FIVE-SPICE POWDER IS A TRADITIONAL CHINESE SEASONING. THE ACTUAL SPICES USED TO MAKE IT UP VARY FROM REGION TO REGION, BUT THREE OF THEM ARE ALWAYS PRESENT: CASSIA BARK (CHINESE CINNAMON), STAR ANISE, AND SICHUAN PEPPER.

Serves 8
Working time: about 45 minutes
Total time: about 16 hours (includes marinating)

Calories **225**
Protein **32g.**
Cholesterol **75mg.**
Total fat **9g.**
Saturated fat **4g.**
Sodium **140mg.**

one 3-lb. half leg of lamb, shank end, trimmed of fat
1 tbsp. apple jelly
1¼ lb. small carrots, peeled
32 pearl onions, blanched and peeled
½ tsp. arrowroot
Five-spice marinade
¾ oz. cassia bark (Chinese cinnamon), or 6 cinnamon sticks
12 star anise
12 cloves
1½ tsp. Sichuan peppercorns
3 strips fresh orange zest
1 or 2 dried chili peppers (cautionary note, page 125)
¼ cup low-sodium dark soy sauce
¼ cup low-sodium light soy sauce
2 cups Chinese rice wine or dry sherry
2 tsp. brown sugar
4 garlic cloves, unpeeled
one 1-inch piece fresh ginger, unpeeled and cut into quarters
½ tsp. arrowroot

To make the marinade, put the cassia bark or the cinnamon sticks, star anise, cloves, Sichuan pepper-corns, orange zest, and chili peppers into a small piece of cheesecloth, and tie it up with cotton string, leaving one long end. Mix the dark and the light soy sauce, the rice wine or sherry, and the sugar with 2 cups of water in a large saucepan. Bring the liquid to a simmer, stirring to dissolve the sugar, then add the garlic, gin-ger, and the spice bag, tying its string to the handle of the pan. Cover the pan and let the marinade simmer for 30 minutes, skimming off any scum from time to time. At the end of this period, add the leg of lamb and boil it, uncovered, for six to seven minutes, turning it once. Reduce the heat to very low and skim the mar-inade, then cover the pan and simmer the lamb for 30 minutes. Turn the meat after 15 minutes and skim again if necessary. Let the lamb cool in the liquid, then marinate it in the refrigerator for 12 to 24 hours, turning it several times.

Preheat the oven to 450° F. Remove the leg of lamb from the pan, reserving half of the marinade for bast-ing and deglazing, and the other half for the sauce. Place the meat on a rack over a roasting pan and roast it for 10 minutes. Lower the heat to 350° F., put a pan of cold water on the bottom shelf, and continue cook-ing for one hour to one hour and 20 minutes for medium to well-done meat; baste the meat several times with the marinade. Ten minutes before the end of roasting time, glaze the meat: Mix the apple jelly with 1 teaspoon of boiling water, brush this solution evenly over the leg, and return it to the oven.

While the lamb is roasting, begin to make the sauce. Strain the remaining half of the marinade into a sauce-pan through a fine sieve, bring it to a boil, and add the carrots. Let the liquid return to a boil, lower the heat, and simmer the carrots for five minutes; then add the onions and simmer the vegetables until they are ten-der—about 15 minutes. Remove the pan from the heat and leave the vegetables in the liquid for 10 minutes to absorb its color. Remove them with a slot-ted spoon and keep them warm. Strain the liquid into a saucepan and set it aside.

When the meat is cooked, turn off the oven and transfer the leg to a large platter. Let it rest for 15 minutes in the oven with the door slightly ajar. Mean-while, skim off any fat from the roasting pan, set the pan over high heat, and add about 3 tablespoons of the marinade. Stir the liquid as it comes to a boil, scraping off any browned bits from the bottom of the pan. Strain the pan juices and add them to the veg-etable cooking liquid. Boil the liquid rapidly for one to two minutes. Add ½ cup of water. Mix the arrowroot with 1 tablespoon of water and add it to the sauce. Return it to a boil, and cook until the sauce thickens and clears—two to three minutes. Transfer it to a serving bowl.

Arrange the vegetables around the meat and carve at the table.

SUGGESTED ACCOMPANIMENTS: *rice; apple jelly.*

EDITOR'S NOTE: *All the spices required for this recipe can be purchased in Asian markets.*

Parslied Leg of Lamb Baked in a Casing of Dough

IN THIS RECIPE, A PASTE OF FLOUR AND WATER WORKS
IN THE SAME WAY THAT A CLAY OVEN DOES,
SEALING IN THE FLAVORS AND KEEPING THE MEAT
MOIST AND TENDER.

Serves 10
Working time: about 30 minutes
Total time: about 2 hours and 30 minutes

Calories **210**	one 5-lb. leg of lamb, trimmed of fat
Protein **30g.**	6 garlic cloves, peeled
Cholesterol **80mg.**	¾ tsp. salt
Total fat **10g.**	freshly ground black pepper
Saturated fat **4g.**	¼ cup chopped fresh parsley
Sodium **185mg.**	1 tbsp. virgin olive oil
	6 cups unbleached all-purpose flour

Preheat the oven to 400° F.

Work the garlic cloves and salt into a creamy paste with a mortar and pestle. Mix in some freshly ground black pepper, the parsley, and the oil. Rub this mixture evenly all over the leg of lamb.

Put the flour into a large mixing bowl and make a well in the center. Add 2 cups of cold water and mix to make a soft dough. Lightly knead the dough on a floured work surface until it is smooth, then roll it out into a rectangle large enough to completely encase the leg of lamb.

Place the lamb upside down in the center of the dough. Bring the short sides of the rectangle up and over each end of the leg, then fold in the long edges to encase the lamb completely. Mold the dough neatly around the leg and press the edges well together to seal the casing.

Place the lamb in a large roasting pan with the seams in the dough underneath. Sprinkle the dough lightly with flour. Cook the lamb for two hours.

To serve, break open and discard the casing, by now baked to hardness, then carve the leg in the usual way.

SUGGESTED ACCOMPANIMENTS: *braised leeks; glazed carrots; creamed potatoes.*

Lamb with Eggplant and Parmesan

Serves 4
Working time: about 40 minutes
Total time: about 1 hour

Calories **450**
Protein **34g.**
Cholesterol **80mg.**
Total fat **10g.**
Saturated fat **4g.**
Sodium **235mg.**

1 lb. lean lamb (from the leg or loin), cut into ½-inch cubes
½ lb. pasta shells
1 tsp. olive oil
½ lb. pearl onions, blanched in boiling water for 2 minutes and peeled
½ lb. small fresh mushrooms, wiped clean
¾ lb. eggplant, cut into ½-inch cubes
1 tsp. fresh thyme, or ½ tsp. dried thyme leaves
freshly ground black pepper
½ oz. Parmesan cheese, shaved with a vegetable peeler or grated (about ¼ cup)

Add the pasta to 3 quarts of boiling water with 1½ teaspoons of salt. Start testing the pasta for doneness after six minutes and cook it until it is *al dente*. Drain the pasta, rinse it under cold running water to prevent the shells from sticking together, and set it aside.

Heat a large, nonstick skillet over high heat. Add the pieces of lamb to the skillet and sauté them until they are browned on all sides —about three minutes. Lower the heat to medium and cook the lamb for three minutes more. Remove the lamb from the skillet and set the meat aside.

Add the olive oil and onions to the skillet. Place the cover on the skillet and cook the onions, stirring occasionally, until they are browned—about 15 minutes. Add the mushrooms and eggplant, then increase the heat to high, and sauté the vegetables until all are browned and the mushrooms and eggplant are soft—six to eight minutes.

Return the lamb to the skillet; add the pasta, the thyme, and a generous grinding of pepper. Sauté the mixture until the pasta is heated through—about three minutes. Spoon the mixture into a serving dish and top it with the cheese.

Serve immediately.

SUGGESTED ACCOMPANIMENT: *curly endive salad.*

Lamb Shanks with Orange and Cinnamon

Serves 4
Working time: about 45 minutes
Total time: about 2 hours and 40 minutes

Calories **285**	4 lamb shanks (about ¾ lb. each), trimmed of fat
Protein **20g.**	⅓ cup all-purpose flour
Cholesterol **52mg.**	freshly ground black pepper
Total fat **10g.**	2 tbsp. chopped fresh oregano, or 2 tsp. dried oregano
Saturated fat **2g.**	1½ tbsp. safflower oil
Sodium **255mg.**	1 onion, chopped
	2 garlic cloves, finely chopped
	½ cup red wine
	¼ cup fresh orange juice
	¼ tsp. salt
	1 bay leaf
	1 cinnamon stick, or ¼ tsp. ground cinnamon
	2 cups pearl onions (about 10 oz.), blanched for 2 minutes in boiling water and peeled
	1 lb. carrots, cut crosswise into 2-inch-long pieces
	1 tbsp. julienned orange zest
	¼ cup finely chopped parsley

Put the flour, some pepper, and half of the oregano into a large plastic bag. Add the shanks and shake the bag to coat the meat with the mixture.

Heat the oil in a large, heavy-bottomed skillet over medium-high heat. Sauté the shanks in the skillet, turning them from time to time, until they have browned. Add the chopped onion, reduce the heat to low, and cover the skillet. Cook the lamb and onion for five minutes, stirring occasionally.

Increase the heat to medium high and add the garlic, wine, orange juice, and 3 cups of water. Bring the liquid to a simmer, scraping the bottom of the skillet with a wooden spoon to dissolve any caramelized juices. Add the salt, bay leaf, cinnamon, and the remaining oregano. Lower the heat, cover the skillet, and continue simmering the meat until it is barely tender—one and a half to two hours.

Skim any fat from the surface of the liquid; add the pearl onions, carrots, and orange zest. Simmer, partially covered, until the vegetables are tender—about 30 minutes. Skim off any more fat, stir in the parsley, and serve the lamb with the vegetables and the sauce.

SUGGESTED ACCOMPANIMENT: rice.

Roast Leg of Lamb with Pear Mustard

Serves 10
Working time: about 1 hour
Total time: about 2 hours and 15 minutes

Calories **225**
Protein **24g.**
Cholesterol **75mg.**
Total fat **9g.**
Saturated fat **3g.**
Sodium **430mg.**

one 5-lb. leg of lamb, trimmed of fat, the pelvic and thigh bones removed, the shank bone left in place
½ tbsp. Dijon mustard
1 tbsp. safflower oil
¼ tsp. salt
3 bunches scallions, trimmed and cut into 1-inch lengths
Pear mustard
½ tbsp. safflower oil
1½ lb. pears (preferably Comice), peeled, cored, and coarsely chopped
1 cup unsalted brown stock or unsalted chicken stock
1½ tbsp. fresh lemon juice
1 shallot, finely chopped, or 1 scallion, white part only, finely chopped
1 garlic clove, finely chopped

1¼ tsp. salt
freshly ground black pepper
1½ tbsp. Dijon mustard

To make the pear mustard, heat the oil in a heavy-bottomed saucepan set over medium-high heat. Add the pears and cook them, stirring frequently, until the juice is syrupy and lightly browned—15 to 20 minutes. Add the stock, lemon juice, shallot or scallion, garlic, salt, some pepper, and the mustard. Lower the heat to medium and simmer the mixture, stirring occasionally, until only about 1½ cups remain—15 to 20 minutes. Transfer the pear mustard to a food processor or a blender, and purée it.

Preheat the oven to 325° F.

While the pear mustard is cooking, prepare the leg of lamb for roasting. Rub the ½ tablespoon of mustard over the exposed inner surface of the leg. Fold the meat over to enclose the mustard, then tie the leg securely with butcher's twine.

Heat the tablespoon of oil in a large, ovenproof skillet set over high heat. When the oil is hot, add the leg of lamb and brown it evenly on all sides—about 10 minutes. Sprinkle the lamb with the salt and transfer the skillet to the oven. Roast the lamb for 20 minutes, then coat it with about one-third of the pear mustard and roast it for 20 minutes more. Brush the lamb with about half of the remaining pear mustard. Increase the oven temperature to 500° F. and cook the lamb until the pear mustard is lightly browned in places—15 to 20 minutes. Remove the leg of lamb from the oven and let it rest for 20 minutes.

Blanch the scallion pieces in boiling water for one minute, then drain them and divide them among 10 warmed dinner plates. Slice the lamb and arrange the pieces on the scallions; dab a little of the remaining pear mustard on top before serving.

SUGGESTED ACCOMPANIMENT: *a gratin of sliced turnips and sweet potatoes.*

Leg of Lamb Roasted with Ginger

Serves 10
Working time: about 25 minutes
Total time: about 4 hours and 30 minutes
(includes marinating)

Calories **185**
Protein **24g.**
Cholesterol **75mg.**
Total fat **7g.**
Saturated fat **3g.**
Sodium **170mg.**

one 5-lb. leg of lamb, trimmed of fat
3 tbsp. finely chopped fresh ginger
3 garlic cloves, finely chopped
2 tsp. low-sodium soy sauce
¼ tsp. dark sesame oil
1 tsp. rice vinegar or distilled white vinegar
⅓ cup mirin or sweet sherry
ground white pepper
Dipping sauce
1 tbsp. low-sodium soy sauce
2 tbsp. mirin or sweet sherry
1 tsp. sesame seeds
2 tsp. rice vinegar or distilled white vinegar
1 scallion, trimmed and thinly sliced
1 small carrot, trimmed, peeled, and thinly sliced
2 tbsp. chopped fresh ginger
½ cup unsalted brown stock or unsalted chicken stock

With a knife, lightly score the surface of the lamb in a crosshatch pattern. Transfer the lamb to a shallow baking dish. Mix the ginger, garlic, soy sauce, sesame oil, vinegar, mirin or sherry, and some white pepper in a bowl. Pour the marinade over the lamb and refrigerate it for at least three hours, or as long as overnight. From time to time, baste the lamb with the marinade.

Toward the end of the marinating time, preheat the oven to 450° F. Transfer the lamb to a roasting pan, reserving the marinade, and roast the lamb for 15 minutes. Lower the oven temperature to 325° F. and continue roasting the lamb, basting it occasionally

with the reserved marinade, until a meat thermometer inserted in the center registers 140° F.—about 50 minutes more. Let the leg of lamb rest for 20 minutes before you carve it.

While the lamb is resting, combine the dipping-sauce ingredients. Serve the dipping sauce at room temperature with the lamb slices.

SUGGESTED ACCOMPANIMENT: *a cold salad of Asian noodles.*

Pepper Pork with Mozzarella

Serves 4
Working time: about 25 minutes
Total time: about 40 minutes

Calories **240**
Protein **25g.**
Cholesterol **90mg.**
Total fat **14g.**
Saturated fat **5g.**
Sodium **225mg.**

1 lb. pork tenderloin, trimmed of fat	
1 tsp. black peppercorns	
1 tsp. green peppercorns in brine, rinsed, drained, and chopped	
1 tbsp. safflower oil	
1 garlic clove, halved	
½ cup grated part-skim mozzarella	
2 shallots, finely chopped	
hot red-pepper sauce	
Worcestershire sauce	
⅔ cup unsalted chicken stock	
2 tbsp. dry sherry	
4 sprigs flat-leaf parsley	

Lay the pork on a board, and with a knife, cut it at a slightly diagonal angle into 12 slices, each about ¾ inch thick. Crush the black peppercorns using a pestle and mortar. Sprinkle the black and green pepper over one side of the pork slices, and press it into the meat. Cover the slices and set them aside for 15 minutes.

Heat the oil in a heavy-bottomed or nonstick frying pan on medium. Add the garlic and pork, peppered side down, and cook until well browned—about three minutes on each side. Preheat the broiler. Remove the pork from the pan and arrange the slices, peppered side up, in two overlapping rows in a shallow, flame-proof dish. Sprinkle the mozzarella over the pork, and broil until the cheese has melted and begins to brown.

Meanwhile, remove the garlic from the pan and discard it. Add the shallots to the pan and stir well, scraping up any browned bits from the bottom of the pan. Stir in a few drops each of hot red-pepper sauce and Worcestershire sauce, and add the stock and sherry. Simmer the sauce until it is slightly reduced—about three minutes. Spoon the sauce around the pork steaks and serve at once, garnished with the parsley.

SUGGESTED ACCOMPANIMENTS: *new potatoes; green salad.*

Pot-Roasted Pork Loin with Cherry Tomatoes

Serves 6
Working time: about 20 minutes
Total time: about 1 hour and 20 minutes

Calories **260**	1½ lb. boned pork loin, trimmed of fat
Protein **30g.**	1 tbsp. virgin olive oil
Cholesterol **70mg.**	2 tsp. fennel seeds
Total fat **13g.**	1 tsp. green peppercorns
Saturated fat **4g.**	2 tbsp. white wine vinegar
Sodium **90mg.**	2 tbsp. white wine
	¼ tsp. salt
	½ lb. cherry tomatoes, peeled

Heat the oil in a flameproof casserole that is just large enough to hold the pork loin, then, over medium heat, lightly brown the meat all over—about six minutes. Pour off and discard the oil, and add the fennel seeds, peppercorns, vinegar, wine, and salt to the casserole. Cover and cook over low heat for one hour; check the level of the liquid occasionally, and add more vinegar and wine if necessary. About 10 minutes before the end of cooking, add the tomatoes to the casserole.

Carefully remove the meat from the casserole and cut it into ¼-inch-thick slices. Overlap the slices in the middle of a warmed serving dish and arrange the tomatoes along the edges of the dish. Skim the fat from the surface of the liquid in the casserole, then pour the juices over the meat, making sure to include the fennel seeds and peppercorns.

Caper Cutlets

Serves 4
Working (and total) time: about 20 minutes

Calories **190**
Protein **20g.**
Cholesterol **60mg.**
Total fat **10g.**
Saturated fat **4g.**
Sodium **260mg.**

4 pork cutlets (about 3½ oz. each), trimmed of fat
½ tsp. salt
freshly ground black pepper
cayenne pepper (optional)
2 tsp. dry mustard
1 tsp. safflower oil
2 tbsp. Marsala
1 orange, grated zest of half, juice of whole
1 tbsp. capers, rinsed, drained, and chopped
1 tsp. green peppercorns in brine, rinsed and drained
1 tsp. ground cinnamon
2 tbsp. sour cream
½ cup plain low-fat yogurt

Pound the cutlets to tenderize them, season with the salt and some black pepper, and some cayenne, if you wish; dust the cutlets with the mustard.

Brush a heavy-bottomed, nonstick skillet with the oil and heat the pan over medium-high heat. Brown the cutlets briefly and cook them for two minutes on each side; ensure that the meat is cooked through, but do not overcook. Remove the cutlets from the pan and keep them warm.

Deglaze the pan with the Marsala and cook until the wine is almost evaporated. Add the orange juice and zest to the pan, and reduce until it is syrupy. Stir in the capers, peppercorns, cinnamon, and sour cream, bring to a simmer, and cook for one minute. Remove the pan from the heat and stir in the yogurt. Return the pan to the heat to warm the yogurt, but do not allow the sauce to boil. Serve the cutlets with the sauce at once.

SUGGESTED ACCOMPANIMENT: *herbed potatoes.*

Tenderloin with Mushrooms and Water Chestnuts

Serves 4
Working time: about 30 minutes
Total time: about 1 hour and 30 minutes (includes chilling)

Calories **275**
Protein **24g.**
Cholesterol **70mg.**
Total fat **10g.**
Saturated fat **4g.**
Sodium **290mg.**

1 lb. pork tenderloin, trimmed of fat
3½ oz. water chestnuts, fresh or canned
1 cup unsalted vegetable stock, reduced to ⅔ cup
½ lb. button mushrooms, finely sliced
4 tbsp. dry white wine
1 tsp. fresh lemon juice
2-inch piece fresh ginger
1 tbsp. safflower oil
2 garlic cloves, crushed
½ tsp. salt
freshly ground black pepper
3 tbsp. sour cream
½ cup plain low-fat yogurt
finely chopped fresh chives or scallions for garnish (optional)

Chill the tenderloin in the freezer for one hour to make

it easier to cut, then slice it into very thin rounds.

If you are using fresh water chestnuts, scrub and peel them; canned chestnuts will already be peeled. Slice the chestnuts into thin rounds.

In a pan, simmer the water-chestnut slices in the reduced stock for 10 minutes, to allow them to absorb its flavor. In another pan, cook the mushrooms in the wine and lemon juice over medium heat for two minutes. Drain the chestnuts and mushrooms, reserving their cooking liquids separately, and set them aside.

Cut the ginger into four or five pieces, and use a garlic press to extract the juice, or grate the ginger and press it through a fine sieve; discard the ginger solids. In a frying pan, heat half of the oil with one of the garlic cloves and about one-third of the ginger juice over low heat for a minute or two, then discard the garlic and increase the heat to medium high.

Season the meat with the salt and some pepper, and quickly arrange about half of the slices in the hot frying pan. When the upper surface of each slice is nearly translucent—30 to 45 seconds—turn and brown the other side. Lift the slices out of the pan and keep them warm. Heat the rest of the oil with the remaining garlic clove and one-third of the ginger juice as before, and brown the remaining slices of pork.

Once all the meat is cooked, gently wipe excess fat from the frying pan with a paper towel, but retain any browned bits and deglaze the pan over medium-high heat with the wine used to cook the mushrooms. When the wine has all but boiled away, add the stock used to cook the water chestnuts and reduce this mixture until it is slightly syrupy in appearance. Add the sour cream to the pan and cook the sauce for a few seconds more.

Strain the sauce through a fine-mesh sieve and wipe out the pan. Return the sauce to the pan, along with the meat, water chestnuts, and mushrooms. Heat the pan over low heat to warm all the ingredients, then stir in the yogurt, and continue to heat for another 30 seconds—do not allow the mixture to boil, as this will cause the sauce to separate.

Stir in the remaining ginger juice and serve the dish immediately, lightly sprinkled with the chives or scallions, if you are using them.

SUGGESTED ACCOMPANIMENTS: *plain brown rice; snow peas.*

Oriental Pot Roast

Serves 12
Working time: about 30 minutes
Total time: about 2 hours and 45 minutes

Calories **220**
Protein **32g.**
Cholesterol **70mg.**
Total fat **8g.**
Saturated fat **3g.**
Sodium **310mg.**

3 lb. boned pork loin, trimmed of fat and tied into shape
1 tbsp. safflower oil
2 tbsp. very finely chopped fresh ginger
2 tbsp. very finely chopped garlic
1 tbsp. very finely chopped fresh green chili pepper (caution, page 125)
4 tbsp. rice wine or dry sherry
2 tsp. brown sugar
4 tbsp. low-sodium soy sauce
2 sweet red peppers, seeded and deribbed, each cut into 12 strips
24 frozen baby corn
24 small scallions

Brown the meat well on all sides in a very hot, dry wok or a heavy-bottomed skillet. It may seem to stick at first, but if you leave the stuck surface for a few seconds and the heat is high enough, the meat will soon loosen. Keep the wok unwashed for later use.

Heat the oil in a flameproof casserole, then add the ginger, garlic, and chili pepper. Stir until the mixture begins to brown, then add the rice wine or sherry, and bring to a boil. Reduce the heat to low. Stir in the sugar and soy sauce, then place the browned meat in the casserole and turn it in the mixture so that all sides are coated. Ensure that the heat is low enough so that the liquid does not boil, cover the pot, and cook for two and a quarter hours. Add a little stock or water, if necessary, to prevent the meat from sticking.

About 15 minutes before serving, stir-fry first the red-pepper strips, then the corn, and finally the scallions in the wok or skillet over high heat. Transfer each batch to a bowl after stir-frying. The vegetables should be slightly soft and flecked with black, but still crisp.

When the meat has finished cooking, remove the string and slice the meat into 12 portions. Lay the slices on a serving platter. If the liquid in the casserole has not reduced to a dark, glossy syrup, skim off any fat and reduce the liquid over high heat. Toss the vegetables in the syrup left at the bottom of the casserole and make sure they are heated through, then spoon them over the pork and serve immediately.

SUGGESTED ACCOMPANIMENTS: *rice; bok choy in oyster sauce.*

Green Peppercorn Tenderloin

Serves 4
Working time: about 35 minutes
Total time: about 1 hour and 20 minutes

Calories **180**
Protein **19g.**
Cholesterol **60mg.**
Total fat **9g.**
Saturated fat **3g.**
Sodium **240mg.**

¾ lb. pork tenderloin, trimmed of fat
¼ lb. button mushrooms
2 shallots
1 tsp. virgin olive oil
3 tbsp. fresh lemon juice
½ tsp. salt
½ cup green beans, trimmed
1 tsp. green peppercorns packed in brine, rinsed and drained
1 tbsp. chopped fresh marjoram, or 1 tsp. dried marjoram
1 cup unsalted chicken stock
1 cup dry white wine
1 tsp. cornstarch

Preheat the oven to 375° F. Cut a lengthwise slit about halfway into the pork tenderloin, then open the pork out and place it, cut side down, on a board. Cover with a piece of plastic wrap and pound with a wooden mallet until the pork has a rectangular shape and is about ½ inch thick.

Chop the mushrooms and shallots finely in a food processor or by hand. Heat the oil in a nonstick frying pan, and add the mushrooms and shallots and 1 tablespoon of the lemon juice. Cook over medium heat, stirring frequently, until almost all of the moisture has evaporated—about seven minutes. Remove the pan from the heat and stir in the salt. Set aside.

Blanch the beans in boiling water for three minutes. Drain the beans and refresh them under cold water, then drain them again and dry them on paper towels.

Spread the mushroom mixture over the pork, leaving about ¼ inch clear on all sides. Sprinkle the peppercorns evenly over the mushroom mixture, then ar-

range the beans on top, parallel to the long edges of the meat. Press the beans into the mushroom mixture and sprinkle the marjoram over the beans.

Roll up the pork from a long side and tie it into shape with string. Place the pork in a roasting pan and pour the stock over it, along with half of the wine and the remaining lemon juice. Roast the pork for 45 minutes, basting several times with the cooking juices.

Remove the pork from the pan and keep it warm. Bring the cooking liquid to a simmer over medium heat. Mix the cornstarch with the remaining wine and stir this into the simmering liquid. Cook, stirring, for two minutes. Strain the sauce into a gravy boat.

Put the pork on a cutting board, cut away the string, and slice the pork into rounds. Arrange the slices on a heated serving plate and serve with the sauce.

5 *Pasta and the ingredients of numerous pasta dishes await metamorphosis into satisfying meals.*

Pasta

Vermicelli, Onions and Peas

Serves 8 as a side dish
Working time: about 15 minutes
Total time: about 1 hour

Calories **186**	½ lb. vermicelli or spaghettini
Protein **5g.**	2 tbsp. virgin olive oil
Cholesterol **0mg.**	4 cups chopped onion
Total fat **4g.**	1 leek, trimmed, cleaned and thinly sliced
Saturated fat **1g.**	¼ tsp. salt
Sodium **122mg.**	freshly ground black pepper
	1 cup dry white wine
	½ cup peas

Heat the oil in a large, heavy-bottomed skillet over low heat. Add the onion, leek, salt and a generous grinding of pepper. Cover the skillet tightly and cook, stirring frequently to keep the onions from sticking, until the vegetables are very soft — about 45 minutes.

Cook the pasta in 3 quarts of boiling water with 1½ teaspoons of salt. Start testing the pasta after seven minutes and cook it until it is *al dente*.

While the pasta is cooking, finish the sauce: Pour the wine into the skillet and raise the heat to high. Cook

the mixture until the liquid is reduced to about ¼ cup — approximately five minutes. Stir in the peas, cover the pan, and cook for another minute or two to heat the peas through. If you are using fresh peas, increase the cooking time to five minutes.

Drain the pasta and transfer it to a serving dish; pour the contents of the skillet over the top and toss well. Serve immediately.

Lasagne Roll-Ups

Serves 6
Working time: about 45 minutes
Total time: about 1 hour and 10 minutes

Calories **446**
Protein **24g.**
Cholesterol **35mg.**
Total fat **16g.**
Saturated fat **7g.**
Sodium **342mg.**

12 lasagne
1 lb. part-skim ricotta cheese
4 oz. part-skim mozzarella, shredded
2 small broccoli stalks, steamed for 5 minutes, drained and chopped (about 2 cups)
1 cup sliced fresh mushrooms
2 scallions, trimmed and chopped
2 tbsp. chopped fresh basil, or 2 tsp. dried basil
1 tbsp. chopped fresh oregano, or 1 tsp. dried oregano
¼ cup chopped fresh parsley
Tomato sauce
2 tbsp. safflower oil
1 onion, coarsely chopped
2 small carrots, peeled and coarsely chopped
2 celery stalks, trimmed and coarsely chopped
2 garlic cloves, thinly sliced
3 tbsp. chopped fresh basil, or 1 tbsp. dried basil
freshly ground black pepper
1 bay leaf
⅔ cup Madeira
2½ lb. ripe tomatoes, peeled, seeded and chopped, or 28 oz. unsalted canned whole tomatoes, drained and chopped
2 tbsp. tomato paste
½ cup unsweetened applesauce
3 tbsp. freshly grated Parmesan cheese

To make the sauce, pour the oil into a large, heavy-bottomed saucepan over medium-high heat. Add the onion, carrot and celery. Sauté the mixture, stirring frequently, for two minutes. Add the garlic and cook for one minute more. Stir in the basil, pepper, bay leaf and Madeira. Bring the liquid to a boil and cook it until it is reduced by about half — two to three minutes. Add the tomatoes, tomato paste and applesauce. As soon as the liquid returns to a boil, reduce the heat to low and gently simmer the sauce for 30 to 35 minutes. Remove the bay leaf and transfer the sauce to a food processor or blender. Purée the sauce and return it to the saucepan. Stir in the grated Parmesan cheese and set the pan aside.

Preheat the oven to 350° F. Add the lasagne to 4 quarts of boiling water with 2 teaspoons of salt. Start testing the pasta after 12 minutes and cook it until it is *al dente*. Drain the pieces and spread them on a clean dish towel to dry.

In a large bowl, mix the ricotta, mozzarella, broccoli, mushrooms, scallions, basil, oregano and parsley.

To assemble the dish, spread 1 cup of the tomato sauce over the bottom of an 11-by-13-inch baking pan. Spread about ¼ cup of the cheese-and-vegetable mixture over a lasagne strip; starting at one end, roll up the strip. Place the roll, seam side down, in the baking pan. Repeat the process with the remaining lasagne strips and filling. Pour the rest of the sauce over the rolls and cover the pan tightly with aluminum foil. Bake the rolls for 20 minutes, then remove the foil and bake them for 15 to 20 minutes more. Serve the lasagne roll-ups piping hot from the pan.

EDITOR'S NOTE: *To compensate for lasagne that may tear during cooking, add one or two extra strips to the boiling water.*

Vegetable Lasagna

Serves 6
Working time: about 1 hour and 30 minutes
Total time: about 2 hours and 15 minutes

Calories **295**
Protein **13g.**
Cholesterol **55mg.**
Total fat **12g.**
Saturated fat **5g.**
Sodium **280mg.**

1 tbsp. virgin olive oil
1 onion, finely chopped
1 leek, trimmed, washed thoroughly to remove all grit, thinly sliced
2 garlic cloves, crushed
6 oz. broccoli florets (about 2 cups)
¼ lb. green beans, ends removed, cut into 1-inch lengths
6 celery stalks, thinly sliced
1 small yellow pepper, seeded, deribbed, and thinly sliced
1 tsp. mixed dried herbs
1 tbsp. chopped parsley
14 oz. canned tomatoes, sieved
¼ tsp. salt
freshly ground black pepper

Spinach pasta dough

1½ cups unbleached all-purpose flour
3 tbsp. finely chopped spinach (about 5 oz. frozen spinach, thawed, or ½ lb. fresh spinach, washed, stemmed, and blanched in boiling water for 1 minute, squeezed dry)
1 egg
1 egg white
1 tbsp. safflower oil

Nutmeg sauce

2 tbsp. unsalted butter
¼ cup unbleached all-purpose flour
1¼ cups skim milk
½ tsp. freshly grated nutmeg, or ½ tsp. ground nutmeg
⅛ tsp. salt
freshly ground black pepper
¼ cup freshly grated Parmesan cheese

To prepare the vegetable filling, heat the oil in a large, heavy-bottomed saucepan over medium heat. Add the onion and leek, and cook until they are soft—six to eight minutes. Stir in the garlic, all of the remaining vegetables, the dried herbs, chopped parsley, tomatoes, salt, and some black pepper. Bring the mixture to a boil, then lower the heat and partially cover the pan. Cook gently until the vegetables are tender and the liquid has thickened—about 45 minutes.

Meanwhile, make the pasta. Put the flour into a mixing bowl and make a well in the center. Add the spinach, egg, egg white, and oil, and stir them, using a fork or wooden spoon, gradually incorporating the flour. Transfer the dough to a lightly floured surface and knead it for a few minutes. The dough should come cleanly away from the surface; if it is too wet, add flour by the tablespoon until the dough is no longer sticky. If the dough is too dry and crumbly to work with, add water by the teaspoon until it is pliable. Continue kneading the dough until it is smooth and elastic—about 10 minutes. (Alternatively, place the dough ingredients in a food processor and process them for about 30 seconds.) Wrap the dough in wax paper or plastic wrap, and let it rest for 15 minutes before rolling it out.

Using a rolling pin, roll out the dough on a well-floured surface into a rectangle approximately 18 by 24 inches; it should be about 1/16 inch thick. Cut the rectangle lengthwise into three 6-inch strips, then cut each of these strips crosswise into six 4-inch-wide pieces, to make a total of 18 sheets of lasagna.

Preheat the oven to 400° F. Cook the lasagna, three or four sheets at a time, in 3 quarts of gently boiling water for one minute. Lift the sheets out of the water with a slotted spoon and spread them on a clean dishtowel to drain.

Grease a 7-by-11-by-2-inch ovenproof dish and line the bottom with six sheets of lasagna. Pour in half of the vegetable filling and cover it with another six sheets of lasagna. Pour in the rest of the vegetables and arrange the remaining lasagna over the top.

To make the sauce, melt the butter in a saucepan over medium heat. Add the flour, then gradually stir in the milk. Bring the sauce to a boil, stirring continuously until it thickens. Stir in the nutmeg, salt, and some black pepper. Reduce the heat to low and simmer the sauce for five minutes, stirring frequently. Pour the sauce over the top of the lasagna and spread it to cover the entire surface. Sprinkle the Parmesan evenly over the sauce. Cook the dish in the oven for 40 minutes, until it is golden brown and bubbling hot.

SUGGESTED ACCOMPANIMENT: *mixed salad.*

EDITOR'S NOTE: *Instead of kneading and rolling out the pasta by hand, you can use a pasta machine. Dried lasagna strips may be used for this recipe in place of the fresh pasta. Cook them first according to the instructions on the package.*

Penne with Celery and Ricotta Cheese

Serves 8
Working (and total) time: about 30 minutes

Calories **320**
Protein **14g.**
Cholesterol **15mg.**
Total fat **6g.**
Saturated fat **3g.**
Sodium **275mg.**

1 lb. penne, or other short, tubular pasta
½ lb. celery (2 to 3 stalks), trimmed and finely chopped
½ cup part-skim ricotta cheese
¾ cup sour cream
¾ cup plain low-fat yogurt
½ tsp. freshly grated nutmeg, or ½ tsp. ground nutmeg
½ tsp. salt
freshly ground black pepper
1 tbsp. virgin olive oil
4 to 6 shallots, finely chopped
5 tbsp. finely chopped parsley
3 tbsp. fresh lime juice

Add the penne to 5 quarts of boiling water with 1½ teaspoons of salt. Start testing the pasta after 10 minutes and continue to cook until it is *al dente.*

While the pasta is cooking, pour enough water into a saucepan to fill it about 1 inch deep. Set a vegetable steamer in the pan and bring the water to a boil. Put the chopped celery in the steamer, cover the saucepan, and steam the celery until it is tender but still firm —three to four minutes.

Stir the ricotta, sour cream, and yogurt together in a bowl with a fork until smooth, then season with the nutmeg, salt, and some freshly ground black pepper. Set the mixture aside.

Heat the oil in a heavy skillet, add the steamed celery, the shallots, and 4 tablespoons of the chopped parsley, and sauté them over medium heat until they are soft—about five minutes. Drain the pasta and stir it into the celery mixture. Remove the pan from the heat, and gently stir the cheese mixture into the pasta and celery. Return the pan to low heat, cover with a lid, and warm the pasta mixture until it is thoroughly heated—about three minutes. Stir in the lime juice and serve immediately, garnished with the remaining chopped parsley.

SUGGESTED ACCOMPANIMENT: *grilled tomatoes or a tomato salad.*

Spaghetti with Fresh Basil, Pine Nuts and Cheese

Serves 4
Working (and total) time: about 15 minutes

Calories **362**
Protein **14g.**
Cholesterol **15mg.**
Total fat **13g.**
Saturated fat **3g.**
Sodium **414mg.**

8 oz. spaghetti
1 tbsp. virgin olive oil
1 garlic clove, crushed
1 cup shredded basil leaves, plus several whole leaves reserved for garnish
½ cup unsalted chicken stock
¼ cup pine nuts (about 1 oz.), toasted in a small, dry skillet over medium heat
½ cup freshly grated Romano cheese
¼ tsp. salt
freshly ground black pepper

To prepare the sauce, first pour the oil into a skillet set over medium heat. When the oil is hot, add the garlic and cook it, stirring constantly, for about 30 seconds. Reduce the heat to low. Stir in the shredded basil leaves and allow them to wilt — approximately 30 seconds. Pour in the stock and simmer the liquid gently while you cook the pasta.

Add the spaghetti to 3 quarts of boiling water with 1½ teaspoons of salt. Start testing the pasta after 10 minutes and cook it until it is *al dente*.

Drain the pasta and add it to the skillet with the basil. Toss well to coat the pasta. Add the pine nuts, cheese, salt and some pepper, and toss again. Serve at once, garnished with the whole basil leaves.

Gorgonzola Lasagne

Serves 8
Working time: about 45 minutes
Total time: about 1 hour and 30 minutes

Calories **207**
Protein **9g.**
Cholesterol **13mg.**
Total fat **8g.**
Saturated fat **3g.**
Sodium **244mg.**

8 oz. lasagne
4 red peppers
2 red onions (about ¾ lb.), sliced into ½-inch-thick rounds
2 tbsp. fresh lemon juice
3 tsp. fresh thyme, or ¾ tsp. dried thyme leaves
2 tbsp. virgin olive oil
1 small head escarole (about 1 lb.), washed, trimmed and sliced crosswise into 1-inch-wide strips
½ tsp. salt
freshly ground black pepper
¼ cup freshly grated Parmesan cheese
4 oz. Gorgonzola cheese, broken into small pieces

Preheat the broiler. Arrange the peppers in the center of a baking sheet with the onion slices surrounding them. Broil the vegetables until the peppers are blis-tered on all sides and the onions are lightly browned — 10 to 15 minutes. (You will need to turn the peppers a few times, the onions once.) Put the peppers in a bowl, cover it with plastic wrap, and set it aside. Separate the onion slices into rings and reserve them as well.

Cook the lasagne in 3 quarts of boiling unsalted water with the lemon juice for seven minutes — the pasta will be slightly underdone. Drain the pasta and run cold water over it.

Peel the peppers when they are cool enough to han-dle, working over a bowl to catch the juices. Remove the stem, seeds and ribs from each pepper. Set one pepper aside and slice the remaining three into length-wise strips about ¾ inch wide. Strain the pepper juices and reserve them.

Quarter the reserved whole pepper; purée the pieces in a food processor or blender with the pepper juices and 2 teaspoons of the fresh thyme or ½ tea-spoon of the dried thyme. Preheat the oven to 350° F.

Heat the oil in a large, heavy-bottomed skillet over medium-high heat. Add the escarole, ¼ teaspoon of the salt, the remaining teaspoon of fresh thyme or ¼ ▶

teaspoon of dried thyme, and a generous grinding of black pepper. Sauté the escarole until it is wilted and almost all the liquid has evaporated — about five minutes. Remove the pan from the heat.

Line the bottom of a baking dish with a layer of the lasagne. Cover this layer with half of the escarole and sprinkle it with 1 tablespoon of the Parmesan cheese. Spread half of the pepper strips over the top, then cover them with half of the onion rings. Build a second layer of lasagne, escarole, Parmesan cheese, pepper strips and onion rings, this time topping the onion rings with half of the pepper purée. Cover the second level with a final layer of lasagne, and spread the remaining purée over the top. Scatter the Gorgonzola cheese evenly over the pepper sauce and sprinkle the remaining 2 tablespoons of Parmesan cheese over all.

Bake the lasagne for 30 minutes. Let the dish stand for 10 minutes to allow the flavors to meld.

Pasta Salad with Lobster and Snow Peas

THE RADIATORI CALLED FOR HERE IS A PASTA WITH RIDGES THAT RESEMBLE THE HEATING COILS OF A RADIATOR. COOKING THE RADIATORI IN THE LOBSTER WATER INFUSES THE PASTA WITH THE FLAVOR OF THE SHELLFISH.

Serves 4
Working time: about 40 minutes
Total time: about 1 hour

Calories **375**
Protein **17g.**
Cholesterol **41mg.**
Total fat **12g.**
Saturated fat **1g.**
Sodium **271mg.**

8 oz. radiatori (or other fancy pasta)
¼ cup very thinly sliced shallots
1 tbsp. red wine vinegar
3 tbsp. virgin olive oil
2 garlic cloves, lightly crushed
¼ tsp. salt
freshly ground black pepper
1 live lobster (about 1½ lb.)
2 tbsp. lemon juice
½ lb. snow peas, stems and strings removed, sliced in half with a diagonal cut
1 tbsp. chopped fresh basil or Italian parsley

Pour enough water into a large pot to fill it about 1 inch deep. Bring the water to a boil and add the lobster. Cover the pot tightly and steam the lobster until it turns a bright reddish orange — about 12 minutes.

In the meantime, put half of the shallots in a bowl with the vinegar and let them stand for five minutes. Whisk in 2 tablespoons of the oil, then stir in the garlic, ⅛ teaspoon of the salt, and some pepper. Set the vinaigrette aside.

Remove the lobster from the pot and set it on a dish to catch the juices. Pour 2 quarts of water into the pot along with 1 tablespoon of the lemon juice, and bring the liquid to a boil.

When the lobster has cooled enough to handle, twist off the tail and claws from the body. Crack the shell and remove the meat from the tail and claws. Add the shells and the body to the boiling liquid and cook for 10 minutes. Cut the meat into ½-inch pieces and set it aside in a bowl.

Use a slotted spoon to remove the shells from the boiling liquid; then add the pasta. Start testing after 13 minutes and cook the pasta until it is *al dente*.

While the pasta is cooking, pour the remaining tablespoon of oil into a large, heavy-bottomed skillet over medium-high heat. Add the snow peas along with the remaining 2 tablespoons of shallots and ⅛ teaspoon of salt. Cook, stirring constantly, until the snow peas turn bright green — about one and a half minutes. Scrape the contents of the skillet into the bowl with the lobster.

When the pasta finishes cooking, drain it and rinse it briefly under cold water. Remove and discard the garlic from the vinaigrette, then combine the vinaigrette with the pasta. Add the lobster mixture, the basil, the remaining tablespoon of lemon juice and some more pepper, and toss well.

EDITOR'S NOTE: *Although the pasta salad may be served immediately, allowing it to stand for 30 minutes will meld its flavors. Alternatively, the salad may be served chilled.*

Goat Cheese and Parsley Ravioli

Serves 4
Working (and total) time: about 1 hour and 15 minutes

Calories **430**
Protein **23g.**
Cholesterol **75mg.**
Total fat **14g.**
Saturated fat **2g.**
Sodium **490mg.**

1½ cups unbleached all-purpose flour
1 egg
1 egg white
1 tbsp. safflower oil
6 oz. soft goat cheese
¾ cup fine fresh white breadcrumbs
¾ cup loosely packed parsley, finely chopped
2 scallions, finely chopped
Tomato sauce
1 tsp. virgin olive oil
1 small onion, chopped
4 medium tomatoes, peeled and coarsely chopped
½ tsp. salt
freshly ground black pepper

To prepare the dough, put the flour into a mixing bowl and make a well in the center. Add the egg, egg white, and oil, and stir them, using a fork or wooden spoon, gradually mixing in the flour. Transfer the dough to a lightly floured surface and knead it for a few minutes. The dough should come cleanly away from the surface. If it is too wet, add flour by the tablespoon until it is no longer sticky. If it is too dry and crumbly to work with, add water by the teaspoon until it is pliable. Continue kneading the dough until it is smooth and elastic—about 10 minutes. (Alternatively, place the dough ingredients in a food processor and process them for about 30 seconds.) Wrap the dough in wax paper or plastic wrap, and let it rest for 15 minutes.

Meanwhile, make the tomato sauce. Heat the olive oil in a heavy skillet over medium heat, then sauté the onion in the oil until it is soft—about three minutes. Add the tomatoes, and season them with the salt and some black pepper. Bring the contents of the pan to a boil, and cook over high heat until the tomatoes are soft—about five minutes. Lower the heat and simmer, uncovered, for 15 minutes more. Remove the pan from the heat; when the mixture has cooled a little, purée it in a blender. Pass the purée through a coarse sieve into a clean saucepan and set it aside.

To make the ravioli filling, combine the cheese, breadcrumbs, all but 1 tablespoon of the parsley, and the scallions. Divide the dough in half. Cover one portion with plastic wrap or an inverted bowl. Using a rolling pin, roll out the other portion very thinly on a well-floured surface into a rectangle measuring about 30 by 6 inches; it should be about ¹⁄₁₆ inch thick. Then, following the steps opposite, form it into 18 ravioli that are each about 2½ by 2 inches. Repeat the process with the second portion of dough.

Gently reheat the tomato sauce over low heat. Add the ravioli to 3 quarts of boiling water with 1½ teaspoons of salt. Start testing the ravioli after one minute and cook them until they are *al dente,* then drain them. Serve the ravioli immediately, with the sauce and a sprinkling of the remaining chopped parsley.

EDITOR'S NOTE: *Instead of kneading and rolling out the pasta by hand, you can use a pasta machine.*

Making Ravioli

1 *ADDING THE FILLING. Spread the rolled dough sheet on a lightly floured surface. Place 18 dollops of the filling on half of the sheet, taking care to space them evenly, about 1½ inches apart.*

2 *COVERING THE FILLING. Brush the other half of the sheet lightly with water. Then fold it gently over the mounds of filling, matching the edges as closely as possible.*

3 *CUTTING THE RAVIOLI. Starting from the folded edge, use your fingers or the side of your hand to force out the air between the mounds of filling and to seal the dough. Then cut out the ravioli with a fluted pastry wheel.*

Spaghetti with Omelet Strips and Stir-Fried Vegetables

Serves 6
Working (and total) time: about 40 minutes

Calories **290**	2 eggs
Protein **13g.**	¼ tsp. salt
Cholesterol **75mg.**	¼ tsp. cayenne pepper
Total fat **9g.**	2 tsp. chopped cilantro
Saturated fat **2g.**	¾ lb. dried whole-wheat spaghetti
Sodium **100mg.**	2 tbsp. safflower oil
	10 oz. bok choy (Chinese chard), washed and dried, stalks removed and julienned, leaves cut into strips
	1-inch piece fresh ginger, julienned
	12 scallions, white parts only, thinly sliced
	2 large sweet red peppers, seeded, deribbed, and julienned
	2½ tbsp. low-sodium soy sauce

First make two thin, flat omelets. Break the eggs into a bowl, add the salt, cayenne pepper, and cilantro, and whisk well. Pour half of the egg mixture into a hot, lightly oiled nonstick skillet, and cook over medium heat until the underside begins to set—about one minute. Carefully lift the edge of the omelet with a spatula and allow any uncooked egg to run underneath; repeat until there is no liquid left on the surface of the omelet. Flip the omelet over with the spatula and cook it for 30 seconds more. Slide the omelet onto a plate and make another omelet in the same way. Set them aside to cool, then slice them into strips.

Cook the spaghetti in 5 quarts of boiling water with 2 teaspoons of salt. Start testing the spaghetti after 10 minutes and cook it until it is *al dente*. When it is almost ready, heat the oil in a wok or large, heavy skillet and stir-fry the vegetables. At 20-second intervals, stirring after each addition, add the bok choy stalks to the wok, then the ginger, the scallions with the red peppers, and finally the bok choy leaves. Drain the cooked spaghetti thoroughly and add it to the wok together with the omelet strips. Season with the soy sauce, stir well, and serve immediately.

SUGGESTED ACCOMPANIMENT: *salad of carrot strips and cucumber, dressed with a lemon and mint vinaigrette.*

Macaroni Baked with Stilton and Port

Serves 6
Working time: about 20 minutes
Total time: about 45 minutes

Calories **301**
Protein **11g.**
Cholesterol **17mg.**
Total fat **9g.**
Saturated fat **4g.**
Sodium **401mg.**

8 oz. elbow macaroni
1 tbsp. safflower oil
2 shallots, finely chopped
2 tbsp. flour
½ cup ruby Port
1 cup low-fat milk
1 cup unsalted chicken stock
4 oz. Stilton or other blue cheese, crumbled
2 tsp. Dijon mustard
⅛ tsp. white pepper
¼ cup dry bread crumbs
1 tsp. paprika

Preheat the oven to 350° F. Pour the oil into a large, heavy-bottomed saucepan over medium heat. Add the shallots and cook them, stirring occasionally, until they are transparent — approximately two minutes. Sprinkle the flour over the shallots and cook the mixture, stirring continuously, for two minutes more.

Pour the Port into the pan and whisk slowly; add the milk and the stock in the same manner, whisking after each addition, to form a smooth sauce. Gently simmer the sauce for three minutes. Stir in half of the cheese along with the mustard and pepper. Continue stirring until the cheese has melted.

Meanwhile, cook the macaroni in 3 quarts of boiling water with 1½ teaspoons of salt. Start testing the pasta after 10 minutes and cook it until it is *al dente*.

Drain the macaroni and combine it with the sauce, then transfer the mixture to a baking dish. Combine the bread crumbs with the remaining crumbled cheese and scatter the mixture evenly over the top. Sprinkle the paprika over all and bake the dish until the sauce is bubbling hot and the top is crisp — 20 to 25 minutes. Serve immediately.

Ditalini Gratin with Jalapeño Pepper

IN THIS DISH, PASTA AND SAUCE ARE COOKED TOGETHER, WITH THE STARCH IN THE PASTA SERVING AS THE THICKENING AGENT FOR THE SAUCE.

Serves 6 as a side dish
Working time: about 25 minutes
Total time: about 30 minutes

Calories **226**
Protein **10g.**
Cholesterol **12mg.**
Total fat **4g.**
Saturated fat **3g.**
Sodium **183mg.**

8 oz. ditalini (or other small, tubular pasta)
1½ lb. ripe tomatoes, peeled, seeded and chopped, or 14 oz. unsalted canned whole tomatoes, drained and chopped
1 onion, chopped
1 cup low-fat milk
1 jalapeño pepper, seeded, deribbed and finely chopped (caution, page 125)
1 garlic clove, finely chopped
¼ tsp. ground cumin
¼ tsp. salt
freshly ground black pepper
2 oz. Monterey Jack cheese, finely diced

Put the tomatoes, onion and milk in a large, heavy-bottomed skillet, and bring the mixture to a boil. Add the ditalini, jalapeño pepper, garlic, cumin, salt and a liberal grinding of pepper. Stir to mix thoroughly, then cover the pan and reduce the heat to medium. Simmer the mixture for two minutes, stirring from time to time to keep the pasta from sticking to the bottom. Preheat the broiler.

Pour into the skillet just enough water to cover the ditalini. Cook the pasta, removing the lid frequently to stir the mixture and keep it covered with liquid, until the pasta is just tender and a creamy sauce has formed — about seven minutes.

Transfer the contents of the skillet to a gratin dish. Sprinkle the cheese over the top and broil the pasta until the cheese is melted — two to three minutes. Serve the dish immediately.

Warm Sichuan Noodles with Spiced Beef

Serves 6
Working time: about 30 minutes
Total time: about 1 hour

Calories **281**
Protein **29g.**
Cholesterol **28mg.**
Total fat **12g.**
Saturated fat **2g.**
Sodium **340mg.**

1 lb. fresh Asian egg noodles, or 12 oz. dried vermicelli
¾ lb. beef tenderloin or lean sirloin, trimmed of all fat
8 dried shiitake or Chinese black mushrooms, soaked in very hot water for 20 minutes and drained
4 scallions, thinly sliced diagonally
1 ½ tbsp. safflower oil

Sesame-soy marinade

¼ cup low-sodium soy sauce
2 tbsp. Chinese black vinegar or balsamic vinegar
2 tbsp. rice vinegar
1 to 2 tsp. chili paste with garlic
½ tsp. very finely chopped garlic
1½ tsp. very finely chopped fresh ginger
1 tsp. sugar
1 tsp. dark sesame oil
2 tbsp. safflower oil
2 tbsp. toasted sesame seeds, crushed with a mortar and pestle
5 scallions, very finely chopped (about ¾ cup)
½ cup cilantro, coarsely chopped

Garnish

1 small cucumber, scored lengthwise with a fork and thinly sliced
1 tbsp. toasted sesame seeds
cilantro sprigs

Combine the marinade ingredients in a bowl and set the marinade aside.

Cut the beef across the grain into julienne about 1½ inches long and ⅛ inch thick. Cut off and discard the mushroom stems, and slice the caps into strips about ⅛ inch wide. In a bowl, combine the beef, mushrooms and scallions with one third of the marinade. Let the beef marinate for 30 minutes.

At the end of the marinating time, put 4 quarts of water on to boil. Drain and discard any excess marinade from the beef mixture. Heat the 1½ tablespoons of safflower oil in a heavy-bottomed skillet or a wok; add the mushrooms, scallions and beef strips, and sauté them for one minute. Set the beef mixture aside on a large plate, spreading it out so that it cools rapidly.

Add the noodles to the boiling water. Start testing them after three minutes and cook them until they are *al dente*. Drain the noodles and transfer them to a large bowl. Add the remaining two thirds of the marinade and toss it with the noodles.

To serve, arrange the cucumber slices in an overlapping pattern around the edge of a large plate. Arrange the noodles in the center of the plate, partly covering the cucumbers. Make a shallow well in the center of the noodles and spoon the beef mixture into the well. Sprinkle the tablespoon of sesame seeds over all and garnish the top with a few fresh cilantro sprigs. Serve at room temperature.

EDITOR'S NOTE: *A colorful salad of fresh fruit, tossed with unsweetened coconut milk and fresh lemon juice, and garnished with mint, makes a delightful accompaniment.*

Shining Noodle Salad with Beef and Tomato

Serves 6
Working time: about 30 minutes
Total time: about 1 hour

Calories **267**
Protein **16g.**
Cholesterol **28mg.**
Total fat **6g.**
Saturated fat **2g.**
Sodium **339mg.**

8 oz. flat beanthread noodles or rice noodles
two 6-oz. beef tenderloin steaks, trimmed of all fat
½ cup thinly sliced red onion
grated zest of 1 lime
4 tbsp. fresh lime juice
2 tsp. finely chopped cilantro
2 tsp. very finely chopped fresh lemon grass, or 1½ tsp. grated lemon zest
2 tsp. finely chopped fresh mint
½ tsp. finely chopped hot chili pepper (caution, page 125), or ½ tsp. sambal oelek
½ tsp. finely chopped garlic
3 tbsp. low-sodium soy sauce
1 tbsp. safflower oil
½ tsp. sugar
2 small heads Boston lettuce
3 ripe tomatoes, thinly sliced
mint leaves for garnish

Broil the steaks until they are rare and allow them to cool. Cut each steak in half lengthwise. Thinly slice each half into pieces about ⅛-inch thick, and toss the pieces with the onion slices. Set the mixture aside.

In a large bowl, combine the lime zest and juice, cilantro, lemon grass or lemon zest, mint, chili pepper or sambal oelek, garlic, soy sauce, oil and sugar. Pour half of this marinade over the beef and onion slices, reserving the other half of the marinade for the noodles. Toss well, then cover the beef and let it marinate at room temperature for 30 minutes.

Pour enough boiling water over the noodles to cover them. Soak the noodles until they are *al dente* — 10 to 15 minutes, depending on their thickness. Drain the noodles, rinse them in cold water, and drain them ▶

once again. Wrap the noodles in a clean towel and squeeze out most of their moisture. Cut the noodles into 6-inch lengths and toss them with the reserved half of the marinade.

To serve, arrange some lettuce leaves on each of six plates. At one side of each plate, just inside the edge of the leaves, arrange several tomato slices in a crescent. Mound some noodles next to the tomatoes. Arrange the beef slices on top of the noodles, then distribute the onion strips around the beef in a flower pattern. Garnish the salads with the mint leaves and serve them at room temperature.

EDITOR'S NOTE: *To give the onion slices an intriguingly different shape, first halve an onion lengthwise, then cut one of the halves lengthwise into thin strips resembling crescents.*

Nonya Rice Noodles with Shrimp

A BLEND OF CHINESE AND MALAYSIAN INGREDIENTS, NONYA DISHES ARE DISTINCTIVELY RICH AND SPICY. NONYA COOKING DEVELOPED IN THE 19TH CENTURY WITH THE INFLUX OF CHINESE TIN MINERS INTO THE MALAY PENINSULA.

Serves 6
Working (and total) time: about 45 minutes

Calories **349**
Protein **15g.**
Cholesterol **62mg.**
Total fat **8g.**
Saturated fat **3g.**
Sodium **358mg.**

12 oz. flat rice noodles
¾ lb. small shrimp, shelled
2 tsp. very finely chopped fresh lemon grass, or 1½ tsp. freshly grated lemon zest
1 tsp. very finely chopped fresh ginger
½ tsp. very finely chopped garlic
½ tsp. salt
2 tbsp. safflower oil
½ cup unsweetened coconut milk
1½ cups unsalted chicken stock, reduced to 1 cup
6 tbsp. fresh lemon juice
2 tsp. low-sodium soy sauce
2 tsp. sweet chili sauce
2 tsp. ground coriander
1 large onion, halved lengthwise and thinly sliced
1 red bell pepper, seeded, deribbed and thinly sliced
1 lemon, cut into wedges (optional)
1 bunch watercress (optional)

Pour enough boiling water over the rice noodles to cover them, and let them soak for 15 minutes. In a large bowl, combine the shrimp with the lemon grass, ginger, garlic and salt. (If you are using lemon zest in place of the lemon grass, set it aside for later use.)

Heat 1 tablespoon of the oil in a hot wok or a heavy-bottomed skillet over high heat. Add the shrimp mixture and stir fry it until the shrimp are barely cooked — about three minutes. Transfer the shrimp to a plate. Pour out and reserve any juices left in the wok, then wipe the wok clean.

In a saucepan, combine the coconut milk, stock, lemon juice, soy sauce and chili sauce. Bring the liquid just to a boil. Heat the remaining tablespoon of oil in the wok. Add the ground coriander and onion, and gently stir fry them until the onion is limp — about four minutes. Add the red pepper and stir fry the mixture for one minute more.

Drain the noodles and add them to the red pepper and onion in the wok. Pour in the coconut-milk mixture and the reserved juices from the shrimp. Cook over medium heat, stirring, until most of the liquid has evaporated. If you are using lemon zest in place of the lemon grass, add it now. Stir in the shrimp and briefly heat them through. Serve the dish immediately, garnished, if you like, with the lemon wedges and the watercress.

EDITOR'S NOTE: *If canned or frozen unsweetened coconut milk is unavailable, the coconut milk may be made at home: Mix ½ cup of unsweetened dried coconut in a blender with ½ cup of very hot water and strain the mixture.*

Burmese Curried Noodles with Scallops and Broccoli

Serves 6
Working (and total) time: about 35 minutes

Calories **278**
Protein **26g.**
Cholesterol **23mg.**
Total fat **9g.**
Saturated fat **1g.**
Sodium **440mg.**

12 oz. dried rice-noodle squares or other rice noodles
3 tbsp. safflower oil
1 large onion, chopped (about 2 cups)
3 tsp. finely chopped garlic
1 tbsp. finely chopped fresh ginger
1 tsp. ground turmeric
½ tsp. ground cumin
1 tbsp. ground coriander
12 oz. broccoli florets (from about 2 medium stalks)
grated zest of 1 orange (about 1½ tsp.)
¼ cup fresh orange juice
2 tbsp. fresh lemon juice
½ tsp. salt
12 oz. sea scallops, each sliced in half horizontally (about 1½ cups)
4 scallions, trimmed and finely chopped (about ½ cup)
8 oz. fresh water chestnuts, peeled and sliced, or 8 oz. canned sliced water chestnuts, rinsed and drained (about 1 cup)
⅓ cup thinly sliced shallots (optional), stir fried in ¼ cup safflower oil until evenly browned and crisp, drained on paper towels

Heat 1 tablespoon of the oil in a hot wok or a heavy-bottomed skillet over medium heat. Add the onion, 1 teaspoon of the garlic, the ginger, turmeric, cumin and coriander. Cook, adding water as needed to prevent scorching, until the onion is soft and browned — about 15 minutes.

Heat 1 tablespoon of the oil in a skillet over medium heat. Add 1 teaspoon of the garlic and cook it for 30 seconds, stirring. Add the broccoli, cover the skillet, and cook the mixture for three minutes. Uncover the skillet and continue cooking, stirring, until the broccoli is tender — about one minute more.

Meanwhile, discard any noodles that are stuck together. Cook the remaining noodles in 4 quarts of boiling water with 2 teaspoons of salt. Start testing them after five minutes and cook them until they are *al dente*. Drain the noodles, add them to the onion mixture, and toss gently. Add the orange zest, orange juice, lemon juice and salt, and toss thoroughly.

Heat the remaining tablespoon of oil in a wok or a skillet. Add the scallops, the remaining teaspoon of garlic, the scallions and the water chestnuts. Stir fry the scallops and vegetables until they are barely done — one to two minutes.

Arrange the noodles on a serving platter. Distribute the broccoli around them, then spoon the scallops onto the noodles. Garnish the dish with the stir-fried shallots if you are using them, and serve immediately.

Linguine with Mussels in Saffron Sauce

Serves 4
Working (and total) time: about 30 minutes

Calories **474**
Protein **23g.**
Cholesterol **32mg.**
Total fat **8g.**
Saturated fat **2g.**
Sodium **561mg.**

12 oz. linguine
2 lb. large mussels, scrubbed and debearded
1 tbsp. safflower oil
1 shallot, finely chopped
2 tbsp. flour
½ cup dry vermouth
⅛ tsp. saffron threads, steeped in ¾ cup hot water
¼ cup freshly grated Romano cheese
¼ tsp. salt
freshly ground black pepper
1 tbsp. cut chives

Put the mussels and ½ cup of water in a large pan; cover the pan and steam the mussels over high heat until they open — about five minutes. Remove the mussels from the pan with a slotted spoon and set them aside. Discard any mussels that do not open.

When the mussels are cool enough to handle, remove the meat from the shells, working over the pan to catch any liquid; set the meat aside and discard the shells. Strain the liquid left in the bottom of the pan through a very fine sieve. Set the liquid aside.

Heat the safflower oil in a heavy-bottomed skillet over medium-high heat. Add the shallot and sauté it for 30 seconds. Remove the pan from the heat. Whisk in the flour, then the vermouth and the saffron liquid (whisking prevents lumps from forming). Return the

skillet to the heat and simmer the sauce over medium-low heat until it thickens — two to three minutes.

Meanwhile, cook the linguine in 3 quarts of boiling water with 1½ teaspoons of salt. Start testing the pasta after 10 minutes and cook it until it is *al dente*.

To finish the sauce, stir in ¼ cup of the strained mussel-cooking liquid along with the cheese, salt, pepper, chives and mussels. Simmer the sauce for three or four minutes more to heat the mussels through.

Drain the linguine, transfer it to a bowl and toss it with the sauce. Serve immediately.

Linguine Sauced with Capers, Black Olives and Tomatoes

Serves 4
Working (and total) time: about 35 minutes

Calories **302**
Protein **10g.**
Cholesterol **4mg.**
Total fat **6g.**
Saturated fat **1g.**
Sodium **484mg.**

8 oz. linguine
1 garlic clove, very finely chopped
1 tbsp. safflower oil
2½ lb. ripe tomatoes, peeled, seeded and chopped, or 28 oz. canned unsalted whole tomatoes, drained and chopped
2 tsp. capers, drained and chopped
6 oil-cured olives, pitted and cut lengthwise into strips
⅛ tsp. crushed red pepper
¼ tsp. salt
1 tsp. chopped fresh oregano, or ½ tsp. dried oregano
2 tbsp. freshly grated Romano cheese

In a large, heavy-bottomed skillet over medium heat, cook the garlic in the oil for 30 seconds. Add the tomatoes, capers, olives, crushed red pepper and salt. Reduce the heat to low, partially cover the skillet and cook the mixture for 20 minutes. Add the oregano and cook for 10 minutes more.

About 10 minutes before the sauce finishes cooking, add the linguine to 3 quarts of boiling water with 1½ teaspoons of salt. Start testing the linguine after 10 minutes and cook it until it is *al dente*. Drain the pasta and add it to the sauce. Mix well to coat the pasta with the sauce. Sprinkle the cheese on top before serving.

6 *Steamed broccoli clad in a red pepper sauce (recipe, page 167) stands among ceramic, china, and paper renditions of vegetables featured in this section.*

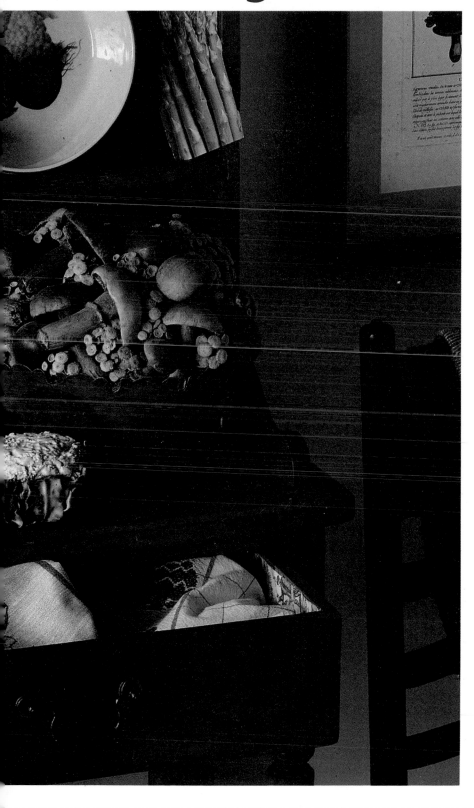

Vegetables and Side Dishes

Fennel with Orange Slices

Serves 6
Working time: about 20 minutes
Total time: about 45 minutes

Calories **27**
Protein **1g.**
Cholesterol **0mg.**
Total fat **0g.**
Saturated fat **0g.**
Sodium **156mg.**

3 heads of fennel, stems cut into 2-inch-long pieces, bulbs quartered lengthwise, feathery green tops reserved
1 orange
1 onion, sliced
1 bay leaf
¼ tsp. salt
freshly ground black pepper

With a small, sharp knife, cut the zest from the orange. In a large skillet, combine the orange zest, fennel stems, onion, bay leaf, salt, pepper and 1 quart of water. Bring the liquid to a boil, and then simmer it over medium heat for 10 minutes.

Put the fennel quarters cut side down into the skillet; cook them until tender — about 15 minutes. With a slotted spoon, transfer the quarters to a serving dish and keep them warm; reserve the cooking liquid.

To make the sauce, strain the cooking liquid into a saucepan and discard the solids left in the strainer. Boil the liquid over high heat until it is reduced to 1 cup — about 10 minutes. Using a small, sharp knife, remove the orange's bitter white pith. Then slice the orange into ¼-inch-thick rounds and cut the rounds in half. Drain off and discard any liquid that may have collected in the serving dish holding the fennel, and pour the reduced sauce over the fennel. Arrange the orange slices on the fennel and garnish the dish with some of the reserved fennel tops.

Sautéed Green Beans with Radishes and Fennel Seed

Serves 6
Working time: about 20 minutes
Total time: about 30 minutes

Calories **60**
Protein **1g.**
Cholesterol **5mg.**
Total fat **5g.**
Saturated fat **2g.**
Sodium **95mg.**

1 lb. green beans, trimmed
1 tbsp. virgin olive oil
1 tbsp. unsalted butter
2 tsp. fennel seeds
4 oz. radishes, trimmed and sliced into ⅛-inch rounds (about 1 cup)
3 scallions, trimmed and thinly sliced
¼ tsp. salt
freshly ground black pepper
1 tbsp. fresh lime or lemon juice

In a large saucepan, bring 2 quarts of water to a rapid boil. Add the beans and, after the water returns to a boil, cook them for four minutes. Remove them from the pan and refresh them under cold running water to preserve their color. Drain the beans and set aside.

In a large, heavy-bottomed skillet, heat the oil and butter over medium-high heat. When the butter has melted, add the beans and the fennel seeds. Sauté for three minutes, stirring frequently. Add the radishes, scallions, salt, pepper, and lime or lemon juice. Sauté, stirring constantly, until the beans are tender but crisp — about three minutes more. Serve immediately.

Honey-Glazed Shallots with Mint

Serves 4
Working time: about 15 minutes
Total time: about 45 minutes

Calories **148**
Protein **5g.**
Cholesterol **8mg.**
Total fat **3g.**
Saturated fat **2g.**
Sodium **167mg.**

1 ¼ lb. shallots, tips and root ends cut off, papery skin and all outer membranes removed to expose the cloves
1 tbsp. unsalted butter
1 tbsp. honey
¼ tsp. salt
freshly ground black pepper
1 cup unsalted chicken or vegetable stock
1 tbsp. chopped fresh mint, or 1 tsp. dried mint

In a heavy-bottomed skillet large enough to hold the shallots in a single layer, melt the butter over medium heat. Stir in the honey and add the shallots, salt and pepper. Pour in the stock and bring the liquid to a simmer. Cook until almost all the liquid has evaporated — about 30 minutes. Stir in the mint, then transfer the shallots to a dish and serve.

Onions Stuffed with Spinach and Pine Nuts

Serves 6
Working time: about 45 minutes
Total time: about 1 hour and 10 minutes

Calories **109**
Protein **5g.**
Cholesterol **1mg.**
Total fat **4g.**
Saturated fat **0g.**
Sodium **132mg.**

6 medium onions (about 1¾ lb.)
¼ cup currants
½ tsp. safflower oil
1 garlic clove, finely chopped
1 lb. spinach, washed and stemmed
¼ tsp. salt
½ cup plain low-fat yogurt
¼ cup pine nuts, toasted
1 tbsp. orange zest
⅛ tsp. grated nutmeg
2 tbsp. fresh whole-wheat bread crumbs

Level the bottoms of the onions by trimming the root end off each one (take care not to remove too much, lest the onions lose their shape while cooking). Discard the ends and peel the onions. Cut a ½-inch-thick slice off the top of each onion and set the tops aside. With a melon baller or a grapefruit spoon, hollow out the onions, forming shells with walls approximately ½ inch thick. Reserve the scooped-out centers.

Pour enough water into a saucepan to fill it about 1 inch deep. Set a vegetable steamer in the pan and bring the water to a boil. Put the onion shells in the steamer, cover the pan, and steam the shells until they are tender when pierced with the tip of a knife — 10 to 15 minutes. Set the shells aside.

Meanwhile, put the currants in a small bowl and pour in just enough water to cover them. Set the bowl aside to allow the currants to plump.

Finely chop the onion tops and centers. In a large, heavy-bottomed skillet, heat the oil over medium-low heat. Add the chopped onion and garlic and cook, stirring occasionally, until the onion is soft but not browned — five to seven minutes.

Add the spinach, cover the skillet, and cook until the spinach is wilted — about three minutes. Uncover the skillet, add the salt, and cook the mixture, stirring occasionally, until all the liquid has evaporated — five to seven minutes more. Transfer the onion-spinach mixture to a large bowl and let it cool.

Preheat the oven to 350° F. Drain the currants and add them to the onion-spinach mixture. Add the yogurt, pine nuts, zest and nutmeg, and mix well. Pour out and discard any liquid that has accumulated in the onion shells, and spoon the stuffing into them.

Spread the remaining stuffing on the bottom of a small baking dish; set the filled onion shells on the stuffing. Sprinkle the bread crumbs over the top of the stuffed onions and bake the onions for 20 to 25 minutes. Remove the baking dish from the oven and preheat the broiler. Broil the onions just long enough to crisp the bread crumbs. Serve the onions with a little stuffing from the bottom of the dish spooned alongside each portion.

Broccoli and Apple Purée

Serves 6
Working (and total) time: about 30 minutes

Calories **113**
Protein **8g.**
Cholesterol **4mg.**
Total fat **4g.**
Saturated fat **1g.**
Sodium **121mg.**

1¾ lb. broccoli, the stalks trimmed to within 2 inches of the florets, the florets separated from the stalks, the stalks then peeled and cut into ½-inch pieces
1 sweet apple, quartered and cored
½ lemon
1 tbsp. safflower oil
2 shallots, coarsely chopped
¼ cup apple juice
½ cup unsalted chicken or vegetable stock
1 tbsp. heavy cream
¼ tsp. cinnamon
¼ tsp. salt
freshly ground black pepper

Pour enough water into a large saucepan to fill it about 1 inch deep. Set a vegetable steamer in the pan and bring the water to a boil. Put the broccoli florets and stalks in the steamer, and steam the broccoli, uncovered, until it is very soft — about 15 minutes. Set the broccoli aside.

Cut four thin slices from one of the apple quarters and reserve them for a garnish in a small bowl. Squeeze the lemon half over the slices to keep them from discoloring. Peel the remaining apple pieces and cut them into thin slices.

In a heavy-bottomed skillet, heat the oil over medium heat. Add the shallots and cook them, stirring occasionally, until they are translucent — two to three minutes. Stir in the peeled apple slices along with the apple juice and stock, and bring the liquid to a boil.

Reduce the heat to medium low and cook the mixture, stirring occasionally, until the apples are soft — three to four minutes. Stir in the broccoli, reserving two florets for a garnish, and heat it through.

Put the broccoli-and-apple mixture into a food processor or blender. Add the cream, cinnamon, salt and pepper, and purée until smooth. (If the mixture does not contain enough liquid to yield a smooth purée, pour in 1 or 2 additional tablespoons of apple juice or stock, and process again.) Serve the purée immediately, garnished with the reserved broccoli florets and apple slices.

Broccoli with Red Pepper Sauce

Serves 4
Working (and total) time: about 15 minutes

Calories **71**
Protein **4g.**
Cholesterol **0mg.**
Total fat **4g.**
Saturated fat **1g.**
Sodium **159mg.**

1 lb. broccoli, stalks cut off 2 inches below the florets and discarded
1 tbsp. virgin olive oil
1 garlic clove, crushed with the flat of a knife
2 red peppers, seeded, deribbed and coarsely chopped
½ cup unsalted chicken or vegetable stock
1½ tsp. white wine vinegar
1 tbsp. chopped fresh tarragon, or 1 tsp. dried tarragon
1 tsp. prepared horseradish
¼ tsp. salt
⅛ tsp. white pepper

Pour enough water into a saucepan to fill it 1 inch deep. Set a vegetable steamer in the pan and bring the water to a boil. Put the broccoli in the steamer, cover the pan tightly, and steam the broccoli until it is tender but still crisp — about seven minutes.

While the broccoli is steaming, make the red-pepper sauce. Heat the oil in a heavy-bottomed skillet over medium heat. Cook the garlic for one minute, then add the peppers and cook until they are soft — about two minutes. Pour in the stock and vinegar, then stir in the tarragon, horseradish, salt and pepper. As soon as the mixture reaches a simmer, remove it from the heat. Purée the mixture in a food processor or blender for about two minutes. Transfer the broccoli to a serving dish and strain the sauce over it. Serve immediately.

Marbled Carrot-and-Zucchini Soufflé

Serves 12 as a side dish, 6 as a main dish
Working time: about 45 minutes
Total time: about 1 hour and 30 minutes

Calories **91**
Protein **6g.**
Cholesterol **31mg.**
Total fat **4g.**
Saturated fat **2g.**
Sodium **170mg.**

5 large carrots (about 2 lb.), peeled and sliced into ¼-inch-thick rounds
2 medium onions, coarsely chopped, plus ¼ cup finely chopped onion
1 tbsp. unsalted butter
3 zucchini (about 1½ lb.), halved lengthwise, seeded and grated
freshly ground black pepper
½ cup low-fat milk
1 cup freshly grated Parmesan or Romano cheese
1 tsp. sugar
1 egg yolk
5 egg whites

Butter a 2-quart soufflé dish and flour it lightly. Put the dish in the refrigerator.

Pour enough water into a saucepan to fill it about 1 inch deep. Set a vegetable steamer in the pan and bring the water to a boil. Put the carrots in the steamer, with the coarsely chopped onions on top of them. Steam the vegetables until the carrots are very soft — about 20 minutes.

While the carrots are steaming, melt the butter in a large, heavy-bottomed skillet over high heat. Add the finely chopped onion, then the zucchini and some pepper. Cook the mixture, stirring frequently, until all of the liquid has evaporated — five to seven minutes. Transfer the mixture to a bowl. Stir in ¼ cup of the milk and ⅓ cup of the cheese. Set the bowl aside.

Transfer the carrots and onions to a food processor and process them for 30 seconds, stopping after 15 seconds to scrape down the sides. Pour in the remaining ¼ cup of milk and the sugar, and purée the mixture for one minute more. Transfer the mixture to a large bowl; add the egg yolk, ½ cup of the cheese and some pepper, and mix well. (To purée the vegetables in a food mill, work them once through the mill into a large bowl. Then add the milk, sugar, egg yolk, cheese and pepper, and mix vigorously.)

Preheat the oven to 450° F. In a clean, dry metal bowl, beat the egg whites just until soft peaks form; do not overbeat them. Fold ½ cup of the whites into the carrot mixture and blend well. Fold another ½ cup of the whites into the zucchini mixture and blend well. Gently fold half of the remaining whites into the carrot mixture; the whites should not be completely incorporated. Repeat the process with the remaining egg whites and the zucchini mixture.

Remove the soufflé dish from the refrigerator. Pour the two vegetable mixtures simultaneously into opposite sides of the dish. Place a spoon in the middle of the zucchini mixture and draw it three quarters of the way around the soufflé to achieve a marbled effect. Sprinkle the remaining cheese over the top. Bake the soufflé for 45 minutes; the top should be golden brown and puffed up. Serve immediately.

Curried Carrots and Raisins

Serves 6
Working time: about 25 minutes
Total time: about 35 minutes

Calories **96**
Protein **1g.**
Cholesterol **3mg.**
Total fat **4g.**
Saturated fat **1g.**
Sodium **34mg.**

1¼ lb. carrots, peeled, halved lengthwise and sliced diagonally into ½-inch-thick pieces
1 tbsp. honey
½ tbsp. fresh lemon juice
1 tsp. Dijon mustard
1½ tsp. curry powder
1 tbsp. safflower oil
½ tbsp. unsalted butter
½ tbsp. brown sugar
⅓ cup raisins

Pour enough water into a saucepan to fill it 1 inch deep. Set a vegetable steamer in the pan and bring the water to a boil. Put the carrots in the steamer, cover the pan, and steam the carrots until they are tender — about 10 minutes. Remove the pan from the heat, uncover it and set it aside.

While the carrots are steaming, combine the honey, lemon juice, mustard and curry powder in a bowl.

Put the oil and butter in a large, heavy-bottomed skillet over medium-high heat. When the butter bubbles, add the carrots and sauté them, stirring often, for two minutes.

Sprinkle the brown sugar over the carrots, add the raisins, and cook the mixture, stirring constantly, for two minutes more. Stir in the honey mixture and continue cooking, stirring constantly and scraping down the sides of the skillet, until the carrots are well glazed — two or three minutes more. Serve at once.

Butternut Squash Purée with Orange and Ginger

Serves 6
Working time: about 30 minutes
Total time: about 1 hour and 30 minutes

Calories **110**
Protein **2g.**
Cholesterol **8mg.**
Total fat **4g.**
Saturated fat **2g.**
Sodium **90mg.**

2 butternut squash (about 3½ lb.), peeled, seeded and cut into ½-inch cubes
1½ tbsp. unsalted butter
¼ tsp. salt
1 cup fresh orange juice with pulp
1 tbsp. fresh lime juice
1½ tbsp. finely chopped fresh ginger

Melt the butter in a heavy-bottomed skillet over medium heat. Add the squash and sprinkle with the salt. Cook for 20 minutes, stirring and scraping the bottom often. Combine the orange juice, lime juice and ginger, and add them to the squash. Continue cooking the squash, stirring frequently, until most of the moisture has evaporated and the mixture has reached a dense, pasty consistency — about 35 minutes.

Transfer the squash to a food processor or blender, and purée it. Alternatively, the squash can be worked through a sieve or food mill. Transfer the purée to a pastry bag fitted with a large star tip and pipe it into a vegetable dish. If you lack a pastry bag, spoon the purée into the dish and use the back of a spoon to make a decorative pattern on its surface.

Butternut Squash and Apple

Serves 6
Working time: about 15 minutes
Total time: about 20 minutes

Calories **162**
Protein **4g.**
Cholesterol **0mg.**
Total fat **1g.**
Saturated fat **0g.**
Sodium **47mg.**

one 3-lb. butternut squash, peeled, seeded and cut into 1-inch cubes
⅛ tsp. salt
freshly ground black pepper
1 apple, peeled, cored and roughly chopped
1 tsp. honey
1 tbsp. fresh lemon juice
⅛ tsp. grated nutmeg

Bring ½ cup of water to a boil in a large saucepan. Add the squash, salt and pepper, cover the pan, and return the water to a boil. Cook the squash until it is tender — about three minutes. Add the apple, put the cover back on and steam until the apple is tender — about two minutes more. With a slotted spoon, transfer the squash and apple pieces to a serving dish. Combine the honey and lemon juice, and drizzle over the squash and apple. Sprinkle with the nutmeg and serve.

Yellow Squash with Peppered Dill Sauce

Serves 6
Working time: about 40 minutes
Total time: about 45 minutes

Calories **55**
Protein **2g.**
Cholesterol **8mg.**
Total fat **3g.**
Saturated fat **2g.**
Sodium **19mg.**

4 medium yellow squash (about 1½ lb.), halved lengthwise, seeded and cut into ½-inch pieces
1½ tbsp. unsalted butter
1½ tbsp. flour
1 cup unsalted chicken or vegetable stock
1 cup fresh dill, coarsely chopped, plus 2 tbsp. finely chopped fresh dill
2 tsp. fresh lemon juice
¼ tsp. cayenne pepper
white pepper

Pour enough water into a saucepan to fill it about 1 inch deep. Set a vegetable steamer in the pan and bring the water to a boil. Put the squash in the steamer, cover the pan, and steam the squash until just tender — about four minutes. Remove the steamer and squash; pour out any water remaining in the pan. Return the squash to the pan and cover to keep it warm.

To prepare the sauce, melt the butter over medium heat in a small, heavy-bottomed saucepan. Add the flour and whisk until the mixture bubbles — about one minute. Stir in the stock and bring it to a boil, stirring constantly. Add the cup of coarsely chopped dill and cook for three minutes more. Stir in 1 teaspoon of the lemon juice along with the cayenne pepper and white pepper. Strain the sauce over the squash in the pan, then stir in the remaining teaspoon of lemon juice and the 2 tablespoons of finely chopped dill. Add more white pepper and serve immediately.

Aromatic Potatoes and Leeks

Serves 6
Working time: about 30 minutes
Total time: about 2 hours

Calories **203**
Protein **5g.**
Cholesterol **1mg.**
Total fat **1g.**
Saturated fat **0g.**
Sodium **127mg.**

3 lb. round white or other boiling potatoes, peeled and sliced into ¼-inch-thick rounds
2 cups unsalted chicken or vegetable stock
3 leeks, trimmed, cleaned and cut into ¼-inch pieces
3 garlic cloves, finely chopped
1½ tsp. fresh rosemary, or ½ tsp. dried rosemary
½ tsp. chopped fresh savory, or ¼ tsp. dried savory
1 tsp. fresh thyme, or ¼ tsp. dried thyme leaves
¼ tsp. salt
freshly ground black pepper
juice of 1 lemon

Preheat the oven to 425° F. In a small saucepan, combine the stock, leeks and garlic; bring the liquid to a boil and simmer it for three minutes. Strain the mixture, reserving both liquid and solids.

Combine the rosemary, savory, thyme, salt and pepper in a small bowl. Arrange one third of the potatoes in a layer in a baking dish. Spread half of the reserved leek mixture over the potatoes, then sprinkle with half of the herb mixture. Arrange half of the remaining potatoes in a second layer on top of the first, and top them with the remaining leek and herb mixtures. Add the rest of the potatoes in a final layer. Pour the lemon juice and the reserved stock over all.

Cover the dish with foil and bake it for 30 minutes. Uncover the dish and return it to the oven until the top turns crisp and golden — about one hour more.

Oven-Baked French Fries

THIS RECIPE USES A MERE 2 TEASPOONS OF OIL TO PRODUCE A
SATISFYING ALTERNATIVE TO FAT-LADEN FRENCH FRIES.

Serves 4
Working time: about 15 minutes
Total time: about 1 hour

Calories **103**
Protein **2g.**
Cholesterol **0mg.**
Total fat **3g.**
Saturated fat **0g.**
Sodium **143mg.**

1½ lb. large russet or other baking potatoes, scrubbed
1 tsp. chili powder
2 tsp. safflower oil
¼ tsp. salt

Put a large baking sheet in the oven and preheat the oven to 475° F. Cut the potatoes lengthwise into slices about ½ inch thick. Cut each slice lengthwise into ½-inch-thick strips and put them in a large bowl. Toss the strips with the chili powder to coat them evenly; sprinkle on the oil and toss again.

Arrange the potato strips in a single layer on the hot baking sheet. Bake the strips for 20 minutes, then turn them and continue baking until they are crisp and browned — about 20 minutes more. Sprinkle the french fries with the salt and serve them hot.

Potato Swirls

Serves 8
Working time: about 20 minutes
Total time: about 1 hour and 30 minutes

Calories **77**
Protein **3g.**
Cholesterol **1mg.**
Total fat **2g.**
Saturated fat **0g.**
Sodium **91mg.**

4 medium russet or other baking potatoes (about 1¾ lb.), scrubbed
1 garlic clove, finely chopped
1 tbsp. virgin olive oil
2 egg whites, lightly beaten
¼ tsp. grated nutmeg
¼ tsp. salt
¼ tsp. white pepper
½ cup plain low-fat yogurt
2 tbsp. finely cut chives

Preheat the oven to 400° F. Prick the potatoes and bake them until they are tender — about one hour. When the potatoes are cool enough to handle, scoop out the flesh and work it through a food mill or a sieve to achieve a smooth purée. (Puréeing the potatoes in a food processor or blender would make them gluey.)

Combine the garlic and oil in a small saucepan over medium heat and cook for one or two minutes (this softens the garlic and mellows its flavor). Add the garlic and oil to the potatoes along with the egg whites, nutmeg, salt and pepper, and mix well. Transfer the mixture to a pastry bag fitted with a large star tip. Pipe eight rounds about 2 inches in diameter onto an oiled baking sheet. Pipe a raised border on the edge of each round. (If you lack a pastry bag, form the potato mixture into eight mounds and make an indentation in the top of each with the back of a spoon.)

Bake the potato swirls until the edges are crisp and brown — seven to 10 minutes. With a spatula, transfer the swirls to a serving platter or individual plates. Combine the yogurt and chives in a small bowl, and spoon this mixture into the center of each swirl. Serve the potato swirls hot.

sor or blender. Purée the mixture, stopping two or three times to scrape down the sides. Transfer the purée to a bowl and stir in the egg yolk.

In a separate metal bowl, beat the egg whites until soft peaks form. Fold the beaten whites into the purée and pour the mixture into a lightly buttered 2-quart gratin dish. Bake the mousse for 30 minutes. Serve the mousse immediately.

Sweet Potato and Pear Mousse

Serves 8
Working time: about 30 minutes
Total time: about 1 hour and 45 minutes

Calories **193**	
Protein **3g.**	2 lb. sweet potatoes (yams)
Cholesterol **38mg.**	2 large ripe pears, peeled, cored and cut into 1-inch cubes
Total fat **3g.**	3 tbsp. fresh lemon juice
Saturated fat **1g.**	½ tsp. curry powder
Sodium **26mg.**	½ tsp. cinnamon
	1 tbsp. unsalted butter
	1½ cups chopped onion
	1 cup apple juice
	freshly ground black pepper
	1 egg yolk
	2 egg whites

Preheat the oven to 450° F. Prick the sweet potatoes and bake them until they have begun to soften — about 30 minutes. Remove the sweet potatoes from the oven and set them aside to cool. Reduce the oven temperature to 350° F.

In a large bowl, combine the pears, lemon juice, curry powder and cinnamon. When the sweet potatoes are cool enough to handle, cut them in half lengthwise. Peel the sweet potatoes, cut them into 1-inch cubes and add them to the bowl.

Heat the butter in a large, heavy-bottomed skillet over medium heat. Add the onion and cook it for five minutes, then stir in the apple juice, the sweet-potato mixture and the pepper. Cover the skillet, leaving the lid slightly ajar, and cook the mixture for 15 minutes, stirring occasionally.

Transfer the contents of the skillet to a food proces-

Spicy Sweet Potatoes and Peas

Serves 6
Working (and total) time: about 30 minutes

Calories **128**	
Protein **2g.**	1¼ lb. sweet potatoes (yams), peeled and cut into ½-inch cubes
Cholesterol **5mg.**	2 tsp. honey
Total fat **6g.**	3 tbsp. cider vinegar
Saturated fat **2g.**	¾ tsp. chili powder
Sodium **98mg.**	½ tsp. cinnamon
	1½ tbsp. safflower oil
	1 onion, chopped (about 1 cup)
	1 tbsp. unsalted butter
	¼ tsp. salt
	¾ cup fresh or frozen peas

In a small bowl, mix together the honey, 2 tablespoons of the vinegar, the chili powder and cinnamon. Set the honey mixture aside.

Heat the oil in a large, heavy-bottomed skillet over medium-low heat. Add the sweet potatoes and cook, stirring occasionally, for five minutes. Raise the heat to medium high and cook for another five minutes, stirring frequently to prevent the sweet potatoes from sticking. Add the onion, butter, salt, the remaining tablespoon of vinegar and ¼ cup of water. If you are using fresh peas, add them at this point. Cook, stirring constantly, until the onion just begins to brown — about five minutes.

Pour the honey mixture over the vegetables; if you are using frozen peas, stir them in now. Cook the vegetables, stirring constantly, for another two minutes and then transfer them to a serving dish.

Lentils with Spinach and Carrots

Serves 4
Working time: about 20 minutes
Total time: about 50 minutes

Calories **330**
Protein **18g.**
Cholesterol **0mg.**
Total fat **10g.**
Saturated fat **1g.**
Sodium **80mg.**

1 cup lentils, picked over and rinsed
1 bay leaf
2 tbsp. safflower oil
1 garlic clove, crushed
1 tbsp. freshly grated ginger
½ lb. carrots (2 to 3 medium), peeled and cut into bâtonnets
12 scallions, cut into 1-inch lengths
¾ lb. spinach, stems discarded, washed, dried, and coarsely chopped
2 tbsp. low-sodium soy sauce
⅓ cup dry sherry
1 tbsp. sesame seeds, toasted

Put the lentils in a large, heavy-bottomed saucepan with 3 cups of water. Bring the water to a boil, then lower the heat to medium, add the bay leaf, cover the pan tightly, and simmer the lentils until they are tender—about 40 minutes. Drain the lentils and remove the bay leaf. Rinse the lentils under cold running water and drain them again.

Heat the oil in a wok or large, heavy skillet over high heat. Add the garlic and ginger, and stir them until the garlic sizzles. Add the carrots and scallions, and stir-fry them for one minute, then transfer them to a plate using a slotted spoon. Place the spinach in the pan and stir it over high heat until it begins to wilt—one to two minutes. Then return the carrots and scallions to the pan, add the cooked lentils, and stir them for two minutes to heat them through. Add the soy sauce and the sherry, and bring the liquid to a boil. Stir the ingredients once more, then transfer them to a heated serving dish. Scatter the sesame seeds over the dish and serve it immediately.

SUGGESTED ACCOMPANIMENT: *long-grain brown rice.*

EDITOR'S NOTE: *To toast sesame seeds, put them in a small, heavy-bottomed skillet over medium-low heat until they are golden—one to two minutes.*

Buckwheat and Lentil Pilaf

Serves 8
Working time: about 1 hour
Total time: about 1 hour and 15 minutes

Calories **355**
Protein **19g.**
Cholesterol **0mg.**
Total fat **7g.**
Saturated fat **1g.**
Sodium **175mg.**

3 lb. peas, shelled, or 1 lb. frozen peas, thawed
1¾ cups lentils, picked over and rinsed
1¼ cups buckwheat groats (kasha)
1 tsp. salt
3 tbsp. virgin olive oil
2 small eggplants, cut into ½-inch cubes
2 sweet red peppers, seeded, deribbed, and sliced
2 sweet green peppers, seeded, deribbed, and sliced
8 garlic cloves, finely chopped
2 large onions, sliced
3 medium tomatoes, peeled, seeded and coarsely chopped
4 tbsp. finely cut fresh chives
2 tbsp. chopped fresh mint, or 1 tsp. dried mint
4 tbsp. chopped parsley
4 tbsp. capers (optional)
freshly ground black pepper

If you are using fresh peas, parboil them until they are barely tender—three to four minutes. Drain them, then refresh them under cold running water. Drain the peas again and set them aside. (Frozen peas do not need parboiling.)

Rinse the lentils and put them in a large, heavy-bottomed saucepan with 2½ quarts of water. Bring the water to a boil, then lower the heat and simmer the lentils until they are tender—approximately 40 minutes. When the lentils have finished cooking, drain them in a sieve.

While the lentils are cooking, add the buckwheat and ½ teaspoon of the salt to a saucepan containing 2½ cups of boiling water. Cook the buckwheat, stirring frequently, until the groats have tripled in size but still have a bite to them—about five minutes. Drain the groats in a sieve, rinse them well, and drain them again. Transfer them to a large bowl.

Heat the olive oil over medium heat in a large, heavy skillet. Add the eggplants, peppers, garlic, and onions, and sauté them, stirring constantly, until they become soft—10 to 15 minutes. Add the lentils, buckwheat, tomatoes, and peas to the eggplant mixture. Gently heat all the ingredients, stirring continuously.

Remove the pan from the heat. Add the chives, mint, and parsley, and if using them, the capers. Season with the remaining ½ teaspoon of salt and some black pepper. Serve immediately.

Polenta Pizza

Serves 4
Working time: about 40 minutes
Total time: about 1 hour

Calories **470**
Protein **19g.**
Cholesterol **25mg.**
Total fat **12g.**
Saturated fat **5g.**
Sodium **390mg.**

½ tsp. salt
3 cups cornmeal
1 tbsp. virgin olive oil
1 red onion, finely sliced
1 large garlic clove, chopped
2 carrots, chopped
4 celery stalks, finely sliced
3 medium tomatoes, peeled, seeded, and chopped
6 tbsp. tomato paste, dissolved in ¾ cup hot water
1 tbsp. chopped fresh basil, or 1 tsp. dried basil
½ tbsp. chopped fresh oregano, or ½ tsp. dried oregano
cayenne pepper
freshly ground black pepper
¼ lb. low-fat mozzarella cheese, very thinly sliced
1 tbsp. freshly grated Parmesan cheese
½ tbsp. finely chopped parsley for garnish

Preheat the oven to 350° F. Thoroughly grease a 13-by-9-by-1-inch baking pan.

Put 9 cups of water into a large saucepan with the salt and bring it to a boil. Sprinkle in the cornmeal, stirring continuously with a wooden spoon. Lower the heat to medium, and cook the polenta, stirring constantly, until all the liquid has been absorbed and the polenta is quite stiff—10 to 15 minutes. Spoon the polenta into the prepared baking pan and spread it out to a uniform thickness. Cover the pan with foil and bake the polenta in the oven for 20 minutes.

Meanwhile, make the sauce. Heat the oil in a heavy-bottomed saucepan, add the onion, and sauté it over medium heat until it is soft and transparent—about 10 minutes. Add the garlic, carrots, celery, and tomatoes. Stir well for a few minutes, then mix the tomato paste solution into the sauce. Finally, add the basil, oregano, and some cayenne and black pepper. Simmer the sauce gently, covered, for 10 to 15 minutes.

When the polenta is ready, spread the sauce over it. Cover the sauce with the mozzarella slices, then sprinkle with the Parmesan cheese. Return the polenta to the oven until the cheese has melted—about 10 minutes. Serve the polenta pizza immediately, garnished with the chopped parsley.

SUGGESTED ACCOMPANIMENT: *steamed purple sprouting broccoli or green broccoli, tossed with lemon juice and freshly ground black pepper.*

Polenta Ring with Pine Nuts and Mozzarella

Serves 6
Working time: about 45 minutes
Total time: about 1 hour and 45 minutes
(includes cooling)

Calories **300**
Protein **13g.**
Cholesterol **20mg.**
Total fat **14g.**
Saturated fat **4g.**
Sodium **265mg.**

5 plum or small tomatoes, peeled
2 tbsp. virgin olive oil
1 tsp. paprika
2 garlic cloves, one crushed, the other chopped
½ tsp. salt
1¼ cup cornmeal
¼ lb. low-fat mozzarella cheese, thinly sliced
1 onion, thinly sliced
1 sweet red pepper, seeded, deribbed, and cut into 1-inch strips
1 sweet green pepper, seeded, deribbed, and cut into 1-inch strips
1 tsp. ground cumin
½ cup pine nuts

Thinly slice three of the tomatoes crosswise and the remaining two tomatoes lengthwise; keep them separate. Grease an 8-inch ring mold with ½ tablespoon of the virgin olive oil.

Bring 3¾ cups of water to a boil in a large saucepan.

Add the paprika, crushed garlic, and salt, then stir in the cornmeal. Lower the heat to medium, and continue to cook, stirring, until the cornmeal has formed a thick porridge—10 to 15 minutes. Remove the pan from the heat and immediately pour half the polenta into the prepared ring mold. Press it down firmly using the back of a spoon. Quickly place the crosswise-sliced tomatoes and the mozzarella on top, and cover them with the remaining polenta. Let the polenta cool completely—at least one hour.

Preheat the oven to 350° F. When the polenta has cooled, carefully loosen all around the edges of the mold, using a small metal knife. Turn out the polenta ring onto a large, flat, heatproof plate, and bake it in the oven until the mozzarella has melted—approximately 15 minutes.

While the polenta is baking, heat the remaining oil in a skillet over low heat. Put the onion and chopped garlic in the pan, and cook gently to soften them—about three minutes. Add the peppers, cover the pan, and cook over very low heat for 10 minutes, then add the remaining tomato slices, the cumin, and half of the pine nuts. Cover the pan again and cook for two minutes more over very low heat.

Spoon some of the vegetables into the center of the polenta ring and the remainder around the edge. Sprinkle the remaining pine nuts over the vegetables and serve the polenta ring hot.

Pumpkin and Pecorino Risotto

Serves 4
Working (and total) time: about 1 hour and 15 minutes

Calories **305**
Protein **6g.**
Cholesterol **5mg.**
Total fat **6g.**
Saturated fat **2g.**
Sodium **280mg.**

1 tbsp. virgin olive oil
2 shallots, finely chopped
1¼ cups Italian rice
1 lb. pumpkin, peeled, seeded, and finely grated
¼ tsp. powdered saffron
⅓ cup dry white wine
1 qt. unsalted vegetable stock
1 tbsp. finely chopped fresh oregano, or 1 tsp. dried oregano
½ tsp. salt
freshly ground black pepper
¼ cup finely grated pecorino or romano cheese
2 tbsp. finely chopped parsley for garnish (optional)

Heat the oil in a large flameproof casserole. Add the shallots, and cook over medium heat, stirring from time to time, until they are soft but not brown—about five minutes. Reduce the heat to low, add the rice, and stir to ensure that each grain is coated with a little oil.

Add the pumpkin and stir well over medium heat until heated through—about three minutes. Stir the saffron into the white wine. Increase the heat and pour the wine into the casserole. Stir constantly until all the liquid has been absorbed—about three minutes. Meanwhile, heat the stock in a separate pan.

Reduce the heat under the rice to low, and pour a ladleful—about 1 cup—of hot stock into the casserole. Stir well, then cover the casserole, leaving the lid ajar. Simmer until the stock has been absorbed—about five minutes. Stir in another ladleful of stock and cover as before. This time, however, stir the contents of the casserole once or twice while the stock is being absorbed, replacing the lid after stirring. Mix in the oregano, then continue to add stock by the ladleful, stirring frequently, until the rice is soft but still a little resilient to the bite, and the pumpkin has all but melted into a sauce—approximately 30 minutes. Once this stage has been reached, stir in the remaining stock, and replace the lid on the casserole. Turn off the heat and let the risotto stand for five minutes, during which time the remaining stock will be absorbed. Meanwhile, warm the serving bowls.

Season the risotto with the salt, some freshly ground black pepper, and the pecorino or romano cheese, stirring well until the cheese melts. If you like, sprinkle ½ tablespoon of chopped parsley over each portion. Serve the risotto immediately.

Pea and Mushroom Risotto

Serves 6
Working time: about 45 minutes
Total time: about 1 hour and 15 minutes

Calories **410**
Protein **12g.**
Cholesterol **20mg.**
Total fat **10g.**
Saturated fat **5g.**
Sodium **430mg.**

¾ lb. peas, shelled, or ¼ lb. frozen peas, thawed
2 tbsp. unsalted butter
4 to 6 shallots, chopped
2½ cups brown rice
¾ cup dry white wine or dry vermouth
2 cups tomato juice
2 cups unsalted vegetable stock
2 medium tomatoes, peeled, seeded, and chopped
½ tsp. salt
½ lb. mushrooms, wiped clean and coarsely grated
½ cup freshly grated Parmesan cheese
freshly ground black pepper
chopped parsley for garnish

If you are using fresh peas, parboil them until they are barely tender—three to four minutes. Drain them, then refresh them under cold running water. Drain the peas again and set them aside. (Frozen peas do not need parboiling.)

In a large, heavy-bottomed saucepan, melt the butter and sauté the shallots over medium heat until transparent, stirring occasionally—three to five minutes. Stir the rice into the shallots and cook for two to three minutes, stirring constantly, to ensure that the grains are coated with the butter.

Pour the wine into the rice and simmer, stirring frequently, until the wine has been absorbed by the rice. Add the tomato juice and 1 cup of the stock, bring the liquid to a boil, then reduce the heat to a simmer. Cover the saucepan and cook the rice, stirring occasionally, for about 20 minutes. Stir the tomatoes and salt into the rice, cover the pan, and simmer for 10 minutes more, adding more stock, a ladleful at a time, if the rice dries out.

Add the mushrooms, peas, and any remaining stock, increase the heat to high, and cook rapidly, stirring constantly, until most of the liquid has been absorbed but the rice is still moist. Stir the Parmesan cheese into the risotto and season generously with some black pepper. Turn the risotto into a warmed serving dish and sprinkle it with chopped parsley.

SUGGESTED ACCOMPANIMENT: *salad of raw spinach leaves with a vinaigrette.*

EDITOR'S NOTE: *If preferred, 1 quart of vegetable stock may be used instead of the combination of tomato juice and stock.*

Lentil and Potato Cakes with Mustard Pickle

Serves 4
Working time: about 40 minutes
Total time: about 1 hour and 40 minutes

Calories **295**
Protein **15g.**
Cholesterol **10mg.**
Total fat **4g.**
Saturated fat **1g.**
Sodium **245mg.**

½ lb. starchy potatoes, peeled and cut into 1-inch cubes
½ tsp. safflower oil
12 scallions, trimmed, white parts chopped, green parts sliced into thin rings
1-inch piece fresh ginger, peeled and finely chopped
¼ tsp. ground cinnamon
¼ tsp. freshly grated nutmeg, or ¼ tsp. ground nutmeg
½ tsp. salt
freshly ground black pepper
¾ cup split red lentils, picked over, rinsed
2 cups unsalted vegetable stock
½ tsp. garam masala
⅓ cup sour cream
⅓ cup plain low-fat yogurt
Mustard pickle
¼ tsp. safflower oil
1 small onion, finely chopped
1 tbsp. mustard seeds, lightly crushed
2 tbsp. white wine vinegar
¼ cup dry white wine
1 tbsp. light brown sugar
1 tbsp. grainy mustard
1 red-skinned mango, peeled and pitted, flesh coarsely diced

First make the mustard pickle. Heat the oil in a small, heavy-bottomed saucepan, add the onion and mustard seeds, and cook over medium heat, stirring, until the onion has softened—about three minutes. Stir in the vinegar, wine, sugar, mustard, and mango. Bring to a boil, then lower the heat, cover, and cook gently until the mango is tender and the mixture thick and pulpy—about 15 minutes. Transfer the contents of the pan to a bowl and set it aside.

Cook the potatoes in boiling water until tender—about 20 minutes. Drain well, then mash them with a potato masher. Heat the oil in a large skillet and add the white parts of the scallions, the ginger, cinnamon, nutmeg, salt, and some black pepper. Cook over medium heat, stirring continuously, for three minutes. Add the lentils and stock, and bring to a boil; then cover the pan, lower the heat, and simmer gently, stirring frequently, until the lentils are completely tender—about 25 minutes. Remove the lid, and increase the heat, stirring continuously, until the mixture is dry—about two minutes. Beat in the mashed potatoes and garam masala, then set the mixture aside to cool. Stir together the sour cream and yogurt.

Preheat the broiler and lightly grease a baking sheet. Shape the lentil mixture into 12 flat cakes about 3 inches in diameter, and place them on the baking sheet. Broil the cakes until they are golden—about five minutes on each side—then transfer them to individual serving plates. Top the cakes with the sour-cream mixture and mustard pickle, and garnish them with the green scallion rings.

SUGGESTED ACCOMPANIMENT: *stir-fried cucumber wedges.*

EDITOR'S NOTE: *Garam masala is a mixture of ground spices used in Indian cookery. It usually contains coriander, cumin, cloves, ginger, and cinnamon. In this recipe, a pinch each of some or all of these spices can be substituted if garam masala is not available.*

Lentils with Cumin and Onion

Serves 4
Working time: about 15 minutes
Total time: about 1 hour

Calories **215**
Protein **9g.**
Cholesterol **0mg.**
Total fat **7g.**
Saturated fat **1g.**
Sodium **225mg.**

1½ cups lentils, picked over and rinsed
1 tsp. ground cumin
½ tsp. salt
⅓ cup brown rice
1 tbsp. virgin olive oil
1 lb. onions, thinly sliced
6 to 8 radishes, thinly sliced
2 tbsp. chopped parsley

In a heavy-bottomed saucepan, bring 1 quart of water to a boil; then add the lentils, cumin, and salt, and boil, uncovered, for 20 minutes. Add the rice, lower the heat, and simmer, covered, until the liquid has been absorbed but the rice is still moist—30 to 40 minutes.

Meanwhile, heat the oil in a skillet and sauté the onions over low heat, partially covered, stirring frequently, until they are soft and golden brown—approximately 15 minutes.

Remove half of the onions and stir them into the lentil mixture. Transfer the mixture to the center of a shallow serving dish. Distribute the remaining sautéed onions around the lentil mixture, then arrange the radishes around the onions on the edge of the dish. Sprinkle the parsley over the lentil mixture. Serve hot.

SUGGESTED ACCOMPANIMENT: *salad of lettuce and cucumber.*

Gingered Black Beans with Saffron Rice

Serves 6
Working time: about 35 minutes
Total time: about 2 hours and 45 minutes
(includes soaking)

Calories **390**
Protein **12g.**
Cholesterol **0mg.**
Total fat **14g.**
Saturated fat **2g.**
Sodium **150mg.**

¾ cup black kidney beans or turtle beans, picked over
2 tbsp. virgin olive oil
3-inch piece fresh ginger, peeled, 2 inches thinly sliced, the remainder grated
1 tbsp. chopped fresh oregano, or 1 tsp. dried oregano
1 tsp. chopped fresh sage, or ¼ tsp. dried sage
1 tsp. saffron threads
½ tsp. salt
1¼ cups long-grain white rice
3 oz. shelled walnuts (about ¾ cup), coarsely chopped
3 garlic cloves, crushed
2 oz. dried cloud-ear mushrooms, soaked in hot water for 20 minutes and drained
¼ lb. button mushrooms, wiped and sliced
2 limes, grated zest and juice
freshly ground black pepper
¼ tsp. paprika for garnish

Rinse the beans under cold running water, then put them into a large, heavy pan and pour in enough cold water to cover them by about 3 inches. Discard any beans that float to the surface. Cover the pan, leaving the lid ajar, and slowly bring the liquid to a boil. Boil the beans for two minutes, then turn off the heat and soak the beans, covered, for at least one hour. (Alternatively, soak the beans overnight in cold water.)

In a large clean saucepan, heat 1 tablespoon of the oil over medium heat; add the sliced ginger, oregano, and sage, and sauté them for one minute. Drain the beans, then add them to the pan. Pour in enough cold water to cover the beans by about 3 inches. Bring the water to a boil, then lower the heat to maintain a strong simmer, and cook the beans until they are tender—at least one hour. Drain the beans, return them to the pan, with all the flavorings, and keep them warm while you prepare the rice.

Bring 2½ cups of water to a boil in a saucepan. Add the saffron, salt, and rice, and stir once. Turn the heat to low, cover the pan, and simmer until the rice is just cooked and the water is absorbed—about 15 minutes. Remove the pan from the heat and stir in the chopped walnuts. Cover the pan again and let it stand for a few minutes while the walnuts warm through.

While the rice is cooking, heat the remaining tablespoon of oil in a wok or large skillet over medium heat, then add the garlic, cloud-ear mushrooms, button mushrooms, and the grated ginger. Increase the heat to high and stir-fry the ingredients until they are soft—five to six minutes. Add them to the beans, together with the lime zest and juice, and some black pepper.

Pile the bean mixture in the center of a large platter and arrange the rice around it. Sprinkle the rice with the paprika and serve at once.

SUGGESTED ACCOMPANIMENT: *watercress, curly endive, and orange salad.*

Tuscan-Style Beans

THIS ADAPTATION OF A TRADITIONAL TUSCAN RECIPE REPLACES
THE USUAL SAUSAGES WITH CEPS
AND USES LESS OIL AND MORE TOMATOES.

Serves 4
Working time: about 45 minutes
Total time: about 3 hours (includes soaking)

Calories **330**
Protein **22g.**
Cholesterol **0mg.**
Total fat **6g.**
Saturated fat **trace**
Sodium **245mg.**

1¾ cups borlotti beans or white beans, picked over
2 bay leaves
1 tbsp. virgin olive oil
2 garlic cloves, crushed
3 sprigs fresh rosemary
6 leaves fresh sage, finely shredded
½ lb. fresh ceps, or ¾ oz. dried ceps, soaked in hot water for 20 minutes, drained, and well rinsed
2½ lb. fresh tomatoes, peeled, seeded, and chopped
1 tbsp. red wine vinegar
1 tbsp. molasses
½ tsp. salt
freshly ground black pepper
12 basil leaves, torn in pieces

Rinse the beans under cold running water, then put them into a large, heavy pan and pour in enough cold water to cover them by about 3 inches. Discard any beans that float to the surface. Cover the pan, leaving the lid ajar, and slowly bring the liquid to a boil. Boil the beans for two minutes, then turn off the heat and soak the beans, covered, for at least one hour. (Alternatively, soak the beans overnight in cold water.)

Drain the beans, place them in a saucepan, and pour in enough water to cover them by about 3 inches. Add the bay leaves, bring the liquid to a boil, then lower the heat to maintain a strong simmer, and cook the beans until they are tender—about one hour. Check the water level in the pan from time to time, and add more hot water if necessary. Drain the beans in a colander and discard the bay leaves. Rinse the beans, drain again, and set them aside.

Heat the oil in a flameproof casserole; sauté the garlic in the oil over medium-low heat for one to two minutes. Add the rosemary, lower the heat to the lowest possible setting, cover the casserole with a lid, and leave it for 10 minutes to allow the rosemary to infuse the oil. Discard the rosemary, and add the cooked beans to the casserole along with the sage, stirring well to coat the beans evenly with oil. Increase the heat to medium-low, add the mushrooms, and cook, stirring constantly, until the contents of the casserole are heated through—about two minutes. Cover the casserole closely, and remove it from the heat while you prepare the tomato sauce.

In a large, shallow saucepan, combine the tomatoes with the vinegar, molasses, salt, and some black pepper. Cook briefly over high heat to allow excess moisture to evaporate as the tomatoes break down into a sauce. Pour the sauce over the beans and mushrooms, add the torn basil leaves, and return the casserole to medium-high heat. Simmer briefly until the beans are just heated through; do not overcook.

SUGGESTED ACCOMPANIMENT: *crusty Italian bread.*

EDITOR'S NOTE: *If you use dried ceps, the soaking liquid can be added to the water in which the beans are cooked to enhance their flavor. Strain the mushroom-soaking liquid through a double layer of cheesecloth or a coffee-filter paper before adding it to the beans. Borlotti beans, an Italian variety of bean, are a speckled, pale tan color. White beans can be substituted for them.*

Wild and Brown Rice Pilaf with Mushroom Ragout

Serves 8
Working time: about 45 minutes
Total time: about 3 hours (includes soaking)

Calories **390**
Protein **14g.**
Cholesterol **5mg.**
Total fat **11g.**
Saturated fat **2g.**
Sodium **265mg.**

1¼ cups flageolets or white beans, picked over
2 bay leaves
⅔ cup wild rice
2 cinnamon sticks
1 tsp. salt
1½ cups brown basmati rice or other brown long-grain rice, rinsed under cold running water until the water runs clear, then soaked in 6 cups of water for 15 minutes
½ tsp. ground mace
2 tsp. light brown sugar
¾ lb. baby corn, fresh or frozen, thickly sliced
4 tbsp. hazelnut, walnut, or safflower oil
½ tsp. freshly grated nutmeg
freshly ground black pepper
Mushroom ragout
1 tbsp. unsalted butter
1 small onion, finely chopped
1 lb. mixed fresh wild mushrooms, such as chanterelles, porcini, or oyster or shiitake mushrooms, wiped clean
2 cups unsalted vegetable stock
2 tbsp. cornstarch
2 tbsp. sour cream
¼ tsp. salt
freshly ground black pepper

Rinse the beans under cold running water, then put them into a large, heavy pan, and pour in enough cold water to cover them by about 3 inches. Discard any beans that float to the surface. Cover the pan, leaving the lid ajar, and slowly bring the liquid to a boil. Boil the beans for two minutes, then turn off the heat and soak the beans, covered, for at least one hour. (Alternatively, soak the beans overnight in cold water.)

Drain the beans, then place them in a saucepan and pour in enough water to cover them by about 3 inches. Add the bay leaves, bring the liquid to a boil, then lower the heat to maintain a strong simmer, and cook the beans, covered, until they are tender—about one hour. If the beans appear to be drying out at any point, add more hot water. Drain the beans, rinse them, and

drain them again. Set the beans aside and keep them warm. Preheat the oven to 325° F.

Place the wild rice with the cinnamon sticks and ½ teaspoon of the salt in a small ovenproof baking dish. Bring 2½ cups of water to a boil and pour it over the rice. Cover the dish with a lid and bake the rice in the oven for one hour. Drain off all but about 1 tablespoon of water. Leave the wild rice, covered, in a warm place for about 15 minutes, in order to allow it to absorb the remaining liquid.

Drain the brown rice, and place it in a large saucepan with the ground mace and the remaining ½ teaspoon of salt. Add 3 quarts of water and bring it to a boil. Reduce the heat to low, cover the pan, and simmer until the rice is tender—approximately 20 minutes. When the rice is cooked, drain it, cover it, set it aside, and keep it warm.

While the brown rice is cooking, prepare the mushroom ragout. Melt the butter in a large saucepan over medium heat, add the onion, and cook it gently until it is soft but not brown—five to six minutes. Add the mushrooms, and cook until they are slightly softened—two to three minutes more. Pour in the vegetable stock and bring it to a boil, then cover the pan and lower the heat. Simmer for 10 minutes, until the mushrooms are soft. Blend the cornstarch with the sour cream, and stir it into the mushrooms along with the salt and some freshly ground black pepper. Continue cooking for three to four minutes more, until the sauce thickens slightly. Transfer the mushroom ragout to a serving bowl and keep it warm.

Meanwhile, pour about 1½ inches of water into a large, nonreactive saucepan. Add the brown sugar and bring the mixture to a boil. Add the corn and bring the water back to a boil, turn down the heat, and simmer, covered, until the corn is just tender—about five minutes (one to two minutes for frozen corn). Drain the corn in a colander.

Place half the oil in a warmed serving bowl. Discard the bay leaves from the beans and the cinnamon sticks from the wild rice. Transfer the beans, rices, and corn to the oiled serving bowl. Pour the remaining oil over the vegetables, add the nutmeg and some black pepper, then toss all the ingredients together. Serve immediately, with the mushroom ragout.

EDITOR'S NOTE: *If wild mushrooms are unavailable, substitute button mushrooms. The pilaf is also delicious served cold as a salad, with a little cider vinegar added.*

Mushrooms in Red Wine

Serves 4
Working time: about 20 minutes
Total time: about 45 minutes

Calories **169**
Protein **4g.**
Cholesterol **0mg.**
Total fat **7g.**
Saturated fat **1g.**
Sodium **157mg.**

1 lb. button mushrooms, stems trimmed and caps wiped clean	
1 cup red wine	
2 tbsp. virgin olive oil	
2 or 3 fresh thyme or rosemary sprigs, or 1 tsp. dried thyme or rosemary leaves	
¼ tsp. salt	
8 garlic cloves, unpeeled	
1 bunch scallions, the white bottoms sliced into ¼-inch pieces, the green tops finely chopped	
2 tsp. finely chopped fresh rosemary, or ¼ tsp. dried rosemary	
freshly ground black pepper	

In a large saucepan, combine the wine, oil, thyme or rosemary sprigs, salt and 1 cup of water. Bring the mixture to a boil over high heat. Reduce the heat to medium, add the garlic cloves and simmer the liquid for 10 minutes. Stir in the mushrooms and the white scallion pieces. Simmer the vegetables, partially covered, until the mushrooms feel soft when pierced with the tip of a sharp knife — about 10 minutes.

With a slotted spoon, transfer the vegetables to a serving bowl. Discard the thyme or rosemary sprigs, and boil the cooking liquid until it is reduced to about ¾ cup — 10 to 12 minutes. Pour it over the vegetables and stir in the scallion tops. Sprinkle the vegetables with the chopped rosemary and the pepper, and mix well. Serve the mushrooms warm or well chilled.

EDITOR'S NOTE: *Preparing this dish a day or two ahead of time will intensify its flavor and impart a deep reddish hue to the mushrooms.*

Mushroom-Walnut Pasta Roll with Yogurt Sauce

Serves 10
Working time: about 1 hour and 15 minutes
Total time: about 2 hours

Calories **214**
Protein **9g.**
Cholesterol **58mg.**
Total fat **11g.**
Saturated fat **2g.**
Sodium **159mg.**

1 ¼ cups unbleached white flour or bread flour	
⅓ cup buckwheat flour	
¼ tsp. salt	
2 eggs, beaten	
1 tbsp. virgin olive oil	
Mushroom-walnut filling	
2 tbsp. virgin olive oil	
1 small onion, finely chopped	
½ cup walnuts, finely chopped	
1 ½ lb. mushrooms, wiped clean, finely chopped	
2 tbsp. light cream	
juice of 1 lemon	
½ cup finely chopped parsley (preferably Italian)	
¼ tsp. salt	
freshly ground black pepper	
Yogurt sauce	
1 ½ cups plain low-fat yogurt	
2 tbsp. finely chopped walnuts	
¼ cup finely chopped parsley (preferably Italian)	
freshly ground black pepper	

To prepare the dough, first sift the flours and salt into a large mixing bowl. Make a well in the center, and pour the eggs and oil into the center of the well. With your fingers, gradually work in the flour to make a stiff paste. Gather the dough into a ball and knead it until it is smooth — 10 to 15 minutes. Cover the dough with a damp cloth and let it rest while you make the filling.

For the filling, heat 1 tablespoon of the oil in a large,

heavy-bottomed skillet over low heat. Add the onion, and cook it until it is soft — 10 to 12 minutes. Stir in the walnuts, and cook them for three or four minutes to toast them lightly; transfer the mixture to a large bowl.

In the same skillet, heat the remaining tablespoon of oil, and cook the mushrooms in it over high heat until all the moisture has evaporated — 12 to 15 minutes. Pour in the cream, and cook for another minute or two; then add the lemon juice, and cook until all the liquid has evaporated — two to three minutes more. Transfer the mixture to the bowl with the onion and walnuts. Stir in the parsley, sprinkle with the salt and some pepper, and set aside to cool.

Roll the pasta dough out on a floured work surface to form a rectangle roughly 15 by 18 inches. As you work, flip the dough over several times and dust it lightly with flour. Spread the filling in an even layer over the pasta, leaving an uncovered border 1 inch wide around the edge. Starting at a shorter edge, tightly roll up the dough and its filling, then wrap the roll in a double thickness of cheesecloth or muslin. Tie each end of the wrapper with string.

Pour enough water into a fish poacher or large oval casserole to fill it 4 inches deep. Bring the water to a boil and lower the pasta roll into the water. Once the water returns to a boil, simmer the roll for 45 minutes. Take the roll from the pot, and allow it to drain for 10 minutes before removing the string and wrapper.

While the roll is draining, gently warm the yogurt — do not let it get too hot or it will curdle. Stir in the walnuts, parsley and pepper.

Slice the roll into rounds about ¾ inch thick and arrange them on a warmed serving platter. Serve the dish with the warmed yogurt sauce.

Ragout of Mushrooms with Madeira

Serves 4
Working time: about 30 minutes
Total time: about 1 hour and 30 minutes

Calories **134**
Protein **5g.**
Cholesterol **0mg.**
Total fat **4g.**
Saturated fat **0g.**
Sodium **156mg.**

1 lb. fresh mushrooms, wiped clean, stemmed and quartered
1 oz. dried shiitake mushrooms, soaked for 1 hour in warm water
1 tbsp. safflower oil
1 shallot, finely chopped
1 garlic clove, finely chopped
½ cup Madeira or sherry
2 tomatoes, peeled, seeded and chopped
½ tsp. dried thyme leaves
¼ tsp. salt
freshly ground black pepper
1 tsp. cornstarch, mixed with 1 tbsp. of the mushroom-soaking liquid
1 tbsp. chopped parsley

Squeeze the excess moisture from the shiitake mushrooms and finely chop them. Heat the oil in a large, heavy-bottomed skillet over medium-high heat. Sauté the fresh mushrooms for one minute, then add the shallot and cook, stirring, for 30 seconds longer. Add the shiitake mushrooms and garlic, and cook for one minute. Pour in the Madeira or sherry, then stir in the tomatoes, thyme, salt and pepper. Cook until the mushrooms have softened — three to four minutes. Stir in the cornstarch mixture, and cook the ragout until it is slightly thickened — one to two minutes. Transfer the ragout to a serving dish and sprinkle with the chopped parsley.

EDITOR'S NOTE: *Although shiitake mushrooms are called for here, any dried wild mushroom — morels or cepes, for example — may be used instead.*

7 *Packed with vitamins, minerals, and flavor, fresh vegetables lie ready for the salad maker's attentions.*

Salads

Basic Dressings with a New Twist

The low-fat, low-calorie dressings that follow were specially developed for this book. Several recipes call for them specifically, but the dressings can also be refrigerated for later use on salads of your own invention.

The vinaigrette suits fresh mixed greens of delicate flavor. The yogurt and buttermilk dressings marry well with assertive vegetables; they also complement meats, grains and pasta. The mayonnaise makes an ideal partner for root vegetables as well as poultry and seafood.

Any of the four may be further enhanced by the addition of herbs, spices or other seasonings. The figures found alongside each recipe give the nutrient analysis for one tablespoon of dressing.

New Mayonnaise

THIS TOFU-BASED MAYONNAISE CONTAINS JUST HALF THE AMOUNT OF EGG YOLKS AND OIL FOUND IN THE TRADITIONAL VERSION.

Makes 1½ cups

¼ lb. firm tofu, cut into small cubes and soaked in cold water for 10 minutes
½ cup plain low-fat yogurt, drained in a cheesecloth-lined colander for 10 minutes
1 egg yolk
1 tsp. dried mustard
½ cup safflower oil
¼ cup virgin olive oil
2 tbsp. white wine vinegar or cider vinegar
½ tsp. salt
½ tsp. sugar
⅛ tsp. white pepper

Calories **70**
Protein **1g.**
Cholesterol **12mg.**
Total fat **7g.**
Saturated fat **1g.**
Sodium **50mg.**

Remove the tofu from its soaking water and drain it on paper towels. Transfer the tofu to a food processor or a blender. Add the yogurt, egg yolk and mustard, and process the mixture until it is very smooth, scraping down the sides at least once.

With the motor still running, pour in the oils in a thin, steady stream, stopping halfway through the process to scrape the sides with a rubber spatula.

Add the vinegar, salt, sugar and pepper, and process the mayonnaise for 15 seconds more. Transfer the mayonnaise to a bowl and refrigerate it; the mayonnaise will keep for at least 10 days.

Vinaigrette

Makes about ½ cup

1 tsp. Dijon mustard
¼ tsp. salt
freshly ground black pepper
2½ tbsp. red wine vinegar
2½ tbsp. safflower oil
2½ tbsp. virgin olive oil

Calories **75**
Protein **0g.**
Cholesterol **0mg.**
Total fat **8g.**
Saturated fat **1g.**
Sodium **75mg.**

In a small bowl, combine the mustard, the salt, a grinding of pepper and the vinegar. Whisking vigorously, pour in the safflower oil in a thin, steady stream; incorporate the olive oil the same way. Continue whisking until the dressing is well combined. Covered and stored in the refrigerator, the dressing will keep for about a week.

Buttermilk Dressing

Makes about ½ cup

½ cup buttermilk
cayenne pepper
¼ tsp. sugar
1 shallot, finely chopped
¼ cup nonfat dry milk
2 tbsp. fresh lemon juice

Calories **15**
Protein **1g.**
Cholesterol **1mg.**
Total fat **0g.**
Saturated fat **0g.**
Sodium **30mg.**

In a small bowl, combine the buttermilk, a pinch of cayenne pepper, the sugar and the shallot. Whisk in the dry milk a tablespoon at a time, then stir in the lemon juice. To allow the dressing to thicken, cover the bowl and refrigerate it for at least 30 minutes. The dressing will keep for three days.

EDITOR'S NOTE: *The inclusion of nonfat dry milk makes for a thick, creamy dressing.*

Creamy Yogurt Dressing

Makes about ½ cup

2 tbsp. cream sherry
2 garlic cloves, finely chopped
1½ tsp. Dijon mustard
½ cup plain low-fat yogurt
1 tbsp. sour cream
⅛ tsp. white pepper

Calories **20**
Protein **1g.**
Cholesterol **2mg.**
Total fat **1g.**
Saturated fat **0g.**
Sodium **25mg.**

Put the sherry and garlic into a small saucepan. Bring the mixture to a simmer over medium heat and cook it until nearly all the liquid has evaporated — about three minutes. Transfer the mixture to a bowl. Stir in the mustard, then the yogurt, sour cream and pepper. Cover the bowl and store the dressing in the refrigerator; it will keep for two to three days.

A Potpourri of Vegetables Bathed in Balsamic Vinegar

Serves 8 as a first course
Working time: about 40 minutes
Total time: about 50 minutes

Calories **80**
Protein **3g.**
Cholesterol **0mg.**
Total fat **4g.**
Saturated fat **1g.**
Sodium **135mg.**

2½ tbsp. virgin olive oil
3 shallots, thinly sliced
1 garlic clove, finely chopped
1 bunch beet greens with stems, washed and thinly sliced (about 2 cups)
¼ tsp. salt
freshly ground black pepper
⅓ cup balsamic vinegar
2 carrots, halved lengthwise and sliced diagonally into ½-inch pieces
2 small turnips, peeled and cut into bâtonnets
2 cups small broccoli florets
2 small zucchini (about ½ lb.), halved lengthwise and sliced diagonally into ½-inch pieces
1 small yellow squash (about ¼ lb.), halved lengthwise and sliced diagonally into ½-inch pieces

Pour 3 quarts of water into a large pot; add 1 teaspoon of salt and bring the water to a boil.

In the meantime, heat 1½ tablespoons of the oil in a large, heavy-bottomed skillet set over medium heat. Add the shallots and garlic, and cook them for two minutes. Stir in the beet greens and their stems, the ¼ teaspoon of salt and some pepper. Cook the mixture, stirring frequently, for seven minutes. Pour the vinegar over the mixture, stir well, and remove the skillet from the heat.

Put the carrots into the boiling water and cook them for one minute. Add the turnips and broccoli to the carrots in the pot, and cook them for two minutes. Add the zucchini and yellow squash to the pot, and cook all the vegetables together for only 30 seconds more. Immediately drain the vegetables and refresh them under cold running water; when they are cool, drain them on paper towels.

Transfer the vegetables to a bowl and pour the contents of the skillet over them. Drizzle the remaining tablespoon of oil over the top, add a liberal grinding of pepper, and toss the salad well. Chill the salad for at least 10 minutes. Toss it once more before presenting it at the table.

Celeriac in a Creamy Mustard Dressing

SALADS OF CELERIAC TOSSED IN A CREAMY SAUCE APPEAR THROUGHOUT FRANCE AS FIRST COURSES FOR FAMILY MEALS AND ON RESTAURANT MENUS.

Serves 4
Working (and total) time: about 15 minutes

2 tsp. golden mustard seeds
½ tsp. Dijon mustard
1½ tsp. balsamic vinegar, or 1½ tsp. red wine vinegar, plus ½ tsp. honey
½ cup plain low-fat yogurt
1 celeriac (about 1 lb.), peeled and cut into thin strips

Calories **45**
Protein **3g.**
Cholesterol **0mg.**
Total fat **2g.**
Saturated fat **1g.**
Sodium **30mg.**

In a small, heavy-bottomed frying pan, heat the mustard seeds for a few seconds, until they begin to pop. Transfer the mustard seeds to a small bowl; then mix in the Dijon mustard, vinegar, and yogurt to make a creamy dressing.

Place the celeriac strips in a serving bowl, and toss them with the mustard dressing until they are thoroughly coated. Either serve the salad immediately or place it in the refrigerator until serving time; toss the salad again just before serving.

Grated Carrot Salad

A SALAD OF GRATED RAW CARROTS MAKES A CRISP, REFRESHING APPETIZER, RICH IN VITAMIN A. IT IS PARTICULARLY WELCOME IN WINTER, WHEN MANY FRESH SALAD INGREDIENTS ARE HARD TO COME BY.

Serves 4
Working (and total) time: about 10 minutes

¼ cup plain low-fat yogurt
1 tbsp. fresh lemon juice
½ tsp. grainy mustard
2 tsp. fresh tarragon leaves, chopped, or ½ tsp. dried tarragon
½ lb. carrots, grated in a mouli julienne or in a food processor

Calories **30**
Protein **2g.**
Cholesterol **0mg.**
Total fat **2g.**
Saturated fat **1g.**
Sodium **15mg.**

In a small bowl, whisk together the yogurt, lemon juice, mustard, and the fresh or dried tarragon. Arrange the grated carrots in a large dish, spoon the dressing over them, and serve the salad immediately.

Green Beans with Anchovies and Lemon

Serves 4
Working (and total) time: about 25 minutes

½ lb. green beans, trimmed
3 anchovy fillets, soaked in milk for 15 minutes, drained, and patted dry
2 tbsp. virgin olive oil
1 tbsp. fresh lemon juice
½ lemon, coarsely chopped zest only
freshly ground black pepper
½ garlic clove
1 tbsp. chopped chives

Calories **95**
Protein **3g.**
Cholesterol **0mg.**
Total fat **8g.**
Saturated fat **1g.**
Sodium **100mg.**

Bring a saucepan of water to a boil, and blanch the green beans for two minutes. Drain the beans in a colander, refresh them under cold running water, and then drain them a second time. With a sharp knife, cut the anchovy fillets lengthwise into thin strips, then cut the strips horizontally to make 1-inch pieces.

To make the dressing, whisk together the oil and lemon juice in a small bowl. Stir in the lemon zest and some pepper. Rub a salad bowl with the garlic. Place the beans, anchovies, and chopped chives in the bowl, and toss the beans with the dressing until they are well coated. Serve immediately.

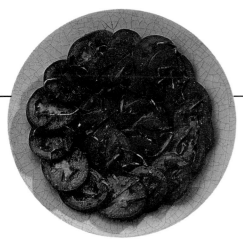

Tomatoes with Basil

A SIMPLE TOMATO SALAD MAKES A WONDERFUL APPETIZER IN HIGH SUMMER, WHEN TOMATOES ARE AT THEIR PEAK OF COLOR AND FLAVOR.

Serves 4
Working (and total) time: about 10 minutes

4 ripe tomatoes
6 basil leaves, cut into chiffonade
¼ tsp. salt
1 tbsp. white wine vinegar
2 tbsp. virgin olive oil
freshly ground black pepper

Calories **80**
Protein **1g.**
Cholesterol **0mg.**
Total fat **8g.**
Saturated fat **1g.**
Sodium **100mg.**

With a sharp knife, cut the four tomatoes into thin slices. Arrange the slices on a serving plate, slightly overlapping, and sprinkle the shredded basil leaves over them.

In a small bowl, stir the salt and vinegar together until the salt dissolves. Whisk in the olive oil, beating until the oil and vinegar are thoroughly blended. Pour the vinaigrette over the tomato slices, add some black pepper, and serve the salad immediately.

Baby Zucchini Vinaigrette

Serves 4
Working (and total) time: about 15 minutes

1 lb. baby zucchini
1 garlic clove, finely chopped
¼ tsp. salt
1 tsp. grainy mustard
½ tsp. Dijon mustard
freshly ground black pepper
1 tbsp. white wine vinegar
2 tbsp. virgin olive oil
7 purple basil leaves, torn

Calories **90**
Protein **1g.**
Cholesterol **0mg.**
Total fat **8g.**
Saturated fat **1g.**
Sodium **200mg.**

With a sharp knife, slice the zucchini diagonally into 1-inch pieces, and plunge the slices into a saucepan filled with boiling water. Boil the zucchini until it is just tender — about five minutes.

While the zucchini cooks, prepare the dressing. Place the garlic and the salt in a mortar, and pound them with a pestle until the garlic has broken down into a puree. Mix in the two mustards, some pepper, and the vinegar, then whisk in the olive oil.

Drain the zucchini in a colander, and refresh it quickly under cold running water to arrest its cooking. Drain it thoroughly again.

Transfer the zucchini to a shallow serving dish. Toss with the mustard dressing and the basil leaves, and serve the salad immediately.

EDITOR'S NOTE: *If purple basil is unavailable, use ordinary fresh basil leaves instead.*

Fennel Salad

Serves 4
Working (and total) time: about 10 minutes

½ tsp. salt
1 tbsp. white wine vinegar
2 tbsp. virgin olive oil
3 tbsp. finely chopped parsley
ground white pepper
2 small fennel bulbs, sliced (about ½ lb.)

Calories **75**
Protein **1g.**
Cholesterol **0mg.**
Total fat **8g.**
Saturated fat **1g.**
Sodium **265mg.**

In a small bowl, stir the salt and vinegar together until the salt dissolves. Add the olive oil, parsley, and some white pepper, whisking until the dressing is well blended.

Place the fennel slices in a serving bowl. Toss them with the vinaigrette dressing just before serving.

Artichoke and Potato Salad

Serves 4
Working time: about 20 minutes
Total time: about 1 hour and 20 minutes
(includes chilling)

Calories **150**
Protein **2g.**
Cholesterol **0mg.**
Total fat **10g.**
Saturated fat **2g.**
Sodium **35mg.**

3 tbsp. fresh lemon juice or vinegar
¾ lb. baby artichokes, stems cut off flush with base, tough outer leaves removed and discarded
½ lb. small new potatoes, scrubbed
1 small head radicchio, washed and dried
1 small head Bibb or Boston lettuce, washed and dried
2 tbsp. fresh chives, cut into 1-inch pieces
Balsamic vinaigrette
1 tbsp. balsamic vinegar
¼ tsp. dry mustard
½ garlic clove, very finely chopped
freshly ground black pepper
2½ tbsp. virgin olive oil

Add the lemon juice or vinegar to a large saucepan of boiling water, and drop in the artichokes. Submerge the artichokes by weighting them down with a heavy plate or the lid from a smaller saucepan, and cook them until tender—20 to 25 minutes. Drain the artichokes in a colander and set them aside to cool. Mean-while, cut the potatoes in half and cook them in boiling water until tender—about 12 minutes.

To make the dressing, put the balsamic vinegar into a small jar that has a tight-fitting lid, and add the mustard, garlic, and some pepper. Shake or stir the ingredients to combine them, then add the oil. Cover the jar and shake it to mix everything well.

When the potatoes are cooked, transfer them to a large bowl. Shake the jar of dressing again, and add half of the vinaigrette while the potatoes are hot. Toss the potatoes to coat them thoroughly.

Cut off the top 1 inch of the cooked artichokes, and remove any outer leaves that are still fibrous. Cut the artichokes in half lengthwise, and remove the fuzzy choke if there is one. Add the artichoke halves to the potatoes. Shake the jar of dressing again, and add the remaining vinaigrette to the salad. Toss the vegetables carefully to combine them. Cover the salad with plastic wrap, and refrigerate it for about 30 minutes.

Line a salad bowl with the radicchio and green let-tuce, scatter the potatoes and artichokes over them, and sprinkle the salad with chives before serving.

EDITOR'S NOTE: *The dressing for the salad may also be made with a good-quality wine vinegar, although the resulting vinaigrette will be less aromatic than with balsamic vinegar.*

Caesar Salad

PREREQUISITES FOR THE CLASSIC CAESAR SALAD INCLUDE DEEP-FRIED CROUTONS AND A RAW EGG IN THE DRESSING. IN THIS LIGHTER VERSION, THE FRIED CROUTONS ARE REPLACED BY CUBES OF TOASTED WHOLE WHEAT BREAD.

Serves 4
Working (and total) time: about 30 minutes

Calories **120**
Protein **6g.**
Cholesterol **35mg.**
Total fat **8g.**
Saturated fat **2g.**
Sodium **400mg.**

¼ lb. escarole, washed and dried	
¼ lb. romaine lettuce, washed and dried	
1 cup radicchio, washed and dried	
2 thin slices whole wheat bread	
1 oz. anchovy fillets (about 4 anchovies)	
2 tbsp. freshly grated Parmesan cheese	

Egg and lemon dressing

½ small egg, beaten
1 tbsp. virgin olive oil
1 tbsp. fresh lemon juice
1 tbsp. finely grated lemon zest
1 small garlic clove, crushed

Tear the salad leaves and put them into a large salad bowl. Cover the bowl with plastic wrap, and place it in the refrigerator for 20 to 30 minutes to crisp the lettuce leaves.

Meanwhile, toast the slices of whole wheat bread until they are golden brown. Remove the crusts and cut the toast into small dice. Drain the anchovy fillets thoroughly on paper towels, then chop them coarsely.

Just before serving, put the ingredients for the dressing into a bowl, and whisk them until they are thoroughly blended. Remove the salad leaves from the refrigerator, and sprinkle them with the diced toast, chopped anchovy fillets, and grated Parmesan cheese. Pour the dressing over the salad, toss it thoroughly, and serve immediately.

Mix the scallops and the shrimp with the lemon juice, basil, horseradish and cayenne pepper. Set them aside while you roast the vegetables.

Toss the mushrooms, fennel, celery, carrot, red pepper, green beans, shallots and garlic with the oregano, thyme, salt, olive oil and some black pepper. Spread the vegetables out in a single layer in a large shallow pan and roast them in a preheated 450° oven, stirring frequently, until the shallots are translucent — 10 to 12 minutes. Add the scallops and shrimp, their liquid, and the snow peas; stir to combine all the ingredients and cook them, stirring from time to time, until the seafood is opaque — five to seven minutes. Transfer the mixture to a shallow nonreactive dish to cool at room temperature for 30 minutes.

Arrange the lettuce and endive on a platter or individual plates. Using a slotted spoon, set the vegetables and seafood atop the greens. Pour the liquid left in the dish into a small bowl.

Make the dressing by whisking the lemon juice, Dijon mustard, grainy mustard and yogurt into the reserved liquid. Serve the dressing with the salad.

Oven-Roasted Vegetable Salad with Shrimp and Scallops

Serves 4 as a main course at lunch
Working time: about 45 minutes
Total time: about 1 hour and 15 minutes

Calories **250**
Protein **23g.**
Cholesterol **86mg.**
Total fat **9g.**
Saturated fat **1g.**
Sodium **450mg.**

½ lb. bay scallops, the bright white connective tissue removed
½ lb. medium shrimp, peeled, and deveined if necessary
3 tbsp. fresh lemon juice
1 cup coarsely chopped fresh basil
½ tsp. drained prepared horseradish
¼ tsp. cayenne pepper
½ lb. mushrooms, trimmed and wiped clean
1 small fennel bulb, thinly sliced
2 celery stalks, cut into 2-inch lengths, then into ¼-inch sticks
1 carrot, cut into 2-inch lengths, then into ¼-inch sticks
1 sweet red pepper, seeded, deribbed and cut into thin strips
¼ lb. green beans, trimmed
4 shallots, thinly sliced
1 tbsp. finely chopped garlic
1 tbsp. chopped fresh oregano, or 1 tsp. dried oregano
1 tbsp. fresh thyme, or 1 tsp. dried thyme leaves
½ tsp. salt
2 tbsp. virgin olive oil
freshly ground black pepper
¼ lb. snow peas, stems and strings removed
1 head of green-leaf lettuce, washed and dried
1 head of Belgian endive, leaves separated
¼ cup fresh lemon juice
2 tsp. Dijon mustard
1 tsp. grainy mustard
2 tbsp. plain low-fat yogurt

Clam Salad on Nappa Cabbage

Serves 4 as a main course
Working time: about 1 hour
Total time: about 1 hour and 30 minutes

Calories **235**
Protein **12g.**
Cholesterol **34mg.**
Total fat **8g.**
Saturated fat **1g.**
Sodium **180mg.**

3 scallions, trimmed and finely chopped
1 shallot, finely chopped
1 cup dry sherry
3 tbsp. fresh lemon juice
½ tsp. saffron threads
36 small hard-shell clams, scrubbed
5 round red potatoes or other boiling potatoes
2 tbsp. red wine vinegar
1 tbsp. grainy mustard
freshly ground black pepper
2 tbsp. safflower oil
1 lb. Nappa cabbage, cut into chiffonade
2 tbsp. thinly sliced fresh basil, or 2 tsp. dried basil
2 tbsp. finely chopped red onion
½ lb. cherry tomatoes, halved lengthwise

Combine the scallions, shallot, sherry, lemon juice and saffron threads in a large, nonreactive pot. Bring the liquid to a simmer, then reduce the heat to low, cover the mixture, and cook it for one minute.

Add the clams and cover the pot. Increase the heat to medium high and cook the clams, stirring occasionally, until they open — about three minutes. Using a slotted spoon, transfer the clams to a large bowl; discard any clams that remain closed. Strain the clam broth through a sieve lined with cheesecloth into a bowl, taking care not to pour any of the accumulated sand into the sieve. Rinse out the cheesecloth and set it aside. Discard the solids.

When the clams are cool enough to handle, remove them from their shells. Dip each clam into the broth to rinse off any residual sand; reserve the broth. Place the rinsed clams in a bowl, cover the bowl, and refrigerate the clams.

Put the potatoes into a saucepan and pour in enough water to cover them by about 2 inches. Bring the water to a boil and simmer the potatoes until they are tender — about 15 minutes. Drain them and set them aside until they are cool enough to handle.

Cut the potatoes into quarters and transfer them to a nonreactive bowl. Reline the sieve with the cheesecloth and strain the clam broth through it. Pour the strained broth over the potatoes. Gently toss the potatoes and let them stand for 20 minutes.

Remove the potatoes from the broth and set them aside. To prepare the vinaigrette, whisk the vinegar, mustard and some pepper into the broth. Then, whisking constantly, pour in the oil in a thin, steady stream; continue whisking until the oil is fully incorporated.

Toss the cabbage with the basil, onion and about half of the vinaigrette. In a separate bowl, mix the clams and tomatoes with the remaining vinaigrette.

To assemble the salad, spread the cabbage-onion mixture on a platter. Mound the clam-and-tomato mixture in the center and arrange the potatoes around it. Pour any remaining vinaigrette over the potatoes and serve at once.

the bowl and marinate the chicken for two hours in the refrigerator.

At the end of the marinating period, remove the thighs from the liquid and pat them dry with paper towels. Reserve the marinade. Heat the oil in a large, heavy-bottomed pot over medium heat. Add the thighs and cook them until they are browned on all sides — about 10 minutes. Stir in the barley, the stock and ½ cup of the reserved marinade. Bring the liquid to a boil, reduce the heat, and simmer the mixture until the barley is tender and most of the liquid has evaporated — about 30 minutes.

Remove the thighs and set them aside; when they are cool enough to handle, pull the meat from the bones and chop it coarsely. Add the chicken to the barley, then add the parsley, the remaining mint and the remaining 2 tablespoons of lemon juice. Mix the salad well and serve it on a bed of iceberg lettuce, garnished with the mint sprigs.

Chicken Salad with Barley and Mint

Serves 6 as a main course
Working time: about 45 minutes
Total time: about 3 hours and 20 minutes
(includes marinating)

Calories **410**
Protein **30g.**
Cholesterol **81mg.**
Total fat **15g.**
Saturated fat **3g.**
Sodium **320mg.**

2 lb. chicken thighs, skinned and trimmed of fat
½ cup plus 2 tbsp. fresh lemon juice
½ tsp. ground cumin
½ tsp. dry mustard
½ tsp. paprika
½ tsp. ground cinnamon
½ tsp. cayenne pepper
½ tsp. salt
freshly ground black pepper
3 tbsp. chopped fresh mint, or 1 tbsp. dried mint
1 garlic clove, finely chopped
2 tbsp. safflower oil
1⅓ cups pearl barley
4 cups unsalted chicken stock
1 tbsp. chopped fresh parsley, preferably Italian
1 small head of iceberg lettuce
several mint sprigs

Put the chicken thighs in a large bowl. In a smaller bowl, combine ½ cup of the lemon juice, the cumin, mustard, paprika, cinnamon, cayenne pepper, salt, some black pepper, 1 tablespoon of the fresh mint or 1 teaspoon of dried mint, and the garlic. Pour this marinade over the thighs, and stir to coat them. Cover

Chicken and Avocado Salad with Tomatillo Sauce

Serves 4 as a main course
Working time: about 25 minutes
Total time: about 45 minutes

Calories **310**
Protein **29g.**
Cholesterol **72mg.**
Total fat **18g.**
Saturated fat **3g.**
Sodium **215mg.**

1 tsp. safflower oil
4 chicken breast halves, skinned and boned (about 1 lb.)
¼ tsp. salt
freshly ground black pepper
⅓ lb. tomatillos, husked and washed
1½ tbsp. virgin olive oil
¼ cup chopped onion
1 garlic clove, thinly sliced
1½ tbsp. fresh lemon juice
5 fresh basil leaves, thinly sliced
1 head of radicchio or red-leaf lettuce, washed and dried
1 ripe avocado, peeled, pitted and rubbed with 1 tbsp. fresh lemon juice
1 tomato, seeded and finely chopped

Heat the safflower oil in a large, heavy-bottomed skillet over very low heat. Sprinkle the chicken breasts with ⅛ teaspoon of the salt and some pepper, and place them in the skillet. Set a heavy plate atop the chicken breasts to weight them down so that they will cook evenly. Cook the breasts on one side for five minutes; turn them over, cover them with the plate, and cook the breasts for three to four minutes more. The meat should feel firm but springy to the touch, with no traces of pink along the edges. Transfer the chicken breasts to a plate and refrigerate them while you finish the salad.

Finely dice two of the tomatillos and set the pieces aside; cut the remaining tomatillos into quarters. Heat the olive oil in the skillet over medium heat, then add the onion and garlic, and cook them for two minutes. Stir in the tomatillo quarters, the lemon juice, basil and the remaining ⅛ teaspoon of salt. Cook the mixture, stirring often, until the tomatillos are soft — about seven minutes. Transfer the contents of the skillet to a food processor or blender and purée the mixture. Pour the sauce into a bowl and stir in the diced tomatillos. Chill the sauce for at least 20 minutes.

Arrange a few radicchio or lettuce leaves on four plates. Slice the breasts diagonally and fan out each one on the leaves. Cut the avocado into thin slices and tuck them between the chicken slices. Spoon a large dollop of the tomatillo sauce onto the base of each fan, then sprinkle chopped tomato over the sauce. Grind fresh pepper over all, if you wish, and serve.

Curried Chicken Salad with Raisins

Serves 6 as a main course
Working time: about 20 minutes
Total time: about 1 hour

Calories **250**
Protein **20g.**
Cholesterol **55mg.**
Total fat **9g.**
Saturated fat **2g.**
Sodium **190mg.**

1 tsp. safflower oil
6 chicken breast halves, skinned and boned (about 1½ lb.)
¼ tsp. salt
½ cup raisins
1 large carrot, grated
1 onion, grated
1 celery stalk, chopped
3 tbsp. fresh lemon juice
1 tbsp. curry powder
1 tbsp. honey
¼ cup mayonnaise
¾ cup julienned radish
½ tbsp. virgin olive oil
1 small head of romaine lettuce, washed and dried
2 ripe tomatoes, cored and sliced into wedges

Heat the safflower oil in a large, heavy-bottomed skillet over low heat. Sprinkle the chicken breasts with the salt and place them in the skillet. Set a heavy plate atop the chicken breasts to weight them down so that they will cook evenly. Cook the breasts on the first side for five minutes; turn them over, weight them down again with the plate, and cook them on the second side for three to four minutes. The meat should feel firm but springy to the touch, with no traces of pink along the edges. Transfer the breasts to a plate and chill them. When the chicken is cool enough to handle, cut it into 1-inch cubes.

In a large mixing bowl, toss the chicken cubes with the raisins, carrot, onion, celery, lemon juice, curry powder, honey and mayonnaise. Chill the salad for at least 30 minutes.

Toss the radish julienne with the olive oil in a small bowl. Mound the chicken salad on the lettuce leaves, and garnish each plate with the radish julienne and the tomato wedges. Serve immediately

Parsley and Bulgur Salad

IN THIS MIDDLE EASTERN PARSLEY SALAD, THE
BULGUR—CRACKED WHEAT—NEEDS ONLY BRIEF SOAKING AND
REQUIRES NO COOKING.

Serves 6
Working time: about 10 minutes
Total time: about 1 hour (includes soaking and cooling)

Calories **155**
Protein **4g.**
Cholesterol **0mg.**
Total fat **8g.**
Saturated fat **1g.**
Sodium **75mg.**

¾ cup bulgur
2 cups chopped parsley leaves
1 cup chopped fresh mint leaves
4 scallions, chopped
4 tbsp. fresh lemon juice
3 tbsp. virgin olive oil
¼ tsp. salt
freshly ground black pepper
1 tomato, cut into thin wedges

Place the bulgur in a bowl, cover it with 2 cups of boiling water, and let it soak for 30 minutes. Drain the soaked wheat through a colander lined with cheesecloth or muslin, and squeeze it dry, a handful at a time, extracting as much water as possible.

Place the drained bulgur in a mixing bowl. Add the parsley, mint, scallions, lemon juice, oil, salt, and some pepper. Mix the ingredients thoroughly, and leave the salad in a cool place for 15 to 20 minutes to allow its flavors to blend.

Transfer the salad to a shallow dish or platter, and serve it garnished with the tomato wedges.

Middle Eastern Spiced Carrot Salad

Serves 6
Working time: about 10 minutes
Total time: about 1 hour (includes cooling)

Calories **75**
Protein **1g.**
Cholesterol **0mg.**
Total fat **5g.**
Saturated fat **1g.**
Sodium **190mg.**

2 lb. carrots, peeled and sliced into thick rounds
2 garlic cloves, sliced
2 tbsp. virgin olive oil
¼ tsp. cayenne pepper
2 tsp. ground cumin
2 tsp. fresh lemon juice
¼ tsp. salt

Put the carrots and garlic into a saucepan. Cover them with hot water and boil them until they are soft—about 15 minutes. Drain the vegetables and mash them thoroughly.

In a small frying pan, heat the olive oil, and sauté the cayenne pepper and ground cumin for one minute. Stir the spices and oil into the carrot mixture, mix in the lemon juice and the salt, and set the salad aside to cool to room temperature before serving.

SUGGESTED ACCOMPANIMENT: *strips of warm pita bread.*

Creamed Tahini Spread

THIS APPETIZER, BASED ON A MIDDLE EASTERN DISH, SHOULD
BE SERVED WITH THIN SLICES OF WHOLE WHEAT TOAST OR
WARM PITA BREAD.

Serves 12
Working (and total) time: about 10 minutes

Calories **110**
Protein **5g.**
Cholesterol **0mg.**
Total fat **7g.**
Saturated fat **1g.**
Sodium **55mg.**

¼ cup parsley, stems removed
1 small garlic clove, sliced
2 slices whole wheat bread, crusts removed and discarded, cut into cubes
⅔ cup tahini (sesame paste)
4 tbsp. fresh lemon juice
1½ cups plain low-fat yogurt
¼ tsp. salt
freshly ground black pepper

Place the parsley, garlic, and bread in a food processor or a blender, and process the mixture until it breaks down into coarse crumbs. Add the tahini, lemon juice, yogurt, salt, and some pepper, and blend until they form a thick paste. Adjust the seasoning, adding more lemon juice or black pepper if necessary.

Transfer the mixture to a small serving bowl.

8 Sunlight greets a leisurely Sunday breakfast. Nutritionists say breakfast should supply a quarter of the day's calories.

Breakfasts and Brunches

Swiss Oatmeal

THE SWISS CEREAL KNOWN AS MUESLI, ON WHICH THIS
RECIPE IS BASED, GENERALLY CONTAINS DRIED FRUIT.
HERE FRESH FRUIT IS USED, AND THE CEREAL IS MOISTENED
WITH BOTH APPLE CIDER AND YOGURT.

Serves 6
Working (and total) time: about 10 minutes

Calories **160**
Protein **5g.**
Cholesterol **2mg.**
Total fat **3g.**
Saturated fat **0g.**
Sodium **29mg.**

1 red apple, quartered, cored and coarsely chopped
1 yellow apple, quartered, cored and coarsely chopped
½ cup apple cider or unsweetened apple juice
1 cup quick-cooking rolled oats
1 tbsp. honey
1 cup plain low-fat yogurt
2 tbsp. sliced almonds
2 tbsp. raisins
1 tbsp. dark brown sugar

Put the chopped apples into a large bowl. Add the
cider or apple juice and toss the apples to moisten
them. Stir in the oats and honey, then add the yogurt,
almonds and raisins. Stir to combine the mixture well.

Serve the Swiss oatmeal in individual bowls; sprinkle
each serving with ½ teaspoon of the brown sugar.

EDITOR'S NOTE: *If you wish, Swiss oatmeal can be made
ahead and kept in the refrigerator, covered with plastic wrap,
for up to two days.*

Homemade Granola

WITH MILK ADDED, THIS GRANOLA BECOMES
A BREAKFAST IN ITSELF.

Serves 8
Working (and total) time: about 30 minutes

Calories **255**
Protein **6g.**
Cholesterol **0mg.**
Total fat **10g.**
Saturated fat **1g.**
Sodium **102mg.**

1 cup rolled oats
½ cup wheat bran
¼ cup untoasted sunflower seeds (about 1 oz.)
½ cup whole blanched almonds (about 2 oz.)
2 tbsp. sesame seeds
2 tsp. safflower oil
¼ tsp. salt
1 cup raisins
10 pitted dates, chopped
2 tbsp. honey
1 tsp. vanilla
grated zest of 1 orange

Preheat the oven to 400° F. Combine the oats, bran,
sunflower seeds, almonds, sesame seeds, oil and salt
in a large bowl. Spread the mixture evenly on a jelly-
roll pan and toast it in the oven, stirring the mixture every five minutes, until it is lightly browned —
about 15 minutes.

Return the toasted mixture to the bowl. Stir in the
raisins, dates, honey, vanilla and orange zest. Let the
granola cool completely before storing it in an airtight
container. Serve the granola in individual bowls, with
low-fat milk poured over it if you like.

Apricot-Orange Breakfast Couscous

Serves 4
Working time: about 5 minutes
Total time: about 10 minutes

Calories **220**
Protein **6g.**
Cholesterol **0mg.**
Total fat **2g.**
Saturated fat **1g.**
Sodium **203mg.**

1 cup fresh orange juice
12 dried apricot halves, thinly sliced
¼ tsp. salt
1 cup couscous
3 tbsp. unsweetened dried coconut
fresh fruit (optional)
low-fat milk (optional)

Put the orange juice, 1 cup of water, all but 1 tablespoon of the apricots and the salt into a medium saucepan. Bring the mixture to a boil. Stir in the couscous and remove the pan from the heat; cover the pan and let it stand for five minutes.

Toast the coconut by putting it in a small, heavy-bottomed saucepan and cooking it, stirring constantly, until it is lightly browned — about five minutes. Spoon the couscous into individual serving bowls. Top each portion with some of the reserved tablespoon of sliced apricot and some coconut. You may garnish the hot cereal with fresh fruit such as raspberries, orange segments, or sliced pineapple or mango. Serve the cereal at once; accompany it with low-fat milk if you like.

Apple-Cinnamon Breakfast Bulgur

Serves 4
Working time: about 5 minutes
Total time: about 20 minutes

Calories **208**
Protein **5g.**
Cholesterol **0mg.**
Total fat **1g.**
Saturated fat **0g.**
Sodium **137mg.**

1 tart apple, preferably Granny Smith, cut in half and cored
1 cup plus 1 tbsp. apple cider or unsweetened apple juice
1 tbsp. currants or raisins
¼ tsp. ground cinnamon
¼ tsp. salt
1 cup bulgur
low-fat milk (optional)

Cut one half of the apple into thin slices. Put the apple slices into a small bowl and toss them with 1 tablespoon of the cider or apple juice. Set the bowl aside.

Cut the remaining apple half into small chunks. Put the chunks into a heavy-bottomed saucepan. Add the remaining cup of cider or apple juice, 1 cup of water, the currants or raisins, the cinnamon, and the salt, and bring the mixture to a boil. Stir in the bulgur, then cover the pan and reduce the heat to medium low. Simmer the bulgur mixture until all of the liquid is absorbed — about 15 minutes.

Spoon the bulgur into individual serving bowls and decorate each portion with some of the reserved apple slices. If you like, serve the cereal with low-fat milk.

Wheat Berry Bread

Makes 3 loaves
Working time: about 45 minutes
Total time: about 5 hours (includes rising)

Per slice:
Calories **105**
Protein **4g.**
Cholesterol **6mg.**
Total fat **1g.**
Saturated fat **0g.**
Sodium **38mg.**

1 cup wheat berries
1 envelope fast-rising dry yeast (about 1 tbsp.)
2 tsp. sugar
¼ cup nonfat dry milk
¼ cup honey
¼ cup molasses
½ cup wheat germ
¼ tsp. salt
7 to 8 cups bread flour
1 egg, beaten
½ tsp. coarse salt

Put the wheat berries and 3 cups of water into a saucepan and bring the water to a boil. Lower the heat and simmer the wheat berries until tender—one and a half to two hours. Let the wheat berries cool in the liquid, then drain them over a bowl; reserve the liquid.

Combine the yeast, sugar, dry milk, honey, molasses, wheat germ, salt and drained wheat berries with 6 cups of the flour in a large bowl. Measure the reserved cooking liquid and add enough water to make 3 cups of liquid. Heat the liquid just until it is hot to the touch (130° F.). Pour the hot liquid into the flour mixture and stir them together with a wooden spoon.

Gradually incorporate up to 2 cups of additional flour, working it in with your hands until the dough becomes stiff but not dry. Turn the dough out onto a floured surface and knead the dough until it is smooth and elastic — five to 10 minutes. Place the dough in a clean, oiled bowl; turn the dough over to coat it with the oil, cover the bowl with a damp towel or plastic wrap, and let the dough rise in a warm, draft-free place until it is doubled in size — about 45 minutes.

Punch the dough down and divide it into three pieces. Knead one piece of the dough and form it into a ball. Knead and form the remaining two pieces of dough into balls. Put the balls of dough onto a large baking sheet, leaving enough space between the loaves for them to expand. Cover the loaves and let them rise until they are doubled in volume again — about 30 minutes.

About 10 minutes before the end of the rising time, preheat the oven to 350° F.

Bake the loaves for 25 minutes. Remove the baking sheet from the oven, brush each loaf with some of the beaten egg, then sprinkle each with a little of the coarse salt. Return the loaves to the oven and continue to bake them until they are brown and sound hollow when tapped on the bottom — 25 to 30 minutes more. Let the loaves cool to room temperature; each yields 16 slices.

EDITOR'S NOTE: *If you plan to store the bread, it is preferable to keep it in the freezer. Refrigeration causes bread to dry out.*

Pear Butter

Makes 1½ cups
Working time: about 25 minutes
Total time: about 2 hours and 30 minutes
(includes chilling)

Per tablespoon:
Calories **30**
Protein **0g.**
Cholesterol **0mg.**
Total fat **0g.**
Saturated fat **0g.**
Sodium **1mg.**

2 lb. ripe pears, peeled, quartered, cored and cut into 1-inch pieces
1 cup apple cider or unsweetened apple juice
1 tbsp. light or dark brown sugar
¼ tsp. ground allspice
⅛ tsp. ground cinnamon
1½ tbsp. pear liqueur or brandy

Combine the pears, cider or apple juice, brown sugar, allspice and cinnamon in a large, heavy-bottomed saucepan. Bring the mixture to a simmer over medium heat, then reduce the heat to maintain a slow simmer. Cook the pears, stirring occasionally, until they are very soft and all the liquid has evaporated — about 1½ hours.

Put the pear mixture into a blender or a food processor, and add the liqueur or brandy. Process the mixture until the pears are smoothly puréed. Spoon the pear butter into a serving bowl and serve it at room temperature. Pear butter can be made up to a week in advance; cover it and store it in the refrigerator.

Apricot Spread

Makes 1½ cups
Working time: about 10 minutes
Total time: about 25 minutes

Per tablespoon:
Calories **29**
Protein **0g.**
Cholesterol **0mg.**
Total fat **0g.**
Saturated fat **0g.**
Sodium **1mg.**

½ lb. dried apricots
1½ cups apple cider or unsweetened apple juice
⅛ tsp. ground allspice
½ tsp. ground cumin

Put the apricots, cider or apple juice, allspice and cumin into a nonreactive saucepan. Bring the mixture to a simmer and cook it, stirring occasionally, until only about ½ cup of liquid remains — 10 to 15 minutes. Purée the mixture in a food processor for five seconds, then scrape down the sides, and process again to make a thick, chunky spread — about 10 seconds. The spread may be kept refrigerated for up to two weeks.

Apple-Rhubarb Butter

Makes 4 cups
Working (and total) time: about 45 minutes

Per tablespoon:
Calories **12**
Protein **0g.**
Cholesterol **0mg.**
Total fat **0g.**
Saturated fat **0g.**
Sodium **0mg.**

1 lb. fresh rhubarb, cut into 1-inch pieces, or 1 lb. frozen rhubarb, thawed
2 large McIntosh or other sweet, tangy apples (about ¾ lb.), peeled, cored and sliced
grated zest and juice of 1 orange
½ cup sugar

¼ tsp. ground mace or grated nutmeg

Put the rhubarb, apples, orange zest, orange juice and sugar into a heavy-bottomed saucepan. Cook the mixture over medium-low heat, stirring occasionally with a wooden spoon to break up the pieces of fruit, until the mixture is very thick — 25 to 30 minutes. Stir in the mace or nutmeg, and serve the apple-rhubarb butter warm with pancakes or French toast, or chilled with muffins or biscuits.

Fresh Yogurt Cheese

Makes 1½ cups
Working time: about 20 minutes
Total time: about 8 hours

Per tablespoon:
Plain:
Calories **18**
Protein **0g.**
Cholesterol **2mg.**
Total fat **0g.**
Saturated fat **0g.**
Sodium **10mg.**

3 cups plain low-fat yogurt

Line a large sieve with a double layer of cheesecloth or a large, round paper coffee filter. Place the lined sieve over a deep bowl so that the yogurt can effectively drain; spoon the yogurt into the sieve. Cover the bowl and sieve with plastic wrap. Put the bowl in the refrigerator and let the yogurt drain overnight.

Discard the whey that has collected in the bowl and transfer the yogurt cheese to another bowl; the cheese should be very thick. Cover the bowl with plastic wrap and refrigerate the cheese until you are ready to use it. Yogurt cheese will keep in the refrigerator for two weeks.

Dill-and-Chive Spread

Makes 1½ cups
Working (and total) time: about 15 minutes

Per tablespoon:
Dill:
Calories **18**
Protein **2g.**
Cholesterol **2mg.**
Total fat **0g.**
Saturated fat **0g.**
Sodium **32mg.**

1½ cups yogurt cheese (recipe, page 212)
2 tbsp. finely cut fresh dill
2 tbsp. finely cut fresh chives
¼ tsp. salt
freshly ground black pepper

Combine the yogurt cheese with the dill, chives, salt and a generous grinding of pepper. The spread may be served at once or covered and refrigerated until you are ready to use it.

Savory Vegetable Spread

Makes 2 cups
Working time: about 30 minutes
Total time: about 2 hours and 30 minutes
(includes chilling)

Per tablespoon:
Veg:
Calories **15**
Protein **1g.**
Cholesterol **1mg.**
Total fat **0g.**
Saturated fat **0g.**
Sodium **42mg.**

1 small carrot, finely shredded or grated (about ¼ cup)
1 small sweet red pepper, seeded, deribbed and quartered, the flesh finely grated and the skin discarded
3 radishes, finely grated
½ small onion, finely grated
½ tsp. salt
2 garlic cloves, finely chopped
2 tsp. fresh thyme, finely chopped, or ½ tsp. dried thyme leaves
1½ cups yogurt cheese (recipe, page 212)

Put the carrot and red pepper into a small, nonstick skillet, and cook them over low heat until most of their moisture has evaporated — three to four minutes. Let the vegetables cool.

Stir the cooled carrot and red pepper, along with the radishes, onion, salt, garlic and thyme, into the yogurt cheese. So that the flavors can meld, refrigerate the spread for at least two hours before serving it.

Transforming Yogurt into Tangy Cheese Spreads

Yogurt plays an important role in a healthy, low-fat diet. In cooking, it provides a tasty alternative to sour cream and heavy cream. And with the simple cheese-making technique presented at left, yogurt can even take the place of cream cheese in your breakfast or brunch menu, especially when it is combined with other ingredients to yield savory spreads.

Yogurt cheese made from plain low-fat yogurt has all the delectability of cream cheese, but has 64 percent fewer calories and 90 percent less saturated fat. Its lighter texture (yogurt cheese contains no gum arabic, a thickener found in most commercial cream cheeses) and its tart, fresh flavor recommend it for morning meals and snacks. Furthermore, yogurt cheese is more easily digested than cream cheese and can be readily eaten by many who have lactose intolerance.

Smoked Salmon Spread

Makes 1½ cups
Working time: about 15 minutes
Total time: about 2 hours and 15 minutes
(includes chilling)

Per tablespoon:
Salmon:
Calories **21**
Protein **2g.**
Cholesterol **3mg.**
Total fat **1g.**
Saturated fat **0g.**
Sodium **21mg.**

1½ cups yogurt cheese (recipe, page 212)
3 tbsp. finely cut fresh chives or scallions
1½ oz. smoked salmon, very finely chopped
¼ tsp. white pepper
⅛ tsp. paprika, preferably Hungarian
1 tsp. fresh lemon juice
⅛ tsp. salt

Combine the yogurt cheese with the chives, salmon, pepper, paprika, lemon juice and salt. So that the flavors can meld, refrigerate the spread for at least two hours before serving it.

Caramel-Orange-Pecan Sticky Buns

Serves 12
Working time: about 25 minutes
Total time: about 45 minutes

Calories **185**
Protein **3g.**
Cholesterol **1mg.**
Total fat **4g.**
Saturated fat **1g.**
Sodium **165mg.**

2 tbsp. dark brown sugar
1½ cups plus 1 tbsp. unbleached all-purpose flour
½ tsp. ground cinnamon
½ cup whole-wheat flour
1 tbsp. granulated sugar
1 tbsp. baking powder
¼ tsp. salt
¾ cup low-fat milk
2 tbsp. safflower oil
grated zest of 1 orange
¼ cup raisins
Caramel-pecan topping
½ cup dark brown sugar
2 tbsp. fresh orange juice
2 tbsp. honey
¼ cup chopped pecans (about 1 oz.)

Preheat the oven to 375° F.

To make the caramel-pecan topping, combine the ½ cup brown sugar, the orange juice and the honey in a small saucepan. Bring the mixture to a boil, then reduce the heat and simmer the liquid for one minute. Stir in the pecans and then pour the topping into a 10-inch ring mold or an 8-inch-round cake pan.

Combine the 2 tablespoons of brown sugar, 1 tablespoon of the all-purpose flour and the cinnamon in a small bowl; set the bowl aside.

In a larger bowl, combine the remaining 1½ cups all-purpose flour, the whole-wheat flour, granulated sugar, baking powder and salt. Add the milk, oil and orange zest; stir the ingredients together just until they are blended; do not overmix. Turn the dough out onto a floured surface and gently knead it just until it is smooth. Roll the dough into an 8-by-12-inch oblong. Sprinkle the dough evenly with the reserved cinnamon mixture, then with the raisins.

Beginning with a long side, roll the dough into a log. Cut the log into 12 slices. Set the slices in the pan, on top of the pecan mixture. Bake the coffeecake until it is brown and the pecan mixture is bubbly — 20 to 25 minutes. Remove the pan from the oven and invert it immediately onto a large serving platter. Serve the coffeecake warm.

Spiced Sweet Potato Quick Bread

Serves 12
Working time: about 20 minutes
Total time: about 2 hours and 20 minutes
(includes cooling)

Calories **155**
Protein **3g.**
Cholesterol **24mg.**
Total fat **5g.**
Saturated fat **1g.**
Sodium **86mg.**

1 cup unbleached all-purpose flour
½ cup whole-wheat flour
1 tsp. baking powder
½ tsp. baking soda
1 tsp. ground cinnamon
½ tsp. ground allspice
1 egg
½ cup light or dark brown sugar
¼ cup safflower oil
½ cup low-fat milk
1 cup peeled, grated, firmly packed sweet potato (about 6 oz.)
½ cup currants or raisins (optional)

Preheat the oven to 350° F. Lightly oil an 8-by-4-inch loaf pan.

Sift the two flours, baking powder, baking soda, cinnamon and allspice into a bowl; set the bowl aside. Put the egg and the sugar into a large bowl and beat the mixture until it is light and fluffy. Gradually add the oil and the milk and continue beating for one minute. Stir in the grated sweet potato and the currants or raisins, if you are using them. Add the sifted flour mixture, ½ cup at a time, mixing the batter after each addition just until the flour is blended. Spoon the batter into the pan.

Bake the loaf until it has shrunk from the sides of the pan and a cake tester inserted into the center comes out clean — 55 to 60 minutes. Let the bread stand for 10 minutes before turning it out onto a rack. Cool the bread completely before slicing it.

Pear Pizza

Serves 8
Working time: about 45 minutes
Total time: about 1 hour and 45 minutes

Calories **212**
Protein **4g.**
Cholesterol **4mg.**
Total fat **2g.**
Saturated fat **1g.**
Sodium **35mg.**

1¾ cup bread flour
½ cup sugar
1 tsp. grated lemon zest
⅛ tsp. salt
1 package fast-rising dry yeast (about 1 tbsp.)
1 tbsp. unsalted butter
⅓ cup currants or raisins, coarsely chopped
3 pears (about 1¼ lb.), quartered, cored, peeled and thinly sliced
2 tbsp. fresh lemon juice
2 tbsp. cornmeal

In a large bowl, combine ½ cup of the flour, 2 tablespoons of the sugar, the lemon zest, salt and yeast. In a small saucepan, heat ¾ cup of water just until it is hot to the touch (130° F.), then pour it into the yeast-flour mixture, and mix the dough thoroughly with a wooden spoon. Gradually stir in enough of the remaining flour to make a dough that can be formed into a ball.

Transfer the dough to a floured surface and knead it until it is smooth and elastic — five to 10 minutes. Put the dough into a large, lightly oiled bowl and turn the dough over to coat it with the oil. Cover the bowl with a damp towel or plastic wrap. Place the bowl in a warm, draft-free place and let the dough rise until it has doubled in bulk — 30 to 45 minutes.

In the meantime, heat the butter in a large, heavy-bottomed skillet over medium-high heat. Add the currants or raisins and the pears, and cook the fruit, stirring frequently, for five minutes. Add the lemon juice and all but 1 tablespoon of the remaining sugar; continue cooking the mixture until the pears are soft and the sugar begins to brown — about five minutes more.

Preheat the oven to 450° F. Lightly oil a baking sheet and sprinkle it with the cornmeal. When the dough has risen, return it to the floured surface and knead it again for one minute. Flatten the dough into a 10-inch disk and transfer it to the baking sheet.

Spread the pear topping over the dough, leaving a ½-inch border of dough all around. Sprinkle the reserved tablespoon of sugar over the pear topping, then bake the pizza until the crust is well browned — about 20 minutes. Remove the pizza from the oven and let it stand for about five minutes before slicing it into wedges and serving it.

EDITOR'S NOTE: *This pizza can be stored for up to one day, wrapped in aluminum foil, and then reheated, unwrapped, in a 400° F. oven for 10 minutes.*

Applesauce-and-Prune Bread

Serves 12
Working time: about 45 minutes
Total time: about 2 hours and 30 minutes
(includes cooling)

Calories **271**
Protein **3g.**
Cholesterol **0mg.**
Total fat **6g.**
Saturated fat **1g.**
Sodium **184mg.**

¾ cup pitted prunes, halved
6 large McIntosh apples, or other sweet, tangy cooking apples, peeled, quartered and cored
2 cups unbleached all-purpose flour
½ cup plus 1 tbsp. oat bran
1 tbsp. unsweetened cocoa powder
2 tsp. baking soda
¼ tsp. salt
1 tsp. ground cinnamon
½ tsp. grated nutmeg
¼ tsp. ground cloves
½ cup plus 1 tbsp. sugar
½ cup honey
¼ cup safflower oil

Put the prunes into a small bowl, pour 1 cup of boiling water over them, and set the bowl aside.

Put the apples into a large, heavy-bottomed sauce-pan and simmer them over low heat, stirring occasionally, until nearly all of the liquid has evaporated and the apples have cooked down to a smooth, thick paste — about 30 minutes. Set the applesauce aside.

While the apples are simmering, mix the flour, ½ cup of the oat bran, the cocoa powder, baking soda, salt, cinnamon, ¼ teaspoon of the nutmeg and the cloves in a large bowl. In another bowl, combine ½ cup of the sugar, the honey and the oil.

Preheat the oven to 350° F. Lightly oil a 9-by-5-inch loaf pan.

Stir the applesauce into the sugar-honey mixture; add the sweetened applesauce to the flour mixture and stir well to make a smooth batter. Drain the prunes well, fold them into the batter, and spoon the batter into the prepared pan.

In a small bowl, mix the remaining 1 tablespoon of oat bran, the remaining 1 tablespoon of sugar and the remaining ¼ teaspoon of nutmeg; sprinkle this topping over the batter.

Bake the bread until a cake tester inserted into its center comes out clean — one hour to one hour and 10 minutes. Remove the bread from the oven and let it stand for five minutes. Run a knife blade around the sides of the pan, then invert the pan onto a cake rack, and rap it sharply to unmold the bread. Let the bread stand for 30 minutes before slicing and serving it.

Poppy-Seed Twist

Serves 12
Working time: about 1 hour
Total time: about 4 hours

Calories **240**
Protein **6g.**
Cholesterol **30mg.**
Total fat **10g.**
Saturated fat **4g.**
Sodium **80mg.**

| 1 cake (.6 oz.) fresh yeast, or |
| 1 envelope (¼ oz.) active dry yeast |
| 6 tbsp. scalded, tepid milk |
| 2 cups bread flour |
| ⅛ tsp. salt |
| 2 tbsp. unsalted butter, melted |
| 2 tbsp. sugar |
| 1 egg, beaten |
| ½ lemon, finely grated zest only |
| 3 tbsp. confectioners' sugar |
| 1 tbsp. fresh lemon juice |

Poppy-seed and raisin filling

| ⅔ cup poppy seeds |
| ⅔ cup raisins, chopped |
| 1 cup milk |
| 2 tbsp. cornstarch |
| 1 egg yolk |
| 2 tbsp. unsalted butter |
| ½ cup hazelnuts, toasted and chopped |

Mix the fresh yeast with the milk and about 1 table-spoon of the flour in a bowl, or reconstitute the active dry yeast according to the manufacturer's instructions, adding the milk and 1 tablespoon of the flour. Leave the mixture in a warm place until it froths—about 10 to 15 minutes.

Sift the remaining flour into a bowl with the salt. Add the butter, sugar, egg, lemon zest, and yeast mixture, and work the combination into a soft dough. Knead the dough on a lightly floured surface for five minutes. Put the dough in an oiled bowl, cover it with oiled plastic wrap, and leave it in a warm place to rise until doubled in volume—one to two hours.

Meanwhile, preheat the oven to 400° F., grease a 9-inch springform pan, and make the filling. Put the poppy seeds and raisins in a saucepan with half the milk and simmer gently for five to seven minutes, until the poppy seeds have swelled and most of the milk has been absorbed. Mix the cornstarch and egg yolk with the remaining milk, and add the mixture to the pan.

Cook, stirring, until the mixture thickens. Remove the pan from the heat and stir in the butter. Allow the filling to cool, then stir in the hazelnuts.

To make the twist, roll out the dough on a lightly floured surface, forming a rectangle about 15 by 18 inches. Spread it with the poppy-seed and raisin filling. Roll up the dough into a cylinder, cut it in half lengthwise, and twist the two halves together (below).

Place the dough in the prepared pan and join the ends of the braid to make a circle. Bake the poppy-seed twist for about 35 minutes, until golden brown. Transfer it to a wire rack. Mix the confectioners' sugar and lemon juice together and brush them over the cake. Let the poppy-seed twist cool a little; it is best served slightly warm.

EDITOR'S NOTE: *To toast hazelnuts, place them on a baking sheet in a preheated 350° F. oven for 10 minutes.*

Twisting the Dough

1 ROLLING AND SLICING. *Spread the poppy-seed filling evenly over the dough, leaving about 1 inch of dough uncovered around the edge. Roll up the dough from one side, enclosing the filling.*

2 DIVIDING THE ROLL. *With a sharp knife, trim the ends of the dough to make a neat cylinder, then slice the cylinder down the middle, cutting it in half lengthwise.*

3 TWISTING THE DOUGH. *With the cut sides facing up, lay one length of poppy-seed dough across the middle of the other. Twist the two lengths over each other, working outward from the center in one direction, then in the other.*

4 LAYING THE CAKE IN THE PAN. *Keeping the filling side up, lift the dough carefully into the pan. Press the ends together, forming a circle.*

Filled Whole-Wheat Monkey Bread

THIS IS A REDUCED-FAT VERSION OF MONKEY BREAD, BALLS OF
SWEET YEAST DOUGH BAKED IN A TUBE PAN.

Serves 8
Working time: about 30 minutes
Total time: about 2½ hours (includes rising)

Calories **352**
Protein **7g.**
Cholesterol **10mg.**
Total fat **7g.**
Saturated fat **3g.**
Sodium **157mg.**

2 cups unbleached all-purpose flour
1 cup whole-wheat flour
½ cup plus 1 tbsp. granulated sugar
½ tsp. salt
1 package fast-rising dry yeast (about 1 tbsp.)
1 cup low-fat milk
¼ cup dark raisins
¼ cup golden raisins or chopped dried apricots

¼ cup chopped walnuts
1 tsp. unsweetened cocoa powder
¼ cup dark brown sugar
2 tbsp. honey
1½ tsp. ground cinnamon
2 tbsp. unsalted butter, melted

To make the bread dough, mix the all-purpose flour, the whole-wheat flour, 1 tablespoon of the granulated sugar, the salt and the yeast together in a large bowl and make a well in the center of the dry ingredients. In a small saucepan, heat the milk just until it is hot to the touch (130° F.). Stir the hot liquid into the flour mixture.

Turn the dough out onto a floured surface and knead the dough until it is smooth and elastic — about 10 minutes. Put it into a large bowl, cover the bowl, and let the dough rise in a warm place until it has doubled in bulk — about 45 minutes.

For the filling, combine the dark raisins, golden raisins or apricots, walnuts, cocoa powder, brown sugar, honey and ½ teaspoon of the cinnamon in a bowl. In another bowl, combine the remaining ½ cup of granulated sugar and the remaining 1 teaspoon of cinnamon. Set the bowls aside.

Punch the dough down and turn it out onto a lightly floured surface. Form the dough into a log shape and cut the dough into 16 pieces. Flatten the pieces into 4-inch rounds.

Put about 2 tablespoons of the filling in the middle of each dough round and form a ball (technique, below). Lightly dip the ball into the melted butter, then roll it in the cinnamon-sugar mixture. Repeat this process with the remaining dough rounds and filling. Arrange the balls in a nonstick or lightly oiled 8-cup Bundt or tube pan with the pinched edges of the balls toward the inside. Cover the pan and let the dough rise until it has again doubled in bulk — about 30 minutes.

Preheat the oven to 375° F.

Bake the bread until it is browned and sounds hollow when tapped — 35 to 45 minutes. Put a serving plate on top of the pan and turn both over to invert the bread onto the plate. Serve the monkey bread warm.

Preparing Monkey Bread

1 FILLING AND FORMING A BALL. After placing about 2 tablespoons of filling onto the middle of a dough round (recipe, left), gather up the sides of the round with your fingers. Pinch the rim together firmly to seal the filling inside.

2 COATING THE BALL. Dip the ball into the small container of melted butter. Then roll the ball in the prepared cinnamon-sugar mixture until it is completely coated.

3 ARRANGING THE BREAD. Put the ball into a nonstick or lightly oiled 8-cup Bundt or tube pan, with the pinched edge facing the hole of the pan. Fill, form and place the other balls in the same manner, packing them into the pan side by side. Cover the pan and bake as directed in the recipe.

Cheese Pinwheels

Makes 8 pastries
Working time: about 30 minutes
Total time: about 45 minutes

Per pinwheel:
Calories **212**
Protein **7g.**
Cholesterol **2mg.**
Total fat **4g.**
Saturated fat **1g.**
Sodium **271mg.**

1 ½ cups unbleached all-purpose flour
¾ cup whole-wheat flour
3 tbsp. granulated sugar
2 tsp. baking powder
½ tsp. baking soda
⅛ tsp. salt
¼ tsp. ground mace or ground cinnamon
1 cup low-fat yogurt
2 tbsp. safflower oil
¼ cup confectioners' sugar, sifted
2 tsp. low-fat milk
Cheese-and-lemon filling
½ cup low-fat cottage cheese
2 tsp. granulated sugar
grated zest of 1 lemon

To make the filling, purée the cottage cheese in a food processor until no trace of curd remains. Add the 2 teaspoons of granulated sugar and the lemon zest; process the mixture until the ingredients are blended. (Alternatively, press the cheese through a fine sieve, add the sugar and the lemon zest, and stir well.) Set the filling aside.

Preheat the oven to 400° F.; lightly oil a baking sheet. Combine the flours, the 3 tablespoons of granulated sugar, the baking powder, baking soda, salt, and mace or cinnamon in a large bowl. In a smaller bowl, whisk together the yogurt and the oil; stir this mixture into the dry ingredients with a wooden spoon. Turn the dough onto a floured surface and knead it once or twice to fully incorporate the ingredients and make a soft dough.

Divide the dough in half. Roll one half of the dough into an 8-inch square, then cut the square into four 4-inch squares. Form a pinwheel, using 1 tablespoon of the cheese filling *(technique, right)*. With a spatula,

transfer the pinwheel to the baking sheet. Repeat the procedure with the remaining dough.

Bake the pinwheels until they are golden brown — 10 to 12 minutes. Just before the pastries are done, mix the confectioners' sugar and the milk in a small bowl. Drizzle or brush the sugar glaze over the pinwheels as soon as they are removed from the oven. Serve the pinwheels hot.

Forming Pinwheels

1 SQUARING THE DOUGH. Onto a lightly floured work surface, roll out half of the dough into a sheet about 9 by 9 inches. With a sharp, small knife, trim the edges to straighten them, then divide the square into quarters (as shown). Discard the trimmings.

2 CUTTING CORNERS. Working with one dough square at a time, use the knife tip to slit each corner diagonally to within an inch of the center.

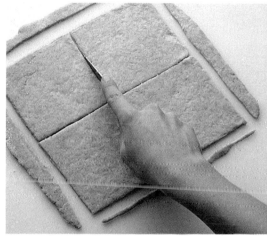

3 FILLING THE SQUARE. Place a heaping spoonful of the prepared cottage-cheese filling (recipe, left) onto the center of the dough square.

4 FORMING THE PINWHEEL. With your fingers, lift and fold every other point over the filling. Press the last point down upon the others to keep them in place. Repeat the procedures to make the other pinwheels.

Potato Pancakes with Apple-Mustard Compote

Serves 8
Working time: about 45 minutes
Total time: about 1 hour and 10 minutes

Calories **204**
Protein **3g.**
Cholesterol **42mg.**
Total fat **4g.**
Saturated fat **2g.**
Sodium **162mg.**

1 medium russet or other baking potato (about ½ lb.), peeled and diced
1 egg, separated, plus 1 egg white
1 tsp. sugar
¼ tsp. salt
⅛ tsp. grated nutmeg
½ cup unbleached all-purpose flour
Apple-mustard compote
6 firm, tart apples that will hold their shape when cooked, preferably Granny Smith, quartered, cored, peeled and cut into eighths
⅓ cup sugar
⅓ cup apple cider or unsweetened apple juice
2 tbsp. butter
¼ cup golden raisins
grated zest and juice of 1 lemon
½ tsp. ground cinnamon
2 tbsp. grainy mustard

Put the potato into a saucepan and cover it with water. Bring the water to a boil, then reduce the heat, and simmer the potato until it is soft — 10 to 15 minutes.

While the potato is cooking, prepare the apple-mustard compote. Put the apples, sugar, cider or apple juice, butter, raisins, lemon zest and lemon juice into a heavy-bottomed skillet over medium-high heat. Cook the mixture, stirring frequently, until the apples are heated through and tender — about five minutes. Stir in the cinnamon and mustard, and keep the compote warm while you make the pancakes. (If you like, you can make the compote a day ahead and reheat it.)

Drain the cooked potato, reserving 1 cup of the cooking liquid. Put the potato into a bowl and mash it with a potato masher or a fork until it is smooth; alternatively, work the potato through a food mill. Stir in the reserved cooking liquid and let the mashed potato cool to lukewarm.

Stir the egg yolk, sugar, salt and nutmeg into the mashed potatoes. Sift in the flour and stir the mixture just until it is blended.

Put the egg whites into a bowl and beat them until they form soft peaks. Stir about one fourth of the egg whites into the potato mixture and then gently fold in the remaining egg whites.

Heat a large griddle or skillet over medium heat until

a few drops of cold water dance when sprinkled on the surface. Spoon about ¼ cup of the batter at a time onto the hot griddle or skillet, and use the back of the spoon to spread the batter into rounds. Cook the pancakes until they are covered with bubbles and the undersides are golden — one to three minutes. Flip the pancakes and cook them until the second sides are lightly browned — about one minute more. Transfer the pancakes to a platter and keep them warm while you cook the remaining batter.

Serve the pancakes immediately together with the apple-mustard compote.

Cornmeal Buttermilk Pancakes

Serves 6
Working (and total) time: about 20 minutes

Calories **286**
Protein **8g.**
Cholesterol **94mg.**
Total fat **7g.**
Saturated fat **1g.**
Sodium **245mg.**

1 ¼ cups unbleached all-purpose flour
3 tbsp. sugar
½ tsp. baking soda
¼ tsp. salt
1 cup cornmeal
2 eggs
1 ½ cups buttermilk
2 tbsp. safflower oil

Sift the flour, sugar, baking soda and salt into a bowl; stir in the cornmeal. In another bowl whisk together the eggs, buttermilk and oil.

Pour the buttermilk mixture into the dry ingredients and whisk them quickly together until they are just blended; do not overmix.

Heat a large griddle or skillet over medium heat until a few drops of cold water dance when sprinkled on the surface. Drop 2 tablespoons of the batter onto the hot griddle or skillet, and use the back of the spoon to spread the batter into a round. Repeat to fill the skillet with pancakes, cook them until the tops are covered with bubbles and the undersides are golden — one or two minutes. Flip the pancakes over and cook them until the second sides are lightly browned — about one minute more.

Transfer the pancakes to a platter and keep them warm while you cook the remaining batter.

Serve the pancakes immediately, accompanied by a topping of your choice.

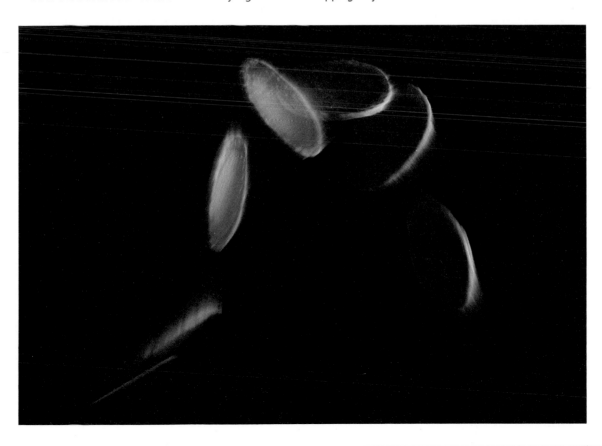

Orange French Toast

Serves 8
Working time: about 30 minutes
Total time: about 45 minutes

Calories **385**
Protein **10g.**
Cholesterol **103mg.**
Total fat **6g.**
Saturated fat **1g.**
Sodium **375mg.**

¼ cup sliced almonds
1 loaf (about 1 lb.) unsliced day-old dense white or whole-wheat bread, the ends trimmed
3 eggs, plus 3 egg whites
¼ cup granulated white sugar
¼ tsp. salt
grated zest of 1 orange
1 tsp. pure vanilla extract
1½ cups fresh orange juice

Orange syrup

1 cup light brown sugar
6 oz. frozen orange-juice concentrate

Preheat the oven to 375° F. In a small, heavy-bottomed skillet set over medium heat, toast the sliced almonds, stirring constantly, until they are golden brown — about five minutes. Remove the almonds from the pan and set them aside.

Cut the bread into 16 slices about ½ inch thick. In a shallow dish, whisk together the eggs, egg whites, granulated sugar, salt, orange zest and vanilla, then stir in the fresh orange juice.

Dip the bread slices into the juice mixture, turning them once or twice, until they are thoroughly soaked with the liquid; transfer the slices to a large plate or baking sheet as you work. After all the slices have been soaked, drizzle any remaining liquid over them.

Heat a large griddle or skillet over medium heat until a few drops of cold water dance when sprinkled on the surface. Cook the slices until the undersides are golden — about three minutes. Turn the slices and cook them until the second sides are lightly browned — two to three minutes more. Transfer the French toast to a clean baking sheet. Brown the remaining slices and transfer them to the baking sheet, too. Bake the French toast until it is cooked through and has puffed up — about 10 minutes.

While the toast is baking, make the orange syrup. Pour 1 cup of water into a small saucepan and stir in the brown sugar; bring the liquid to a boil. Reduce the heat to medium low and simmer the mixture to dissolve the sugar — about one minute. Add the orange-juice concentrate and cook the syrup, stirring, until it is hot — about one minute more. Pour the syrup into a pitcher.

Divide the French toast among eight warmed plates and sprinkle each serving with some of the toasted almonds. Pass the syrup separately.

Pumpernickel Pancakes

Serves 8
Working (and total) time: about 30 minutes

Calories **157**
Protein **10g.**
Cholesterol **80mg.**
Total fat **3g.**
Saturated fat **1g.**
Sodium **315mg.**

2 eggs, plus 2 egg whites
⅔ cup low-fat milk
2 large scallions, trimmed and finely chopped
¼ tsp. salt
freshly ground black pepper
4 cups fresh pumpernickel bread crumbs (made from about ½ loaf of pumpernickel bread)

Accompaniments

1 cup yogurt cheese (recipe, page 212)
1 tbsp. red lumpfish caviar
1 scallion, sliced on the diagonal
1 lemon, thinly sliced (optional)

Whisk together the eggs, egg whites, milk, finely chopped scallions, salt and a generous grinding of pepper in a bowl. Stir in the bread crumbs to make a smooth mixture.

Heat a large griddle or skillet over medium heat until a few drops of water dance when sprinkled on the surface. Drop the batter 1 generous tablespoon at a time onto the griddle or skillet, and use the back of a spoon to spread the batter into ovals. Cook the pancakes until they are covered with bubbles — one to three minutes. Turn each pancake and cook the second side for one minute more. Transfer the pancakes to a platter and keep them warm while you cook the remaining batter.

Accompany each serving with a dollop of yogurt cheese topped with some caviar and sliced scallions; if you wish, garnish with a slice of lemon.

EDITOR'S NOTE: *Plain low-fat yogurt may be substituted for the yogurt cheese.*

Griddle Cheesecakes with Cranberry Sauce

Serves 8
Working (and total) time: about 30 minutes

Calories **222**
Protein **10g.**
Cholesterol **71mg.**
Total fat **2g.**
Saturated fat **1g.**
Sodium **301mg.**

2 cups low-fat cottage cheese
2 eggs
¼ cup sugar
1 cup unbleached all-purpose flour
1 tsp. baking powder
grated zest of 1 lemon
Cranberry sauce
½ cup sugar
1 tbsp. cornstarch
1½ cups fresh orange juice
2 cups fresh or frozen cranberries, picked over

To make the cranberry sauce, combine the sugar and cornstarch in a heavy-bottomed saucepan. Gradually pour in the orange juice, stirring continuously. Add the cranberries and bring the mixture to a boil over medium heat, stirring constantly. Reduce the heat and simmer the mixture until all the cranberries have burst — about 15 minutes. Purée the cranberry mixture in a food processor or a blender and then pass it through a sieve into a bowl. Set the sauce aside in a warm place.

Rinse out the food processor or blender and purée the cottage cheese in it. Add the eggs and blend them into the purée. Transfer the mixture to a bowl and stir in the sugar, flour and baking powder, beating just long enough to produce a smooth batter. Stir the lemon zest into the batter.

Heat a large griddle or skillet over medium heat until a few drops of cold water dance when sprinkled on the surface. Drop a generous tablespoon of the batter onto the hot griddle or skillet, and use the back of the spoon to spread the batter to a thickness of ¼ inch. Form several more batter rounds the same way, then cook the griddle cheesecakes until they are covered with bubbles and the undersides are golden — about three minutes. Flip the cheesecakes and cook them until the second sides are lightly browned — about one minute more. Transfer the cheesecakes to a platter and keep them warm while you cook the remaining batter.

Serve the griddle cheesecakes accompanied by the cranberry sauce.

Paprika Blintzes

Serves 4
Working time: about 50 minutes
Total time: about 1 hour and 30 minutes (includes
standing time for crepe batter)

Calories **223**
Protein **14g.**
Cholesterol **78mg.**
Total fat **10g.**
Saturated fat **3g.**
Sodium **419mg.**

½ cup unbleached all-purpose flour
⅛ tsp. salt
1½ tsp. paprika, preferably Hungarian
1 egg
¾ cup low-fat milk
1 tbsp. olive oil, preferably virgin
1½ tsp. fresh thyme, or ½ tsp. dried thyme leaves
¼ tsp. safflower oil
Cheese-scallion filling
1½ tsp. olive oil, preferably virgin
1 garlic clove, finely chopped
2 bunches scallions, trimmed and cut into 1-inch pieces
1½ tsp. fresh thyme, or ½ tsp. dried thyme leaves
freshly ground black pepper
⅛ tsp. salt
¾ cup low-fat cottage cheese
½ cup plain low-fat yogurt
2 tbsp. freshly grated Parmesan cheese

To make the crepes for the blintzes, sift the flour, salt and paprika into a bowl. Make a well in the center, then add the egg, milk, olive oil and thyme. Whisk the mixture, gradually incorporating the flour. Cover the bowl and let it stand for one hour, or refrigerate it overnight. If the batter has thickened at the end of the refrigeration period, stir in water, 1 tablespoon at a time, to restore the original consistency.

To make the filling, heat the olive oil in a heavy-bottomed saucepan over medium-high heat. Add the garlic, scallions, thyme, some pepper and the salt. Cook the mixture, stirring frequently, until the scallions are soft — four to five minutes. Transfer the scallion mixture to a bowl.

Put the cottage cheese, the yogurt and the Parmesan cheese into a food processor or a blender and purée them. Add the puréed cheese mixture to the bowl containing the scallions. Stir the cheese-scallion mixture well, then set it aside.

Heat a 6-inch crepe pan or a nonstick skillet over medium-high heat. Add the ¼ teaspoon of safflower oil and spread it over the entire surface with a paper towel. Ladle about 3 tablespoons of the crepe batter into the hot pan and immediately swirl the pan to coat the bottom with a thin, even layer of batter. Pour any excess batter back into the bowl. Cook the crepe until the bottom is browned — about 2 minutes and 30 seconds. Lift the edge with a spatula and turn the crepe over. Cook the crepe on the second side until it, too, is browned — 15 to 30 seconds. Slide the crepe onto a plate. Repeat the process with the remaining batter to form eight crepes in all.

Preheat the oven to 400° F. Spoon about ¼ cup of the cheese-scallion mixture onto a crepe, near its edge. Fold the edge of the crepe over the filling, then fold in the sides of the crepe, forming an envelope around the filling. Roll up the crepe to enclose the filling completely. Repeat the process with the remaining crepes and filling to form eight blintzes. Lightly oil a baking sheet, set the blintzes on it, and bake them until they are crisp and lightly browned around the edges — about eight minutes. Serve the blintzes immediately.

Toasted Turkey-and-Provolone Sandwiches with Strawberry-Cranberry Jam

Serves 6
Working (and total) time: about 45 minutes

Calories **447**	12 slices white sandwich bread
Protein **31g.**	2 tsp. Dijon mustard
Cholesterol **61mg.**	¾ lb. sliced roast turkey breast
Total fat **12g.**	6 oz. sliced provolone cheese
Saturated fat **6g.**	1 large red onion, thinly sliced
Sodium **582mg.**	½ cup low-fat milk
	1 egg white
	¼ tsp. ground white pepper
	Strawberry-cranberry jam
	1 cup fresh or frozen cranberries
	1 orange, the zest julienned, the juice reserved
	1 lemon, the zest julienned, the juice reserved
	½ cup sugar
	1 cup fresh strawberries, hulled and halved, or frozen whole strawberries, thawed and halved

To make the jam, combine the cranberries, orange zest and juice, lemon zest and juice, and sugar in a nonreactive saucepan. Bring the mixture to a boil, reduce the heat, and simmer the fruit for five minutes. Add the strawberries to the saucepan, stir well, and cook the jam for an additional five minutes. Transfer the jam to a bowl and chill it.

Preheat the oven to 350° F.

Lay 6 of the bread slices out on a work surface and brush them with the mustard. Divide the turkey, provolone cheese and onion among these 6 slices. Set the remaining slices of bread on top.

In a small bowl, whisk together the milk, egg white and pepper. Brush both sides of the sandwiches with this mixture. Heat a large griddle or skillet over medium heat until a few drops of cold water dance when sprinkled on the surface.

Put the sandwiches on the griddle or in the skillet and cook them until the undersides are well browned — about five minutes. Turn the sandwiches and cook them until the second sides are browned — two to three minutes more. Serve the sandwiches immediately, accompanied by the jam.

Puffy Fruit Omelet

Serves 4
Working (and total) time: about 40 minutes

Calories **200**
Protein **10g.**
Cholesterol **139mg.**
Total fat **5g.**
Saturated fat **1g.**
Sodium **250mg.**

2 eggs, separated, plus 2 egg whites
2 tbsp. unbleached all-purpose flour
½ tsp. baking powder
⅛ tsp. salt
½ cup low-fat milk
5 tsp. sugar
1 tsp. safflower oil
1 sweet red apple, preferably Stayman or Winesap, quartered, cored and cut into ½-inch pieces
1 pear, preferably Bosc, quartered, cored and cut into ½-inch pieces
1 tsp. fresh lemon juice
¼ tsp. ground cinnamon
2 tbsp. raspberry preserves
2 tbsp. apple cider or unsweetened apple juice

Preheat the oven to 450° F. In a bowl, whisk together the egg yolks, flour, baking powder, salt and 3 table-spoons of the milk until the mixture is well blended — five to seven minutes. Whisk in the remaining milk.

In another bowl, beat the egg whites with 3 tea-spoons of the sugar until they form soft peaks. Stir half of the whites into the yolk mixture and then gently fold in the remaining whites just until the mixture is blend-ed; do not overmix. Set the egg mixture aside.

Heat the oil in a large, ovenproof skillet over medium-high heat. Add the apple and the pear, the remaining 2 teaspoons of sugar, the lemon juice and the cinnamon and cook the fruit, stirring frequently, until it is tender — about five minutes. Remove the skil-let from the heat and pour the egg mixture over the fruit; smooth the top of the mixture with a spatula. Place the skillet in the oven and bake the omelet until the top is golden brown — 10 to 15 minutes.

While the omelet is baking, mix together the rasp-berry preserves and the cider or unsweetened apple juice in a small dish. When the omelet is ready, drizzle this syrup over it, slice it into quarters and serve the omelet immediately.

Spicy Shrimp Griddlecakes

Serves 6
Working (and total) time: about 30 minutes

Calories **246**
Protein **12g.**
Cholesterol **68mg.**
Total fat **6g.**
Saturated fat **3g.**
Sodium **294mg.**

1 ¼ cups cornmeal
½ cup unbleached all-purpose flour
2 tsp. baking powder
1 tsp. dried thyme leaves
1 tsp. dried oregano
¼ tsp. salt
¼ tsp. ground white pepper
¼ tsp. cayenne pepper
3 large garlic cloves, finely chopped
1 scallion, finely chopped
1 small sweet red pepper, seeded, deribbed and finely chopped
2 tbsp. unsalted butter, melted
1 ⅔ cups low-fat milk
½ lb. cooked, peeled baby shrimp
1 lemon, cut into wedges, for garnish
several parsley sprigs for garnish

Combine the cornmeal, flour, baking powder, thyme, oregano, salt, white pepper and cayenne pepper in a bowl. Stir in the garlic, scallion and red pepper. Whisk in the melted butter and the milk, mixing until all the ingredients are just blended. Stir in the shrimp.

Heat a large griddle or skillet over medium heat until a few drops of cold water dance when sprinkled on the surface. Drop the batter a generous tablespoon at a time onto the griddle and use the back of the spoon to spread the batter into rounds. Cook the griddlecakes until they are covered with bubbles and the undersides are golden — one to three minutes. Flip the griddlecakes and cook them until the second sides are lightly browned — about one minute more.

Transfer the griddlecakes to a platter and keep them warm while you cook the remaining batter.

Serve the griddlecakes piping hot, garnished with the lemon wedges and parsley sprigs.

Tropical Puffed Pancake

Serves 4
Working time: about 30 minutes
Total time: about 45 minutes

Calories **349**
Protein **9g.**
Cholesterol **141mg.**
Total fat **8g.**
Saturated fat **2g.**
Sodium **265mg.**

3 tbsp. granulated white sugar
¼ tsp. ground cinnamon
¼ cup unbleached all-purpose flour
¼ cup whole-wheat flour
½ tsp. baking powder
¼ tsp. salt
2 eggs, separated, plus 1 egg white
1 tbsp. light or dark rum
1 tbsp. safflower oil
grated zest of 1 lemon
¾ cup low-fat milk
2 bananas, sliced diagonally into ¼-inch-thick ovals

Rum-pineapple topping

1 pineapple, peeled, cored and coarsely chopped (about 2 cups), or 2 cups canned unsweetened pineapple chunks, drained and coarsely chopped
2 tbsp. dark brown sugar
2 tbsp. raisins
juice of 1 lemon
2 tbsp. light or dark rum

To make the rum-pineapple topping, put the pineapple into a heavy-bottomed saucepan, then stir in the brown sugar, raisins and lemon juice. Bring the mixture to a boil, then reduce the heat, and simmer the mixture for five minutes. Remove the pan from the heat and stir in the rum. Keep the topping warm while you prepare the puffed pancake.

In a small bowl, mix 2 tablespoons of the granulated white sugar with the cinnamon; set the cinnamon sugar aside. Preheat the oven to 425° F.

Sift the two flours, the baking powder, the salt and the remaining tablespoon of white sugar into a bowl. In a separate bowl, whisk the egg yolks with the rum and the oil; stir in the lemon zest and the milk. Whisk the flour mixture into the milk mixture to make a smooth, thin batter.

Beat the egg whites until they form soft peaks. Stir half of the egg whites into the batter and then fold in the remaining egg whites.

Heat a 12-inch ovenproof skillet over medium heat. Ladle the batter into the skillet. Cook the pancake for two minutes; top it with the sliced bananas and sprinkle it with the cinnamon sugar. Put the skillet into the oven and bake the pancake until it puffs up and is golden brown — 10 to 12 minutes. Slide the puffed pancake out of the pan onto a warmed serving plate. Cut the pancake into four wedges and serve it immediately with the rum-pineapple topping.

Buckwheat Crepes with Mushroom-Tomato Filling

Serves 8
Working time: about 1 hour
Total time: about 2 hours
(includes standing time for crepe batter)

Calories **174**
Protein **10g.**
Cholesterol **43mg.**
Total fat **6g.**
Saturated fat **2g.**
Sodium **226mg.**

1 egg
1 ½ cups low-fat milk
½ tsp. sugar
⅛ tsp. salt
1 tbsp. unsalted butter, melted
½ cup buckwheat flour
½ cup unbleached all-purpose flour
¼ tsp. safflower oil
Mushroom-tomato filling
1 tbsp. safflower oil
1 lb. mushrooms, wiped clean, trimmed and quartered
2 shallots, thinly sliced
1 tbsp. unbleached all-purpose flour
½ cup unsalted brown stock, or 1 cup unsalted chicken stock reduced by half
¼ cup dry vermouth
4 garlic cloves, finely chopped
2 large tomatoes, peeled, seeded and chopped
1 tbsp. Dijon mustard
2 tbsp. chopped fresh parsley
parsley sprigs, for garnish
Creamy cheese topping
1 cup low-fat cottage cheese
2 tbsp. buttermilk

Put the egg into a bowl and beat it until it is light and foamy. Whisk in the milk, sugar, salt and butter and then gradually whisk in the two flours. Cover the bowl and let it stand for one hour. (Alternatively, you may refrigerate the batter, covered, overnight.) If the batter has thickened at the end of the refrigeration period, stir in additional milk, 1 tablespoon at a time, until the batter has thinned to its original consistency.

While the batter is resting, make the mushroom-tomato filling. Heat the oil in a heavy-bottomed skillet over medium-high heat. Add the mushrooms and shallots and sauté them until the mushrooms begin to exude their liquid — about five minutes.

Add the flour to the mushrooms and cook the mixture, stirring, for one minute. Add the brown stock or reduced chicken stock, vermouth, garlic and half of the tomatoes; reduce the heat and simmer the mixture for three minutes, stirring frequently. Stir in the mustard and the parsley and remove the pan from the heat.

When the crepe batter is ready, heat a 6-inch crepe

pan or nonstick skillet over medium-high heat. Add the ¼ teaspoon of oil and spread it over the entire surface with a paper towel. Pour about 3 tablespoons of the batter into the hot pan and immediately swirl the pan to coat the bottom with a thin, even layer of batter. Pour any excess batter back into the bowl. Cook the crepe until the bottom is browned — about one minute. Lift the edge with a spatula and turn the crepe over. Cook the crepe on the second side until it, too, is browned — 15 to 30 seconds. Slide the crepe onto a plate. Repeat the process with the remaining batter, brushing the pan lightly with more oil if the crepes begin to stick. Stack the cooked crepes on the plate as you go. Cover the crepes with a towel and set them aside. There should be about 16 crepes.

Preheat the oven to 350° F. Spoon 2 tablespoons of the filling down the center of a crepe. Roll the crepe to enclose the filling, then transfer it to a lightly oiled shallow baking dish. Continue filling and rolling the remaining crepes, transferring them to the baking dish as you work. Bake the filled crepes for 15 minutes.

While the crepes are baking, make the cheese topping. Put the cottage cheese into a food processor or a blender and purée it. Add the buttermilk and process the mixture until it is blended.

Garnish the crepes with the remaining chopped tomato and the parsley sprigs and serve them with the cheese topping.

EDITOR'S NOTE: *Canned beef broth or bouillon may be substituted for the brown stock, but if you do use it, be sure to eliminate the salt from the recipe.*

Apple-Filled Buckwheat Crepes with Cider Syrup

Serves 4
Working time: about 1 hour
Total time: about 1 hour and 30 minutes

Calories **322**
Protein **4g.**
Cholesterol **71mg.**
Total fat **11g.**
Saturated fat **2g.**
Sodium **93mg.**

2 cups unsweetened apple cider
1 lb. sweet apples
¼ tsp. ground cinnamon
2 tbsp. sour cream
Crepe batter
¼ cup buckwheat flour
½ cup unbleached all-purpose flour
⅛ tsp. salt
1 egg
2 tbsp. plus ¼ tsp. safflower oil

To prepare the crepe batter, sift together the buckwheat flour, all-purpose flour and salt. In a large bowl, whisk together the egg, 2 tablespoons of the oil and ¼ cup of water. Gradually whisk in the sifted ingredients until a smooth mixture results. Cover the bowl and refrigerate the batter for at least one hour.

Bring 1½ cups of the apple cider to a boil in a heavy-bottomed saucepan. Lower the heat to medium low and boil the cider until it is reduced to ¼ cup — 20 to 30 minutes. Set the apple syrup aside.

Peel, quarter and core the apples, then cut the quarters into ½-inch pieces. Combine the apple pieces with the cinnamon and the remaining ½ cup of apple cider in a large, heavy-bottomed skillet set over medium heat. Cook the apple mixture, stirring occasionally, until almost all of the liquid has evaporated — 15 to 20 minutes. Transfer the apple mixture to a food processor or a blender, and purée it. Return the purée to the skillet and keep it in a warm place.

When the batter is chilled, heat a crepe pan or an 8-inch skillet over medium-high heat. Pour in the remaining ¼ teaspoon of oil; with a paper towel, wipe the oil over the pan's entire cooking surface. Pour 2 to 3 tablespoons of the crepe batter into the hot pan and immediately swirl the pan to coat the bottom with a thin, even layer of batter. Pour any excess batter back into the bowl. Cook the crepe until the bottom is browned — about 2 minutes and 30 seconds — then lift the edge with a spatula and turn the crepe over. Cook the crepe on the second side until it too is browned — 15 to 30 seconds — and slide the crepe onto a warmed plate. Repeat the process with the remaining batter to form eight crepes in all.

Spread about 3 tablespoons of the warm apple purée over each crepe. Fold each crepe in half, then fold it in half again to produce a wedge shape. Arrange two crepes, one slightly overlapping the other, on each of four dessert plates. Drizzle a tablespoon of the apple syrup over each serving; garnish each dessert with ½ tablespoon of the sour cream and serve at once.

Broccoli and Ricotta Pie

Serves 6 as a main dish
Working time: about 1 hour
Total time: about 2 hours

Calories **325**
Protein **17g.**
Cholesterol **63mg.**
Total fat **8g.**
Saturated fat **3g.**
Sodium **284mg.**

1 envelope fast-rising dry yeast (about 1 tbsp.)
2½ cups bread flour
¼ tsp. salt
1 tbsp. olive oil, preferably virgin
1½ cups chopped onion
½ tsp. caraway seeds, or 2 tsp. dried dill
1 egg, plus 2 egg whites
¾ cup part-skim ricotta cheese
¾ cup low-fat milk
freshly ground black pepper
⅛ tsp. grated nutmeg
1 oz. Canadian bacon, finely chopped
1 tbsp. cornmeal
1½ cups broccoli florets, blanched in boiling water for one minute, drained
2 tbsp. freshly grated Parmesan cheese

In a large bowl, mix the yeast with 1 cup of the flour and ⅛ teaspoon of the salt. Heat ¾ cup of water in a saucepan just until it is hot to the touch (130° F.). Pour the hot water into the flour mixture and stir the dough vigorously with a wooden spoon. Stir in 1 teaspoon of the oil and 1 more cup of the flour. Transfer the dough to a floured surface and begin to knead it. If the dough seems too sticky, gradually add up to ½ cup of flour; if it seems too dry, add water, 1 teaspoon at a time, as required. Knead the dough until it is smooth and elastic — about 10 minutes. Transfer the dough to an oiled bowl, turn the dough once to coat it with the oil, and cover the bowl with a damp towel or plastic wrap. Set the bowl in a warm, draft-free place and let the dough rise until it has doubled in volume — about 30 minutes.

While the dough is rising, heat the remaining 2 teaspoons of oil in a heavy-bottomed skillet over medium-high heat. Add the onion and the caraway seeds or dill and cook the mixture, stirring frequently, until the onion is lightly browned — about 10 minutes. Remove the skillet from the heat and set it aside.

Whisk the egg and the egg whites in a large bowl. Whisk in the ricotta, the milk, the remaining ⅛ tea spoon of salt, some pepper, the nutmeg and the Canadian bacon. Stir in half of the onion mixture and set the bowl aside.

Preheat the oven to 400° F. After the dough has finished rising, punch it down. Knead the remaining onion mixture into the dough.

Sprinkle an 8-inch-wide cast-iron skillet or an 11-inch glass pie plate with the cornmeal. Put the dough in the skillet or pie plate and, with your fingertips, gently work some of the dough toward the edge to form a 2-inch-high rim. Allow the dough to stand for 10 minutes.

Place the skillet or pie plate in the oven for 10 minutes to partially bake the dough. Remove the crust from the oven; if the edge is not ¾ of an inch higher than the flat surface of the crust, gently push the dough down to form a depression. Pour in the ricotta-egg mixture. Place the broccoli florets one at a time, bud sides up, in the filling, then sprinkle the Parmesan cheese over the surface of the pie. Return the skillet to the oven and bake the pie until the filling is set and the top is lightly browned — 35 to 40 minutes. Let the pie stand for 10 minutes before cutting it into wedges.

Bread, Cheese, and Onion Pudding

Serves 8
Working time: about 40 minutes
Total time: about 2 hours and 30 minutes

Calories **300**
Protein **12g.**
Cholesterol **60mg.**
Total fat **14g.**
Saturated fat **4g.**
Sodium **485mg.**

5 tbsp. polyunsaturated margarine
2 large onions, thinly sliced
1 lb. zucchini, julienned
2 tsp. Dijon mustard
2 garlic cloves, crushed
24 thin slices white bread, crusts removed
2 eggs
2 egg whites
2½ cups skim milk
freshly ground black pepper
¾ cup grated Cheddar cheese

Heat 1 tablespoon of the margarine in a large, nonstick skillet over medium heat. Add the sliced onions and cook them until they are soft but not brown—about five minutes. Add the zucchini and cook the vegetables for another six minutes, stirring occasionally. Remove the pan from the heat and allow the onions and zucchini to cool for 15 minutes.

Meanwhile, blend the remaining 4 tablespoons of margarine in a small bowl with the mustard and garlic until smooth. Spread the mixture thinly over the sliced bread. Cut each slice into four triangles.

Put the eggs, egg whites, and milk into a mixing bowl, add some black pepper, and whisk them together lightly.

Grease a 12-by-9-inch ovenproof dish. Layer one-third of the bread triangles in the bottom of the dish, and spread half of the onion and zucchini mixture over the top. Sprinkle with one-third of the grated Cheddar cheese. Add another third of the bread, the rest of the onion and zucchini mixture, and another third of the Cheddar cheese. Arrange the remaining triangles of bread decoratively on the top, overlapping them slightly. Pour the whisked eggs and milk over the bread. Scatter the last third of Cheddar cheese evenly over the top of the assembly. Allow the pudding to stand in a cool place for one hour, to allow the bread to soften and soak up the eggs and milk.

Twenty minutes before cooking the pudding, pre-heat the oven to 375° F.

Cook the pudding until it is well puffed up, set, and golden brown—45 to 50 minutes. Serve the bread pudding immediately.

SUGGESTED ACCOMPANIMENT: *red-cabbage salad.*

Fennel, Broccoli, and Okra Croustades

Serves 4
Working time: about 40 minutes
Total time: about 1 hour

Calories **270**
Protein **15g.**
Cholesterol **10mg.**
Total fat **11g.**
Saturated fat **4g.**
Sodium **465mg.**

1 loaf unsliced, whole-wheat sandwich bread (minimum 9 inches long)
1 tsp. safflower oil
1 fennel bulb (about ½ lb.) trimmed and chopped
½ lb. broccoli florets (3 to 4 cups)
1½ tbsp. unsalted butter
4 scallions, trimmed and sliced diagonally
2 oz. okra, trimmed and thinly sliced
⅔ cup plain low-fat yogurt
¼ tsp. salt
⅛ tsp. ground allspice
freshly ground black pepper
¼ cup pine nuts, toasted

Prepare four croustade cases from the loaf of whole-wheat bread, brush them with the oil, and bake them *(technique, below)*. While the croustades are baking, prepare the filling.

Place the fennel in a saucepan with water to cover and cook it until it is just tender—two to three minutes. Add the broccoli florets and cook them until they, too, are just tender—two to three minutes more. Drain the vegetables and keep them warm.

Melt the butter in a heavy-bottomed saucepan, and add the scallions and okra. Cook them over medium-low heat until the okra begins to soften and looks slightly sticky—four to five minutes. Add the yogurt,

salt, allspice, and some black pepper, and bring the mixture to a boil. Lower the heat and simmer gently until the liquid has thickened a little—two to three minutes. Add the fennel, broccoli, and most of the pine nuts, and heat them through.

Divide the mixture among the croustades, piling it up well in the center. Sprinkle with the remaining pine nuts and serve the croustades immediately.

SUGGESTED ACCOMPANIMENT: tomato salad.

EDITOR'S NOTE: *To toast pine nuts, place them in a small, heavy-bottomed skillet over medium-high heat, and cook them, stirring constantly, until they are golden brown and release their aroma—one to two minutes.*

Making Croustades

1 *CUTTING THE CASES. Trim the crust. If the bread is soft, put it in the freezer for a few minutes. Cut the bread into 2-inch-thick slices. Using a sharp knife, cut a square in the top of each slice, ¼ inch from each edge; cut to within ¼ inch of the base.*

2 *LOOSENING THE CENTERS. Insert the knife horizontally ¼ inch above the base of one corner; the knife point should penetrate beyond the square's center. Swivel the knife, withdraw it, then insert it in the diagonally opposite corner, and swivel it to loosen the center.*

3 *HOLLOWING OUT THE CASES. Use the tip of the knife to lift out the center section of each square. Turn the cases upside down and gently shake out any remaining crumbs. Place the cases on a lightly greased baking sheet.*

4 *BAKING THE CASES. Put the oil into a bowl. With a pastry brush, apply a thin coat of oil to the surfaces of the bread cases. Bake the cases in a preheated 325° F. oven until crisp and golden—about 40 minutes—turning occasionally so they color evenly.*

slices. Add the apple slices to the salad along with the oil, salt and some pepper. Toss the salad and serve it immediately.

AUTUMN BRUNCH

Apple-Cabbage Salad
Corn Crepes Filled with Turkey Fricassee
Mashed Sweet Potatoes with Sherry and Chestnuts
Pear and Cranberry Flan

Except for some final steps, all of the work for this autumn brunch can be done a day ahead of time. Make the crepes, the parsley-pepper sauce and the turkey fricassee. Assemble the salad, but do not add the oil, apples, salt and pepper. Combine the mashed sweet potatoes with the sherry and chestnuts so that the dish is ready to bake on the following day. Bake the tart shell and prepare the cranberry filling. Cover everything and store it in the refrigerator overnight.

All that remains to do on the day of the brunch is to bring the crepes to room temperature and then fill them with hot turkey fricassee, bake the sweet potatoes, warm the parsley-pepper sauce, and add the apples, oil, salt and pepper to the salad. To finish the dessert, pour the cranberry filling into the tart shell, arrange the pear slices on top, and bake the tart.

Apple-Cabbage Salad

Serves 6
Working time: about 20 minutes
Total time: about 25 minutes

Calories **71**
Protein **1g.**
Cholesterol **0mg.**
Total fat **2g.**
Saturated fat **0g.**
Sodium **105mg.**

1¼ lb. green cabbage, shredded or thinly sliced
¼ cup distilled white vinegar
1 tbsp. sugar
1 tbsp. mixed pickling spice
2 red apples, preferably Red Delicious
2 tsp. safflower oil
¼ tsp. salt
freshly ground black pepper

Put the cabbage into a large serving bowl. To make the dressing, put the vinegar, sugar and pickling spice into a small saucepan and bring the liquid to a simmer over medium-high heat; stir the mixture several times to help dissolve the sugar. Simmer the dressing for two minutes. Hold a strainer over the cabbage, then pour the dressing through the strainer. Toss the salad well, then refrigerate it.

When you are ready to serve the salad, quarter and core the apples. Cut each quarter crosswise into thin

---

Nestled corn crepes filled with turkey fricassee and topped with parsley-pepper sauce make an attractive main course for this autumn brunch. Mashed sweet potatoes with sherry and chestnuts and an apple-cabbage salad provide seasonal accompaniments. Dessert is a pear and cranberry flan.

Corn Crepes Filled with Turkey Fricassee

Serves 6
Working time: about 35 minutes
Total time: about 1 hour and 15 minutes

Calories **375**
Protein **33g.**
Cholesterol **111mg.**
Total fat **11g.**
Saturated fat **3g.**
Sodium **267mg.**

1½ cups fresh corn kernels (about 2 small ears), or 1½ cups frozen corn kernels, thawed
1¼ cups skim milk
1 egg yolk
⅛ tsp. salt
⅛ tsp. white pepper
1 tbsp. unsalted butter, melted
¾ cup unbleached all-purpose flour
¼ tsp. safflower oil
Turkey fricassee
1½ lb. turkey breast meat, diced
⅛ tsp. salt
freshly ground black pepper
1½ tbsp. safflower oil
1 green pepper, seeded, deribbed and finely chopped
2 onions, finely chopped
½ lb. mushrooms, wiped clean and finely chopped
½ cup dry vermouth or dry white wine
¼ cup unbleached all-purpose flour
1½ cups unsalted chicken stock
1 tsp. fresh thyme, or ½ tsp. dried thyme leaves
Parsley-pepper sauce
1½ cups unsalted chicken stock
1½ tbsp. cornstarch, mixed with 1 tbsp. water
¼ tsp. freshly ground black pepper
⅛ tsp. salt
2 tbsp. chopped fresh parsley

To make the crepe batter, put the corn, milk, egg yolk, salt, pepper and butter into a food processor or a blender and purée them. There should be 1¾ cups of the mixture; if there is less, add enough milk to make 1¾ cups of liquid. Transfer the mixture to a bowl and gradually add the flour, whisking until the batter is smooth. Cover the bowl and let it stand for one hour. Alternatively, you may refrigerate the batter, covered, overnight; if the batter has thickened at the end of the refrigeration period, stir in additional milk, 1 tablespoon at a time, until the batter has thinned to its original consistency.

To prepare the turkey fricassee, toss the turkey, the salt and a generous grinding of pepper together in a bowl. Set the bowl aside.

Heat the oil in a large, heavy-bottomed skillet over medium heat. Add the green pepper, onions and mushrooms and cook the mixture, stirring occasionally, until the onion is translucent and the green pepper ▶

is soft — about seven minutes. Add the vermouth or wine, and cook the mixture until almost all of the liquid has evaporated — three to four minutes. Sprinkle the flour over the vegetables, then pour in the stock. Stir the mixture until it is well blended. Add the turkey and the thyme, then reduce the heat, and simmer the mixture, partially covered, until the turkey firms up and turns white, indicating that it is cooked through — about four minutes. Remove the skillet from the heat; keep it warm while you prepare the sauce.

To make the parsley-pepper sauce, bring the stock to a simmer in a small saucepan. Stir in the cornstarch mixture, pepper and salt, and simmer the liquid for six minutes. Stir in the parsley, then cover the sauce, and keep it warm while you prepare the crepes.

Heat a 6-inch crepe pan or nonstick skillet over medium-high heat. Add the ¼ teaspoon of oil and spread it over the entire surface with a paper towel. Pour about 2 tablespoons of the crepe batter into the hot pan and immediately swirl the pan to coat the bottom with a thin, even layer of batter. Pour any excess batter back into the bowl. Cook the crepe until the bottom is set — about one minute. Lift the edge with a spatula and turn the crepe over, then cook the crepe on the second side until it too is set — 15 to 30 seconds. Slide the crepe onto a warmed plate; cover the crepe and keep it warm. Repeat the process with the remaining batter, brushing the pan lightly with more oil if the crepes begin to stick. Transfer the cooked crepes to the plate as you go, separating them with pieces of wax paper. There should be 12 crepes in all.

Place about 4 tablespoons of the filling in a line down the center of a crepe and roll the crepe to enclose the filling. Transfer the filled crepe to a warmed serving platter. Repeat the process with the remaining crepes and filling. Spoon the warm parsley-pepper sauce over the crepes and serve them at once.

Mashed Sweet Potatoes with Sherry and Chestnuts

Serves 6
Working time: about 20 minutes
Total time: about 1 hour

Calories **263**
Protein **5g.**
Cholesterol **1mg.**
Total fat **3g.**
Saturated fat **0g.**
Sodium **135mg.**

½ lb. fresh chestnuts
2 lb. sweet potatoes (yams), peeled and cut into 1-inch slices
1½ cups skim milk
¼ tsp. salt
⅛ tsp. white pepper
2 tsp. safflower oil
1 tsp. finely chopped shallots
¾ cup dry sherry

Lay a chestnut with its flat side down on a cutting board. Using a sharp paring knife, make an *X* in the rounded side of the shell, cutting through both the shell and the inner skin. Repeat the process with the other chestnuts. Cook the chestnuts in boiling water for 10 minutes. Remove the pan from the heat but do not drain the chestnuts. Alternatively, bake the chestnuts in a 350° F. oven on a baking sheet until the cut shell begins to curl — about 15 minutes.

While the chestnuts are still warm, remove the shells and as much of the brown skin as possible. (Waiting until the chestnuts are cool would make them difficult to peel.) Finely chop the chestnuts and set them aside.

Preheat the oven to 350° F.

Pour enough water into a saucepan to fill it 1 inch deep. Set a steamer in the pan and put the sweet potatoes into the steamer. Bring the water to a boil, and steam the sweet potatoes, covered, until they are tender — about 10 minutes. Transfer them to a bowl.

Pour the milk into a saucepan and bring it just to a simmer. Add the milk to the sweet potatoes. Mash the sweet potatoes until they form a smooth purée, then stir in the salt and white pepper.

Heat the oil in a small, heavy-bottomed skillet set over medium-high heat. Add the shallots and cook them until they are translucent — about one minute. Stir in the chopped chestnuts and the sherry; simmer the mixture until the sherry has reduced by half — about three minutes. Combine this mixture with the sweet potatoes, then transfer them to a baking dish. Smooth the surface of the purée with a spatula. Bake the sweet potatoes until they are heated through — about 15 minutes. Serve at once.

Pear and Cranberry Flan

Serves 6
Working time: about 25 minutes
Total time: about 1 hour

Calories **244**
Protein **3g.**
Cholesterol **10mg.**
Total fat **7g.**
Saturated fat **3g.**
Sodium **112mg.**

1 cup sifted unbleached all-purpose flour
2 tsp. sugar
¼ tsp. salt
2 tbsp. cold unsalted butter, cut into pieces
1 tbsp. cold unsalted margarine, preferably corn oil, cut into pieces
½ tsp. pure vanilla extract
3 cups cranberries, picked over
¼ cup fresh orange juice
5 tbsp. sugar
3 ripe but firm pears, peeled, cored, cut into ¼-inch-thick slices and tossed with the juice of ½ lemon
1 tbsp. chopped filberts (optional)

To prepare the flan pastry, combine the flour, sugar and salt in a food processor or a bowl. If you are using a food processor, add the butter and margarine and cut them into the dry ingredients with several short bursts. With the motor running, slowly pour in the vanilla and 3 tablespoons of cold water, blending the dough just until it begins to form a ball. If you are making the dough in a bowl, use a pastry blender or two knives to cut the butter and margarine into the dry ingredients, then mix in the vanilla and water with a wooden spoon or your hands. Shape the dough into a ball and wrap it in plastic wrap. Chill the dough until it is firm enough to roll — about 20 minutes.

Meanwhile, put the cranberries into a small sauce-pan with just enough water to float the berries; bring the liquid to a simmer and cook the cranberries until they burst — about four minutes. Drain the cranberries to remove any excess liquid and put them in a blender or food processor; add the orange juice and 3 table-spoons of the sugar. Process the cranberries just until they are puréed. (Take care not to overprocess the cranberries. Crushing the seeds can make the purée bitter.) Strain the purée through a fine sieve to remove the seeds and skins; chill the purée.

To form the flan shell, set the chilled dough on a floured surface. Using a rolling pin, flatten the ball of dough into a round, then roll the dough into a 10-inch circle. Transfer the dough to an 8-inch tart pan with a removable bottom, rolling the dough around the rolling pin and then unrolling it onto the tart pan. Gently press the dough into the corners and up the sides of the tart pan. Fold any excess dough back into the pan and press it well into the sides. Chill the flan shell for 10 minutes.

Preheat the oven to 425° F.

To prebake the flan shell, put the tart pan on a baking sheet. Prick the bottom of the dough several times with a fork. Line the flan shell with a round of wax paper and fill it with dried beans; this helps the pastry keep its shape. Bake the pastry for 10 minutes, remove the beans and wax paper, and continue baking until the flan shell is dry and just begins to color — about five minutes more. Remove the shell from the oven and let it cool in the tart pan.

Meanwhile, make a sugar syrup: Heat the remaining 2 tablespoons of sugar with 2 tablespoons of water in a small saucepan over medium-low heat until the sugar is dissolved — three to four minutes.

To assemble the flan, fill the bottom of the cooled flan shell with the cranberry purée. Arrange the pear slices on top in a circular pattern, overlapping the pieces slightly. Brush the pears and the edge of the pastry with the sugar syrup. Sprinkle the top with the filberts if you are using them. Bake the flan until the pears are soft and glazed — about 10 minutes. Remove the flan from the tart pan and serve it hot or cold.

Make the pear butter *(recipe, page 211)* for this buffet brunch up to one week in advance. The pancakes can be made a day or two ahead. The day before the brunch, marinate the pork, cook it, and reduce the sauce to a glaze. Make the dessert and refrigerate it. Store everything in the refrigerator, covered well.

On the day of the brunch, make the broccoli gratin; the gratin can sit for up to one hour, covered, after it is baked. Bring the dessert and the meat to room temperature. Make and chill the dessert topping and bake the biscuits. Make the spinach-onion filling and fill the pancake; cover it with foil and then heat it in a 325° F. oven for about five minutes. Cook the rutabaga and put it on a warmed platter; arrange the sliced meat on the rutabaga, cover the platter with foil, and heat it in the oven with the pancake for about 10 minutes. Warm the glaze. If you like, heat the dessert for 15 minutes at 200° F. to warm it. Make the mocha coffee.

Pork Loin with Cider and Rosemary

Serves 12
Working (and total) time: about 50 minutes

Calories **224**
Protein **22g.**
Cholesterol **64mg.**
Total fat **9g.**
Saturated fat **2g.**
Sodium **110mg.**

1 tbsp. safflower oil
2¾ lb. boneless pork loin roast, trimmed of fat
1 small onion, coarsely chopped
1½ tbsp. fresh rosemary, or 1 tsp. dried rosemary
¼ tsp. salt
freshly ground black pepper
4 cups apple cider or unsweetened apple juice
3 tbsp. cider vinegar
2 lb. rutabagas, peeled and coarsely grated (about 5 cups)
3 fresh rosemary sprigs for garnish (optional)

Heat the oil in a large, heavy-bottomed skillet over medium-high heat. Put the pork into the skillet and brown it lightly on all sides — about seven minutes in all. Add the onion, rosemary, salt and some pepper to the skillet; pour in the cider or apple juice and bring the mixture to a boil. Reduce the heat to medium low, cover the skillet with the lid ajar, and simmer the pork for 10 minutes. Turn the meat over and continue simmering it, partially covered, until the juices run clear when it is pierced with the tip of a sharp knife — about 10 minutes more. Remove the pork from the skillet and keep it warm.

Add the vinegar to the skillet and simmer the cooking liquid over medium-high heat until it is reduced to about ⅔ cup — 15 to 20 minutes.

While the sauce is reducing, pour enough water into

a large saucepan to fill it about 1 inch deep. Set a vegetable steamer in the pan and put the rutabagas into it. Cover the pan, bring the water to a boil, and steam the rutabagas until they are tender — about three minutes. Drain the rutabagas, pressing them lightly with the back of a spoon to release any excess liquid. Transfer the rutabagas to a large serving platter and keep them warm.

Cut the pork into ⅛-inch-thick slices and arrange the slices on top of the rutabagas. Strain the sauce over the pork slices and, if you like, garnish the platter with the rosemary sprigs. Serve at once.

A loaded sideboard awaits guests: Pork loin on a bed of rutabaga is served with squares of broccoli gratin, wedges of spinach-filled pancake torte, wheat biscuits with pear butter, scrambled eggs with salmon in toast-and-lettuce cups and, for dessert, Riesling-simmered apricots and pears.

Scrambled Eggs with Smoked Salmon in Toast Cups

CUTTING DOWN ON THE NUMBER OF EGG YOLKS USED REDUCES THE CHOLESTEROL IN THIS RECIPE.

Serves 12
Working (and total time): about 30 minutes

Calories **115**
Protein **7g.**
Cholesterol **72mg.**
Total fat **5g.**
Saturated fat **1g.**
Sodium **233mg.**

1 head Boston lettuce, or ⅓ lb. radicchio
12 slices whole-wheat bread, crusts removed
3 eggs, plus 6 egg whites
⅛ tsp. salt
freshly ground black pepper
2 tbsp. olive oil, preferably virgin
2 garlic cloves, finely chopped
¾ cup diced sweet red pepper
2 oz. smoked salmon, finely chopped (about ¼ cup)
5 scallions, trimmed and thinly sliced
1 tbsp. fresh lemon juice

Separate the lettuce or radicchio leaves and wash them if necessary. Set the leaves aside. Preheat the oven to 400° F. and lightly oil a muffin pan.

Using a rolling pin, flatten each slice of bread slightly. Gently press one slice of bread into each muffin cup. Bake the bread until it is crisp and lightly browned — 10 to 15 minutes. Keep the toast cups warm.

Whisk together the eggs, egg whites, salt, some pepper and 1½ tablespoons of the oil in a large bowl. Heat the remaining ½ tablespoon of oil in a large, nonstick skillet over medium-high heat. Add the garlic and red pepper and cook them for one minute, stirring constantly. Add the salmon, scallions and lemon juice; cook the mixture for two minutes more. Pour in the egg mixture and cook it, stirring constantly, just until the eggs are set but still moist — about two minutes.

Spoon the scrambled eggs into the toast cups, place each toast cup on a lettuce leaf, and serve at once.

Whole-Wheat Biscuits with Bulgur and Citrus

Makes 16 biscuits
Working time: about 25 minutes
Total time: about 40 minutes

Per biscuit:
Calories **80**
Protein **3g.**
Cholesterol **1mg.**
Total fat **2g.**
Saturated fat **0g.**
Sodium **67mg.**

¼ cup bulgur
1 cup plain low-fat yogurt
2 tsp. grated orange zest
1 tsp. grated lemon zest
2 tbsp. safflower oil
1½ cups whole-wheat flour
3 tbsp. sugar
1½ tsp. baking powder
⅛ tsp. salt

Put the bulgur into a bowl and pour in ⅓ cup of boiling water. Cover the bowl and let the bulgur stand until it is tender — about 15 minutes.

Preheat the oven to 375° F. Lightly oil a baking sheet or line it with parchment paper.

Drain the bulgur thoroughly, put it into a large bowl, and stir in the yogurt, orange zest, lemon zest and oil. Sift the flour, sugar, baking powder and salt over the bulgur mixture and stir them together just until they are combined. The dough will be quite sticky.

Turn the dough out onto a heavily floured surface. Dust your hands and the top of the dough with flour. Flatten the dough with your hands until it is about ¼ inch thick, using flour as needed to keep the dough from sticking. Using a 2½-inch-round cookie cutter, cut out as many biscuits as possible and put them on the baking sheet. Press the scraps of dough together and use them to make more biscuits.

Bake the biscuits until they are lightly browned — 15 to 20 minutes. Serve the biscuits hot.

Pancake Torte with Spinach and Onion Filling

Serves 12
Working (and total) time: about 25 minutes

Calories **88**
Protein **4g.**
Cholesterol **25mg.**
Total fat **4g.**
Saturated fat **1g.**
Sodium **106mg.**

2 lb. fresh spinach, stemmed and washed, or 20 oz. frozen spinach, thawed
2 tsp. olive oil, preferably virgin
2 onions, thinly sliced
1 tbsp. fresh thyme, or 1 tsp. dried thyme leaves
⅛ tsp. salt
freshly ground black pepper
⅓ cup cider vinegar
Pancake batter
¾ cup unbleached all-purpose flour
⅛ tsp. salt
1¼ cups low-fat milk
1 egg, plus 1 egg white
1½ tbsp. olive oil, preferably virgin

To make the pancake batter, sift the flour and salt into a large bowl. In another bowl, whisk the milk, egg, egg white and oil together. Pour the milk mixture into the dry ingredients, stirring just until the batter is blended; do not overmix. Set the batter aside while you make the filling.

If you are using fresh spinach, cook it in 3 quarts of boiling water for one minute, then drain it and run cold water over the spinach to refresh it; thawed frozen spinach does not require cooking. Squeeze the spinach in your hands to extract as much water as possible and coarsely chop it.

Heat the oil in a large, heavy-bottomed skillet over medium heat. Add the onions, thyme, salt and some pepper, and cook the mixture, stirring occasionally, until the onions are translucent — about 10 minutes. Increase the heat to medium high and continue cooking the onions, stirring frequently, until they have browned — five to 10 minutes more. Pour in the vinegar and continue to cook the onions until all the vinegar has evaporated — one to two minutes. Stir the spinach into the onions and cook the mixture for one minute. Keep the spinach mixture warm while you cook the pancakes.

Heat an 8-inch skillet or griddle over medium heat. Pour in half of the pancake batter, and swirl the skillet or griddle to distribute the batter over the bottom. Cook the pancake until the underside is golden — two to three minutes. Turn the pancake and cook it until the second side is lightly browned — two to three minutes more. Transfer the pancake to a plate and keep it warm while you make a second pancake with the remaining batter.

Spread the spinach filling over the first pancake and top it with the second pancake. Cut the pancake torte into 12 wedges and serve the wedges either warm or at room temperature.

EDITOR'S NOTE: *The pancakes for this torte can be made up to two days in advance and kept in the refrigerator, covered with plastic wrap. On the day of the brunch, make the filling and spread it between the pancakes. Cover the torte with foil and heat it in a 350° F. oven for about five minutes.*

Broccoli Gratin

Serves 12
Working time: about 25 minutes
Total time: about 1 hour and 15 minutes

Calories **76**
Protein **6g.**
Cholesterol **35mg.**
Total fat **4g.**
Saturated fat **2g.**
Sodium **135mg.**

2 lb. broccoli, the florets separated from the stems, the stems peeled and cut into ½-inch pieces
½ cup low-fat milk
1 cup part-skim ricotta cheese
¼ cup light cream
1 egg, plus 1 egg white
¼ cup freshly grated Parmesan cheese
2 garlic cloves, finely chopped
¼ tsp. grated nutmeg
¼ tsp. salt
freshly ground black pepper

Preheat the oven to 350° F.

Pour enough water into a large saucepan to fill it about 1 inch deep. Set a vegetable steamer in the pan, bring the water to a boil, and put the broccoli stems into the steamer; cover the pan and steam the stems for three minutes. Add the broccoli florets and steam the florets and stems until both are tender — about five minutes more. Remove the steamer from the saucepan and refresh the broccoli under cold running water; drain it thoroughly.

Put the broccoli into a food processor and pour in the milk; process the broccoli in short bursts until it is coarsely puréed. (Do not overprocess — the mixture should not be smooth.)

In a large bowl, whisk together the ricotta, cream, egg, egg white, 2 tablespoons of the Parmesan cheese, the garlic, nutmeg, salt and some pepper. Mix the broccoli purée into the ricotta mixture.

Spoon the broccoli mixture into an 8-by-12-inch baking dish; sprinkle it with the remaining 2 tablespoons of Parmesan cheese. Bake the broccoli gratin in the oven until it is firm and lightly browned — 35 to 40 minutes. Cut the gratin into 12 squares or diamonds, arrange them on a large plate and serve them at once.

Riesling-Simmered Apricots and Pears with Yogurt Cream

Serves 12
Working time: about 30 minutes
Total time: about 1 hour and 15 minutes
(includes chilling)

Calories **131**
Protein **2g.**
Cholesterol **10mg.**
Total fat **3g.**
Saturated fat **2g.**
Sodium **9mg.**

1½ cups Riesling or other dry white wine
¾ lb. dried apricots
3 ripe pears (about 1¼ lb.), peeled, cored and cut into ¾-inch pieces
Yogurt cream
⅓ cup heavy cream
¼ cup plain low-fat yogurt
1 tbsp. confectioners' sugar
1 tsp. pure vanilla extract

Combine the wine and apricots in a large, nonreactive saucepan and bring the wine to a simmer over low heat. Simmer the mixture, stirring occasionally, until the apricots are soft and the liquid is reduced to about ½ cup — about 15 minutes.

Drain the apricots in a sieve set over a bowl, gently pressing them with a spoon to extract as much liquid as possible. Transfer the apricots to another bowl and set them aside. Pour the liquid back into the saucepan, add the pears, and cook them over low heat, stirring occasionally, until they are soft — about 20 minutes. The liquid should be syrupy. Line an 8-inch cake pan with a round of wax paper or parchment paper.

Add the pears with their liquid to the apricots and gently stir them together. Spoon the mixture into the prepared pan and spread it evenly over the bottom. Chill the fruit until it is firm — about 45 minutes.

Meanwhile, beat the cream until it forms soft peaks; mix in the yogurt, sugar and vanilla just until they are blended. Spoon the cream into a bowl and chill.

When the dish is set, run a knife around the edge of the pan and invert a serving plate on top of it. Turn both over together; lift away the pan and peel off the paper. Serve the dessert chilled or at room temperature topped with the yogurt cream.

*9*Freshly baked ginger snaps, molded while they are hot and pliable, harden into delicate horns as they cool (recipe, page 264).

Desserts

Orange Slices Macerated in Red Wine and Port

Serves 8
Working time: about 20 minutes
Total time: about 2 hours and 20 minutes
(includes chilling)

Calories **145**
Protein **2g.**
Cholesterol **0mg.**
Total fat **1g.**
Saturated fat **1g.**
Sodium **2mg.**

6 large navel oranges
1 cup Beaujolais or other fruity red wine
¼ cup sugar
1 cinnamon stick
⅛ tsp. ground cardamom or allspice
⅓ cup ruby port
2 tbsp. currants
2 tbsp. toasted sweetened dried coconut

With a vegetable peeler, remove the zest from one of the oranges. Put the zest into a small saucepan with the wine, sugar, cinnamon stick, and cardamom or allspice. Bring the mixture to a boil and cook it over medium-high heat until the liquid is reduced to about ⅔ cup — approximately five minutes. Remove the pan from the heat; stir in the port and currants, and set the sauce aside.

Cut away the skins, removing all the white pith, and slice the oranges into ¼-inch-thick rounds. Arrange the orange rounds on a serving dish and pour the wine sauce over them; remove and discard the cinnamon stick. Refrigerate the dish, covered, for two hours.

Just before serving the oranges, sprinkle the toasted coconut over all.

EDITOR'S NOTE: *To toast the coconut, spread it on a baking sheet and cook it in a preheated 325° F. oven, stirring every five minutes, until it has browned — about 15 minutes in all.*

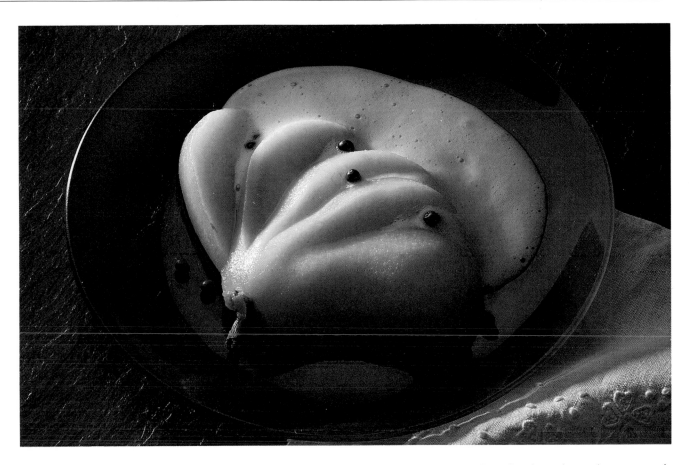

Peppercorn Pears in Sabayon Sauce

Serves 8
Working time: about 1 hour
Total time: about 2 hours

Calories **181**
Protein **2g.**
Cholesterol **69mg.**
Total fat **2g.**
Saturated fat **0g.**
Sodium **19mg.**

1 lemon, halved
4 firm but ripe pears
1 cup sugar
1 cup dry white wine
8 black peppercorns
2 eggs
½ tsp. pure vanilla extract
1 tbsp. vinegar-packed green peppercorns, drained

Prepare acidulated water by squeezing the juice from one of the lemon halves into 1 quart of cold water. Peel, halve, and core the pears, dropping them into the acidulated water to prevent them from discoloring as you work.

In a large, nonreactive skillet, combine the sugar, 1 cup of water, the wine and the black peppercorns. Peel a strip of lemon zest from the reserved lemon half and add it to the skillet. Squeeze the juice of the remaining lemon half into the skillet as well. Bring the liquid to a boil, then reduce the heat to low, and simmer the mixture for five minutes.

Transfer the pears to the sugar syrup and poach them in a single layer for about three minutes on each side. With a slotted spoon, transfer the pears to a plate.

Continue to simmer the poaching liquid over low heat until it is reduced to about 1 cup of heavy syrup — five to 10 minutes. Remove the peppercorns and zest with a spoon. Reserve ⅓ cup of the syrup; pour the remainder over the pears, cover them and refrigerate them until they are chilled — about one hour.

Let the reserved syrup cool for five minutes, then use it to prepare the sabayon sauce. Whisk the eggs in a small, heavy-bottomed saucepan. Pour the syrup into the pan in a thin, steady stream, whisking constantly so that its heat does not curdle the eggs. Cook the mixture over medium heat, stirring constantly until it coats the back of the spoon — three to four minutes. Transfer the custard to a bowl. With an electric mixer set on high, whip the sauce until it has quadrupled in volume and is cool — about five minutes. Blend in the vanilla, then refrigerate the sabayon sauce, covered, until it is chilled — about one hour.

When the pears are chilled, cut them into fans: Set a pear half core side down on the work surface. Holding the knife at a 45-degree angle to the work surface, cut the pear half into five lengthwise slices, leaving the slices attached at the stem end. Gently transfer the pear half to a dessert plate, then spread out the slices in the shape of a fan. Repeat the process to make eight fans in all. Spoon about 1 tablespoon of the chilled sabayon sauce next to each portion. Sprinkle each fan with a few green peppercorns and serve at once.

Apple-Prune Timbales with Lemon Syrup

Serves 6
Working time: about 40 minutes
Total time: about 1 hour and 10 minutes

Calories **142**
Protein **1g.**
Cholesterol **5mg.**
Total fat **2g.**
Saturated fat **1g.**
Sodium **2mg.**

1 tbsp. unsalted butter
1¾ lb. tart green apples, peeled, cored and cut into ½-inch pieces
½ tsp. ground coriander
⅛ tsp. ground cloves
2 tbsp. fresh lemon juice
¼ cup brandy
¼ lb. pitted dried prunes, quartered
⅓ cup golden raisins
¼ cup sugar
zest of 1 lemon, finely julienned

Melt the butter in a large, heavy-bottomed skillet over medium-high heat. Add the apple pieces, coriander and cloves, and cook the mixture, stirring constantly, for five minutes.

Stir in the lemon juice, brandy, prunes, raisins, 3 tablespoons of the sugar and ½ cup of water. Cook the compote, stirring frequently, until nearly all the liquid has evaporated — about 10 minutes.

While the apple compote is cooking, combine the zest, the remaining tablespoon of sugar and ¼ cup of water in a small saucepan. Bring the mixture to a boil, then reduce the heat to low; simmer the mixture until the liquid is thick and syrupy — about seven minutes.

Spoon the apple compote into six 4-ounce ramekins, tamping it down in order to give the timbales a uniform shape when they are unmolded. Let the ramekins stand at room temperature until tepid — approximately 30 minutes.

Unmold the timbales onto individual plates. Garnish each with some of the lemon zest and drizzle the lemon syrup over the top.

Pears with Filberts

Serves 4
Working time: about 30 minutes
Total time: about 45 minutes

Calories **223**
Protein **2g.**
Cholesterol **8mg.**
Total fat **8g.**
Saturated fat **2g.**
Sodium **5mg.**

¼ cup filberts (about 1 oz.)
¼ cup light brown sugar
1 tbsp. cold unsalted butter
4 large ripe pears
1 lemon half
1 tbsp. fresh lemon juice

Preheat the oven to 375° F.

Spread the nuts in a single layer in a small cake pan or a roasting pan. Toast the nuts in the oven for 10 minutes. Test a nut for doneness by rubbing it in a clean kitchen towel; the skin should come off easily. (If it does not, toast the nuts for two minutes more and repeat the test.) When the nuts are done, wrap them in the towel and rub off their skins. Let the nuts cool to room temperature.

Put the nuts, brown sugar and butter into a food processor or a blender, and process them just until the nuts are coarsely chopped. Set the mixture aside.

Preheat the broiler. Peel the pears, then halve them lengthwise, and core them, rubbing them with the lemon half as you work to prevent discoloration. Arrange the pear halves, cored sides up, in a large, shallow baking dish. Moisten the pears with the lemon juice and sprinkle the filbert mixture over them. Broil the pears until the topping browns and bubbles — about two minutes.

Pear and Cranberry Crisp

Serves 8
Working time: about 30 minutes
Total time: about 1 hour and 10 minutes

Calories **188**
Protein **3g.**
Cholesterol **8mg.**
Total fat **5g.**
Saturated fat **2g.**
Sodium **2mg.**

1 lemon
2 cups fresh or frozen cranberries
¼ cup plus 2 tbsp. sugar
4 pears
Oat topping
1½ cups rolled oats
¼ cup unsweetened apple juice
2 tbsp. unsalted butter, melted

With a vegetable peeler, peel the zest from the lemon. Chop the zest finely and set it aside. Squeeze the lemon, straining and reserving the juice.

Combine the cranberries with ¼ cup of the sugar, the lemon zest and ¼ cup of water in a saucepan over medium-high heat. Bring the mixture to a boil and cook it, stirring occasionally, until the berries burst — about 10 minutes. Set the berry mixture aside.

Peel and core the pears, then coarsely chop them. Transfer the pears to a heavy-bottomed saucepan. Dribble the lemon juice over the pears and bring the mixture to a boil. Reduce the heat to maintain a simmer, then cook the mixture, stirring occasionally, until the pears reach the consistency of thick applesauce — 20 to 30 minutes. Set the pears aside.

Preheat the oven to 400° F.

For the topping, mix together the oats, apple juice and butter. Spread the oat mixture on a baking sheet and bake it, stirring occasionally, until it has browned — 20 to 30 minutes. Remove the topping from the oven and reduce the temperature to 350° F.

Spread about 2 tablespoons of the oat mixture in the bottom of a lightly oiled 1½-quart soufflé dish or casserole. Spread half of the pear mixture in the dish, then top it with half of the cranberry mixture in an even layer. Spread half of the remaining oat topping over the cranberry mixture. Repeat the layering process with the remaining pear, cranberry and oat mixtures to fill the dish. Sprinkle the remaining 2 tablespoons of sugar on top. Bake the crisp until the juices are bubbling hot in the center — 20 to 30 minutes.

Apple Brown Betty
with Cheddar Cheese

Serves 6
Working time: about 30 minutes
Total time: about 1 hour and 15 minutes

Calories **253**	
Protein **5g.**	6 firm whole-wheat bread slices, crusts removed
Cholesterol **11mg.**	6 large tart green apples
Total fat **4g.**	½ cup plus 1 tbsp. sugar
Saturated fat **2g.**	½ tsp. ground cinnamon
Sodium **171mg.**	1 tbsp. fresh lemon juice
	½ cup unsweetened apple juice
	⅓ cup grated sharp Cheddar cheese (about 2 oz.)

Preheat the oven to 300° F. Cut the bread slices into ½-inch cubes and spread them out on a baking sheet.

Bake the bread cubes for 10 minutes, stirring them once to ensure that they cook evenly without browning. Remove the bread cubes from the oven and set them aside. Increase the oven temperature to 375° F.

Peel, quarter and core the apples, then cut the quarters into thin slices. In a bowl, gently toss the slices with ½ cup of the sugar, the cinnamon, lemon juice and apple juice. Spoon half of the apple mixture into a 1½-quart soufflé dish. Cover the apple mixture with half of the toasted bread cubes. Form another layer with the remaining apple mixture and bread cubes. Scatter the cheese over the bread cubes and sprinkle the remaining tablespoon of sugar evenly over the top.

Bake the dish until the juices bubble up around the edges and the top browns — about 45 minutes.

Orange Chiffon Cheesecake

Serves 12
Working time: about 1 hour
Total time: about 1 day (includes chilling)

Calories **145**
Protein **7g.**
Cholesterol **12mg.**
Total fat **4g.**
Saturated fat **2g.**
Sodium **130mg.**

1 cup sugar
2 navel oranges, halved lengthwise and cut crosswise into ⅛-inch-thick slices
½ cup fresh orange juice
2½ tbsp. fresh lemon juice
2½ tsp. unflavored powdered gelatin (1 envelope)
1 cup part-skim ricotta cheese
1 cup low-fat cottage cheese
2 oz. cream cheese
grated zest of 1 orange
grated zest of 1 lemon
3 egg whites

Put the sugar and ½ cup of water into a saucepan. Bring the mixture to a boil, then add the orange slices, reduce the heat, and simmer the oranges for 20 minutes. Refrigerate the oranges in the syrup for one hour.

Pour the orange juice and lemon juice into a small saucepan. Sprinkle in the gelatin, then set the pan aside until the gelatin has softened.

Meanwhile, purée the ricotta, cottage cheese, cream cheese, orange zest and lemon zest in a food processor or a blender until they are very smooth. Transfer the cheese mixture to a bowl.

Set the saucepan containing the gelatin mixture over low heat; cook it, stirring continuously, until the gelatin has dissolved. Stir the gelatin mixture into the puréed cheeses.

Remove the orange slices from their syrup and drain them on paper towels. Reserve the syrup.

Pour the egg whites into a deep bowl. Set up an electric mixer; you will need to start beating the egg whites as soon as the sugar is ready.

To prepare the Italian meringue, bring the reserved

syrup to a boil in a small saucepan over medium-high heat. Continue boiling the mixture until the bubbles rise to the surface in a random pattern, indicating that the liquid has nearly evaporated and the sugar itself is beginning to cook.

With a small spoon, drop a bit of the syrup into a bowl filled with ice water. If the sugar dissolves immediately, continue cooking the sugar mixture. When the sugar dropped into the water can be rolled between your fingers into a supple ball, begin beating the egg whites on high speed. Pour the sugar down the side of the bowl in a very thin, steady stream. When all the sugar has been incorporated, decrease the speed to medium; continue beating the egg whites until they are glossy, have formed stiff peaks and have cooled to room temperature. Increase the speed to high and beat the meringue for one minute more.

Mix about one quarter of the meringue into the cheese mixture to lighten it, then gently fold in the rest. Rinse a 6-cup ring mold with cold water and shake out the excess. (Do not wipe the mold dry; the clinging moisture will help the dessert unmold cleanly.) Line the mold with the drained orange slices, then pour in the cheesecake mixture, and chill it in the refrigerator for four hours.

To turn out the cheesecake, invert a chilled platter on top of the mold and turn both over together. Wrap the bottom of the mold in a towel that has been soaked with hot water and wrung out. After five seconds, remove the towel and lift away the mold.

Kugel with Dried Fruit

Serves 12
Working time: about 35 minutes
Total time: about 1 hour and 35 minutes

Calories **327**
Protein **13g.**
Cholesterol **17mg.**
Total fat **6g.**
Saturated fat **3g.**
Sodium **231mg.**

½ lb. dried wide egg noodles
1 cup sugar
1 lb. low-fat cottage cheese
½ lb. farmer cheese
1 cup plain low-fat yogurt
1 tsp. pure vanilla extract
2 tbsp. fresh lemon juice
1 cup golden raisins
½ cup diced dried pears
½ cup diced dried apples
½ cup diced dried prunes
2 tbsp. cornstarch
2 cups low-fat milk
2 tbsp. dry bread crumbs
Cinnamon topping
2 tbsp. unsalted butter, softened
½ cup dry bread crumbs
½ tsp. ground cinnamon
2 tbsp. sugar

Add the noodles to 3 quarts of boiling water. Start testing for doneness after seven minutes and continue cooking the noodles until they are *al dente*. Drain the noodles and rinse them under cold running water, then set them aside.

Preheat the oven to 350° F. In a large bowl, mix together the sugar, cottage cheese, farmer cheese, yogurt, vanilla, lemon juice, raisins, pears, apples and prunes. Dissolve the cornstarch in ½ cup of the milk. Stir the cornstarch mixture and the remaining 1½ cups of milk into the cheese mixture.

Stir the noodles together with the cheese mixture, coating them well. Lightly oil a nonreactive 9- by 13-inch baking dish and coat it with the 2 tablespoons of bread crumbs. Transfer the noodles to the baking dish.

To make the cinnamon topping, mix together the butter, the ½ cup of bread crumbs, the cinnamon and the sugar. Sprinkle the topping over the noodles, then cover the dish with foil, and bake it for 30 minutes. Remove the foil and bake the kugel until it is golden brown — about 30 minutes more.

Lemon-Buttermilk Custard with Candied Lemon Slices

Serves 8
Working time: about 20 minutes
Total time: about 2 hours and 40 minutes
(includes chilling)

Calories **185**
Protein **5g.**
Cholesterol **72mg.**
Total fat **2g.**
Saturated fat **1g.**
Sodium **115mg.**

2 eggs
1 cup sugar
⅓ cup unbleached all-purpose flour
2 tsp. lemon extract
3 cups buttermilk
3 lemons, thinly sliced, for garnish
½ cup blueberries or raspberries for garnish

Preheat the oven to 300° F.

To prepare the custard, first whisk the eggs in a bowl, then whisk in ⅔ cup of the sugar and the flour; when the custard is smooth, stir in the lemon extract and buttermilk. Pour the custard into eight ½-cup custard cups and set them on a baking sheet. Bake the custards until they are puffed up and set, and a knife inserted at the edge comes out clean — 15 to 20 minutes. Let the custards cool slightly, then refrigerate them until they are well chilled — about two hours.

To candy the lemon slices, lightly oil a baking sheet and set it aside. Combine the remaining ⅓ cup of sugar with ¼ cup of water in a small, heavy-bottomed saucepan. Bring the mixture to a boil, then reduce the heat to low, and cook the syrup, stirring occasionally, until the sugar has dissolved and the syrup is clear — about one and a half minutes. Add the lemon slices to the pan; immediately turn the slices over, coating them well, and cook them for about 30 seconds. Transfer the slices to the oiled baking sheet.

To serve, run a small knife around the inside of each custard cup and invert the custards onto serving plates. Garnish each plate with a few candied lemon slices and a sprinkling of fresh berries.

Rice Pudding
with Raspberry Sauce

THIS VARIATION ON AN OLD DESSERT OWES ITS VELVETY
TEXTURE TO THE INCLUSION OF PASTRY CREAM.

Serves 8
Working time: about 50 minutes
Total time: about 3 hours

Calories **224**
Protein **7g.**
Cholesterol **44mg.**
Total fat **3g.**
Saturated fat **2g.**
Sodium **142mg.**

4 cups low-fat milk
½ cup long-grain rice
½ cup plus 2 tbsp. sugar
¼ tsp. salt
1 egg yolk
3 tbsp. unbleached all-purpose flour
½ tsp. grated nutmeg
1 tsp. pure vanilla extract
¼ tsp. almond extract
¼ cup golden raisins
2 cups fresh or frozen whole raspberries, thawed
fresh mint leaves (optional)

Bring 3 cups of the milk to a boil in a heavy-bottomed saucepan over medium heat. Reduce the heat to low and add the rice, ¼ cup of the sugar and the salt. Cook the mixture, stirring frequently, for 50 minutes.

To prepare the pastry cream, whisk together the egg yolk and ¼ cup of the remaining milk. Whisk in the flour and ¼ cup of the remaining sugar; then blend in the remaining ¾ cup of milk. Bring the mixture to a boil over medium heat, stirring constantly, then cook it, still stirring vigorously, for two minutes more. Remove the pan from the heat and stir in the nutmeg, vanilla and almond extract.

When the rice has finished cooking, stir in the raisins, then fold in the pastry cream. Transfer the pudding to a clean bowl. To prevent a skin from forming on its surface, press a sheet of plastic wrap directly onto the pudding. Refrigerate the pudding until it is cold — about two hours.

To prepare the sauce, purée the raspberries and the remaining 2 tablespoons of sugar in a blender or a food processor. Rub the purée through a fine sieve with a plastic spatula or the back of a wooden spoon; discard the seeds.

To serve, divide the sauce among eight serving dishes. Top the sauce with individual scoops of pudding; if you like, sprinkle the scoops with some additional nutmeg and garnish each with a sprig of mint.

Spiced Pumpkin Mousse with Lemon Cream

Serves 6
Working time: about 30 minutes
Total time: about 2 hours (includes chilling)

Calories **140**
Protein **4g.**
Cholesterol **18mg.**
Total fat **5g.**
Saturated fat **3g.**
Sodium **88mg.**

2½ tsp. unflavored powdered gelatin (1 envelope)
⅓ cup sugar
2 tsp. grated lemon zest
¾ tsp. anise seeds, finely ground
⅛ tsp. grated nutmeg
1 tbsp. finely chopped crystallized ginger
⅛ tsp. salt
1 cup canned pumpkin
¼ cup fresh lemon juice
4 egg whites, at room temperature
⅛ tsp. cream of tartar
Lemon cream
¼ cup julienned lemon zest
2 tbsp. sugar
2 tbsp. fresh lemon juice
⅓ cup heavy cream

Put ¼ cup of cold water into a bowl, then sprinkle in the gelatin. Let the gelatin soften for five minutes; pour in ¼ cup of boiling water and stir to dissolve the gelatin. Stir in the sugar, lemon zest, ground anise, nutmeg, ginger and salt. Add the pumpkin and lemon juice, and stir to combine them. Chill the mixture in the refrigerator, stirring occasionally, until it starts to gel — about 30 minutes.

When the pumpkin mixture is ready, beat the egg whites with the cream of tartar in a bowl until they form stiff peaks. Remove the pumpkin mixture from the refrigerator and whisk it vigorously for 15 seconds. Stir in one third of the egg whites and combine them thoroughly, then fold in the remaining egg whites (technique, page 261).

Divide the mousse into six portions, mounding each one in the center, and chill them for one to six hours.

For the lemon cream, first put the zest in a small, nonreactive saucepan with ¼ cup of water, the 2 tablespoons of sugar and the 2 tablespoons of lemon juice. Bring the liquid to a boil, then reduce the heat to low, and simmer the mixture until it becomes a thick syrup — about five minutes. Strain the syrup into a small bowl, reserving the zest. Set half of the cooked zest aside; finely chop the rest.

Just before serving, whip the cream in a small bowl. Fold in the syrup and the finely chopped lemon zest. Garnish each mousse with a dollop of the lemon cream and a few strands of the reserved julienned zest.

Folding Mixtures Together

1 *LIGHTENING THE MIXTURE. To ensure an airy dessert's lightness, add one fourth to one third of the lighter mixture (here, beaten egg whites) to the heavier one (in this instance, pumpkin purée) and whisk them gently together. This will lighten the mixture enough so that the remaining egg whites can be folded in easily.*

2 *ADDING THE EGG WHITES. Scoop the remaining beaten egg whites into the bowl containing the lightened mixture. With the blade of a rubber spatula, cut down through the center.*

3 *FOLDING. Glide the spatula across the bottom of the bowl, then lift and turn over the purée and egg whites as you reach the edge. Give the bowl a quarter turn. Continue cutting, lifting and turning the mixture, rotating the bowl each time, until the egg whites have been evenly incorporated.*

Indian Pudding with Buttermilk Cream

Serves 8
Working time: about 25 minutes
Total time: about 2 hours

Calories **231**
Protein **8g.**
Cholesterol **13mg.**
Total fat **3g.**
Saturated fat **2g.**
Sodium **126mg.**

¾ cup stone-ground yellow cornmeal
1 tsp. ground cinnamon
1 tsp. ground ginger
4 cups low-fat milk
½ cup molasses
1 tsp. pure vanilla extract
Buttermilk cream
2 tbsp. cornstarch
¼ cup sugar
1 cup low-fat milk
1 cup buttermilk
1 tsp. pure vanilla extract

Preheat the oven to 325° F.

Combine the cornmeal, cinnamon, ginger and 1 cup of the milk in a heatproof bowl. Pour the remaining 3 cups of milk into a saucepan and bring the milk to a boil. Stirring constantly, pour the hot milk into the cornmeal mixture in a thin, steady stream.

Transfer the cornmeal mixture to the saucepan; stirring continuously, bring it to a boil. Reduce the heat to medium low and cook the mixture, stirring constantly, until it has the consistency of a thick sauce — about three minutes more. Stir in the molasses and the vanilla extract, then pour the cornmeal mixture into a baking dish, and bake it until it sets — about one hour.

While the pudding is baking, make the buttermilk cream. Mix the cornstarch and sugar in a small saucepan, then whisk in the low-fat milk. Bring the mixture to a boil and cook it for one minute. Remove the pan from the heat and stir in the buttermilk and vanilla. Transfer the buttermilk cream to a bowl and chill it in the refrigerator.

Remove the pudding from the oven and allow it to cool at room temperature for about 45 minutes; just before serving, top the pudding with the chilled buttermilk cream.

Baked Chocolate Custard

Serves 8
Working time: about 30 minutes
Total time: about 2 hours

Calories **108**
Protein **4g.**
Cholesterol **73mg.**
Total fat **3g.**
Saturated fat **1g.**
Sodium **71mg.**

2 eggs
½ cup sugar
2 tbsp. unsweetened cocoa powder
¹⁄₁₆ tsp. salt
2 cups low-fat milk
⅓ cup fresh raspberries (optional)

Preheat the oven to 325° F. Whisk together the eggs, sugar, cocoa powder and salt in a heatproof bowl. Heat the milk in a small saucepan just until it comes to a boil. Whisking continuously, pour the hot milk into the bowl. Thoroughly mix in the milk, then pour the mix-ture into the saucepan.

Cook the mixture over low heat, stirring constantly with a wooden spoon, until it has thickened enough to lightly coat the back of the spoon. Strain the mixture into eight custard cups. Set the custard cups in a roast-ing pan or casserole with sides at least ½ inch higher than the cups. Pour enough boiling water into the pan to come halfway up the sides of the cups. Cover the pan with a baking sheet or a piece of aluminum foil, then put it in the oven, and bake the custards until the center of one barely quivers when the cup is shaken — 20 to 30 minutes.

Remove the pan from the oven and uncover it. Leave the custard cups in the water until they cool to room temperature, then refrigerate them for at least 30 min-utes. If you like, arrange several fresh raspberries on each custard just before serving them.

Amaretto Flan
with Plum Sauce

Serves 6
Working time: about 30 minutes
Total time: about 1 hour and 30 minutes

Calories **249**
Protein **8g.**
Cholesterol **98mg.**
Total fat **7g.**
Saturated fat **2g.**
Sodium **96mg.**

¼ cup sliced almonds
1 ¼ tsp. ground cinnamon
5 tbsp. sugar
2 eggs, plus 2 egg whites
¼ cup amaretto
¼ cup honey
2 ¼ cups low-fat milk
4 ripe red plums, quartered and pitted
2 tsp. fresh lemon juice

Preheat the oven to 325° F. Spread the almonds in a small baking pan and toast them in the oven as it preheats until they are golden — about 25 minutes.

Lightly butter six 4-ounce ramekins. (If you do not have ramekins, you may use ovenproof custard cups.) In a small dish, mix ¾ teaspoon of the cinnamon with 2 tablespoons of the sugar. Put about 1 teaspoon of the cinnamon-and-sugar mixture into each ramekin, then tilt it in all directions to coat its buttered sides and bottom. Put the ramekins into a large, ovenproof baking dish and refrigerate them.

In a large bowl, whisk together the eggs, egg whites, amaretto, honey and the remaining ½ teaspoon of cinnamon. Whisk in the milk, then pour the flan mixture into the chilled ramekins, filling each to within ¼ inch of the top.

Place the baking dish with the filled ramekins in the preheated oven. Pour enough hot tap water into the baking dish to come two thirds of the way up the sides of the ramekins. Bake the flans until a thin-bladed knife inserted in the center of one comes out clean — about 30 minutes. Remove the ramekins from their water bath and let them stand for half an hour.

While the flans cool, prepare the plum sauce: Combine the plums, the remaining 3 tablespoons of sugar and the lemon juice in a food processor or a blender. Process the plums to a smooth purée, then pass the purée through a fine sieve into a bowl to remove the skins. Refrigerate the sauce until it is chilled — about half an hour.

To unmold the cooled flans, run a small, sharp knife around the inside of each ramekin. Invert a serving plate over the top and turn both over together. Lift away the ramekin; the flan should slip out easily. If it does not, rock the ramekin from side to side to loosen it. Ladle some of the plum sauce around each flan; sprinkle the toasted almonds over the top.

Ginger Snaps with Kumquat and Ginger Mousse

Makes about 20 ginger snaps
Working time: about 1 hour and 15 minutes
Total time: about 2 hours and 30 minutes (includes chilling)

Per snap:
Calories **75**
Protein **2g.**
Cholesterol **10mg.**
Total fat **4g.**
Saturated fat **2g.**
Sodium **15mg.**

4 tbsp. unsalted butter
¼ cup light brown sugar
2 tbsp. dark corn syrup
½ cup unbleached all-purpose flour, sifted
1 tsp. fresh lemon juice
½ tsp. ground ginger

Kumquat and ginger mousse

6 oz. kumquats, stems removed
6 tbsp. fresh orange juice
1½ tsp. powdered gelatin
1-inch piece preserved stem ginger
2 tsp. syrup from preserved stem ginger
¾ cup plain low-fat yogurt

First, make the mousse. Purée the kumquats in a food processor or a blender with 4 tablespoons of the orange juice. Pass the purée through a fine sieve and discard the seeds. Put the remaining 2 tablespoons of orange juice into a small bowl, sprinkle on the gelatin, and allow it to soften for two minutes. Place the bowl over a pan of simmering water and stir until the gelatin has completely dissolved.

Return the kumquat purée to the food processor or blender, and add the preserved ginger, ginger syrup, and yogurt. Process until smooth. Add the dissolved gelatin and process for another 20 seconds. Transfer the mixture to a bowl and put it in the refrigerator to set—about one and a half hours.

Preheat the oven to 350° F. Grease two baking sheets, and line them with parchment paper. Heat the butter, sugar, and corn syrup in a small, heavy-bottomed pan over medium-low heat. When the butter has melted and the sugar has dissolved, remove the pan from the heat and stir in the flour. Mix well until smooth, then add the lemon juice and ground ginger.

Drop 4 level teaspoons of the mixture onto each baking sheet, spacing them well apart. Put one sheet in the oven, and bake until the snaps are bubbly and golden brown—about 10 minutes. Halfway through the baking period, put the other sheet in the oven. When the snaps on the first sheet are done, remove them from the oven and let them stand for about one minute to firm up slightly. Then lift the snaps from the parchment with a metal spatula and shape them into cornets around a metal cream-horn mold *(technique, right).* Place the shaped snaps on a wire rack.

Wipe the parchment with paper towels, refill the sheet with 4 more teaspoonfuls of mixture, and return it to the oven. Remove the second sheet of cooked snaps from the oven. Let them rest briefly, then shape them as before. Continue to cook and shape the snaps in batches until all the mixture is used up. If the snaps start to harden before they are all shaped, return them to the oven for a few seconds to soften them again.

Finally, transfer the kumquat and ginger mousse to a pastry bag fitted with a ½-inch plain tip, and fill the snaps. Serve immediately; the snaps will hold the mixture for about an hour before becoming soft.

Chocolate Snaps

Makes 20 snaps
Working and (total time): about 1 hour and 15 minutes

Per snap:
Calories **60**
Protein **1g.**
Cholesterol **5mg.**
Total fat **5g.**
Saturated fat **3g.**
Sodium **5mg.**

4 tbsp. unsalted butter
¼ cup light brown sugar
2 tbsp. dark corn syrup
½ cup unbleached all-purpose flour, sifted
1 tsp. fresh lemon juice
½ tsp. ground cinnamon
5 oz. semisweet chocolate, broken into pieces

Preheat the oven to 350° F. Grease two baking sheets and line them with parchment paper.

Put the butter, sugar, and corn syrup into a small saucepan, and stir them over low heat. When the butter has melted and the sugar dissolved, remove the pan from the heat and stir in the flour. Mix until smooth, then stir in the lemon juice and cinnamon.

Drop 4 level teaspoons of the mixture onto each baking sheet, spacing them well apart to allow the snaps to spread. Put one sheet in the oven, and bake the snaps until they are bubbly and golden—about 10 minutes. Halfway through the baking period, put the other sheet in the oven. When the snaps on the first sheet are done, remove them from the oven and let them stand for a minute or so, to firm up slightly. Lift the snaps off the baking sheet with a metal spatula and roll them around the handle of a wooden spoon *(technique, below)*. Place the shaped snaps on a wire rack.

Wipe the parchment with paper towels, refill the sheet with four more spoonfuls of snap mixture, and return it to the oven. Remove the second sheet of cooked snaps from the oven. Allow them to stand briefly, then shape them as before. Cook and shape the remaining snap mixture in staggered batches, following the same procedure. If the snaps start to harden before they are all shaped, return them to the oven for a few seconds to soften them.

When all the snaps are cooked, shaped, and cooled, melt the chocolate in a flameproof bowl set over a saucepan of hot water. Dip the ends of the snaps in the chocolate, and let them set on parchment paper.

EDITOR'S NOTE: *The snaps can be stored for up to a week in an airtight container.*

Shaping Snaps

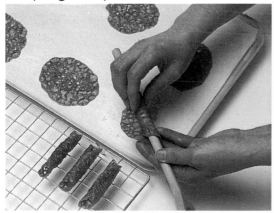

ROLLING CYLINDERS. Remove the snaps from the oven and leave them just long enough to be lifted without tearing—about one minute. Then lift one from the sheet with a metal spatula and quickly roll it around the handle of a wooden spoon. Slide the cylinder off the spoon handle as soon as it has set, and place it on a wire rack. Shape the remaining snaps in the same way.

MOLDING CORNETS. Remove the snaps from the oven and leave them just long enough to be lifted without tearing—about one minute. Then lift one from the sheet with a metal spatula and press it around a metal cream-horn mold to shape it into a cornet. Transfer the cornet to a wire rack as soon as it has set. Shape the remaining snaps in the same way.

hands. Encase the dough in plastic wrap and refrigerate it for 20 minutes.

Scatter several tablespoons of cornmeal over a clean work surface and roll out the dough to a thickness of about ⅛ inch. Alternatively, place the dough between two sheets of parchment paper or wax paper, and roll it out. With a cookie cutter, cut the dough into rounds about 4½ inches in diameter. Use the rounds to line eight 3-inch tartlet molds. Chill the molds in the freezer for at least 10 minutes. While the molds are chilling, preheat the oven to 400° F.

Bake the tartlet shells until they have browned and are crisp — 20 to 25 minutes. Remove them from the pans and cool them on a cake rack.

To prepare the tartlet filling, mix together the blueberries, sugar, lemon juice and lemon zest in a saucepan. Bring the mixture to a boil over medium heat, then continue cooking it until the berries have burst and there is about 1 cup of juice in the pan — five to seven minutes. Stir in the tapioca. Cook the filling, stirring frequently, until it boils and thickens slightly — about 10 minutes more. Set the filling aside to cool.

Spoon the cooled filling into the tartlet shells and let them stand for 10 minutes before serving.

Cornmeal Tartlets with Tapioca-Blueberry Filling

Serves 8
Working time: about 20 minutes
Total time: about 1 hour and 20 minutes

Calories **273**
Protein **3g.**
Cholesterol **7mg.**
Total fat **6g.**
Saturated fat **2g.**
Sodium **171mg.**

1¼ cups unbleached all-purpose flour
½ cup stone-ground cornmeal
½ cup confectioners' sugar
½ tsp. salt
1 tbsp. cornstarch
2 tbsp. cold unsalted butter, cut into 4 pieces
2 tbsp. cold corn-oil margarine, cut into 4 pieces

Tapioca-blueberry filling

4 cups fresh blueberries, picked over and stemmed, or 4 cups frozen whole blueberries, thawed
½ cup sugar
1 tbsp. fresh lemon juice
2 tsp. grated lemon zest
1 tbsp. tapioca

To prepare the tartlet dough, combine the flour, cornmeal, confectioners' sugar, salt and cornstarch in a food processor or a bowl. If you are using a food processor, add the butter and margarine, and cut them into the dry ingredients with several short bursts. With the motor running, pour in 2 tablespoons of cold water in a thin, steady stream, and blend the dough just until it forms a ball. If the dough is too dry and crumbly, blend in up to 1 tablespoon more of water. If you are making the dough in a bowl, use two knives to cut the butter and margarine into the dry ingredients, then incorporate the water with a wooden spoon or your

Pears with a Spiced Walnut Crust

Serves 10
Working time: about 40 minutes
Total time: about 1 hour and 20 minutes

Calories **285**
Protein **3g.**
Cholesterol **6mg.**
Total fat **9g.**
Saturated fat **2g.**
Sodium **34mg.**

½ cup walnuts (about 2 oz.)
1 cup unbleached all-purpose flour
⅓ cup light brown sugar
2 tbsp. unsalted butter
2 tbsp. corn-oil margarine
¼ tsp. ground mace
¼ tsp. ground ginger
grated zest of 1 lemon
½ tsp. pure vanilla extract
6 pears
1 cup apple jelly

Preheat the oven to 375° F.

Spread the walnuts on a baking sheet and toast them in the oven until their skins begin to pull away — about 10 minutes. Then allow the walnuts cool to room temperature.

Put the toasted walnuts, flour, brown sugar, butter, margarine, mace, ginger and lemon zest into a food processor. Process the mixture until it resembles coarse meal. Sprinkle the vanilla and 1 tablespoon of water over the mixture, and process it in short bursts just until it begins to hold together in dough pieces about 1 inch in diameter. (Do not overprocess the dough lest it form a ball.)

Transfer the pieces of dough to a clean work surface. Rub the pieces between your fingers to finish blending the dough, then put the pieces into a 9-inch tart pan with a removable bottom. Spread out the dough with your fingers, coating the bottom and sides of the pan with a very thin layer; crimp the top edge of the dough with your fingers. Put the pan into the refrigerator.

Peel, halve, and core the pears. Thinly slice each pear half crosswise, then arrange 10 of the pear halves around the edge of the tart shell, pointing their narrow ends toward the center. Flatten each half, slightly spreading out the slices. Arrange the two remaining halves in the center of the tart.

Bake the tart until the edges are browned and any juices rendered by the pears have evaporated — about 40 minutes. Set the tart aside to cool.

Cook the apple jelly in a small saucepan over medium-low heat until it melts — about four minutes. Using a pastry brush, glaze the cooled pears with a thin coating of the melted jelly.

EDITOR'S NOTE: *If you do not have a food processor, grind the walnuts in a blender together with 1 tablespoon of sugar, then prepare the dough in a bowl with a pastry blender and a wooden spoon.*

Mile-High Pie with Two Sauces

Serves 12
Working time: about 1 hour
Total time: about 2 hours

Calories **240**
Protein **6g.**
Cholesterol **71mg.**
Total fat **3g.**
Saturated fat **1g.**
Sodium **85mg.**

1 tbsp. safflower oil
1½ cups plus 2 tbsp. sugar
12 egg whites
1 tbsp. pure vanilla extract
¼ tsp. cream of tartar
Vanilla-yogurt sauce
1¼ cups low-fat milk
1 vanilla bean
3 egg yolks
2 tbsp. sugar
1 cup plain low-fat yogurt
Cranberry sauce
2 cups fresh or frozen cranberries, picked over
½ cup sugar
½ cup ruby port
⅓ cup plain low-fat yogurt

Brush the inside of a 9-inch springform pan with the oil. Sprinkle in 2 tablespoons of the sugar; shake and tilt the pan to coat it evenly with the sugar. Preheat the oven to 300° F.

To prepare the meringue, put the egg whites, vanilla extract and cream of tartar into a bowl. Begin beating the whites at low speed, gradually increasing the speed to medium as the whites turn opaque. Add the remaining 1½ cups of sugar a tablespoon at a time, increasing the beater speed all the while. When all the sugar has been incorporated, continue beating the whites on high speed until they are glossy and form stiff peaks when the beater is lifted from the bowl.

Transfer the meringue to the springform pan. Smooth the top of the meringue with a long spatula or the dull side of a knife. Bake the pie until it has risen and is lightly browned — about 40 minutes. It will be moist throughout. Remove the pie from the oven and let it cool to room temperature in the pan.

While the pie is baking and cooling, make the sauces. To make the vanilla-yogurt sauce, heat the milk, vanilla bean, egg yolks and sugar in a small, heavy-bottomed, nonreactive saucepan set over low heat. Cook the mixture, stirring constantly with a wooden spoon, until it is thick enough to coat the back of the spoon. Strain the sauce into a bowl and set it aside; when it has cooled to room temperature, whisk in the yogurt.

To make the cranberry sauce, combine the cranber-ries, sugar and ½ cup of water in a small saucepan over medium-high heat. Cook the cranberries until they burst — six to eight minutes. Continue cooking the berries until they are quite soft — about five minutes.

Press the cooked berries through a sieve into a bowl and set them aside. When they have cooled to room temperature, whisk in the port and the yogurt.

Just before serving the pie, remove the sides of the pan. With a wet knife, cut the pie into wedges; present them with the vanilla-yogurt sauce and the cranberry sauce poured around them. If you like, swirl the two sauces together as shown below.

Two Methods for Swirling Sauces

A Carousel of Hearts

1 PIPING THE SAUCE. Shortly before serving the des-sert, pour sauce into the center of a plate. Tip and swirl the plate to cover the bottom evenly. Pour sauce of a contrasting color into a pastry bag with a very small plain tip, as here, or into a plastic squirt bottle. Pipe a ring of dots onto the first sauce (above).

2 CONNECTING THE DOTS. With one steady motion, draw the blunt end of a wooden skewer or pick from the center of one dot through the center of the next dot in the ring. Continue connecting the dots, without lifting the skewer, until you have formed a wreath of linked hearts. Set the dessert in the middle.

A Rippled Kaleidoscope

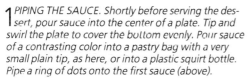

1 CREATING A SPIRAL. Fill a plate with sauce as de-scribed above in Step 1. Pour a sauce of contrast-ing color into a plastic squirt bottle, as here, or into a pastry bag with a very small plain tip. Practice an even flow by squeezing some of the sauce onto a paper towel in a smooth line. Starting at the center of the plate, squeeze out the sauce in a continuous spiral.

2 RIPPLING THE SPIRAL. Draw the blunt end of a wood-en skewer or pick from the center of the spiral to its rim. Lift the skewer from the surface of the sauce, rein-sert it about an inch farther along the rim, and draw the skewer from the rim to the center. Repeat the process to divide the spiral into about a dozen rippled wedges of equal size. Set the dessert in the middle of the design.

Marbled Angel-Food Cake

Serves 12
Working time: about 25 minutes
Total time: about 2 hours and 30 minutes

Calories **128**
Protein **4g.**
Cholesterol **0mg.**
Total fat **0g.**
Saturated fat **0g.**
Sodium **65mg.**

½ cup plus 5 tbsp. unbleached all-purpose flour
3 tbsp. unsweetened cocoa powder
1 ¼ cups sugar
⅛ tsp. salt
10 egg whites
1 tsp. cream of tartar
½ tsp. almond extract
½ tsp. pure vanilla extract
1 tbsp. confectioners' sugar

Sift 5 tablespoons of the flour, the cocoa powder and 2 tablespoons of the sugar into a bowl. Sift the cocoa mixture three more times and set the bowl aside. Sift the remaining ½ cup of flour, the salt and 2 tablespoons of the remaining sugar into a second bowl. Sift this mixture three more times and set it aside too.

Preheat the oven to 350° F. Rinse out a tube pan and shake — do not wipe — it dry.

With an electric mixer, beat the egg whites until soft peaks form when the beater is lifted. Add the cream of tartar, then blend in the remaining cup of sugar a little at a time, beating the egg whites until they form stiff peaks. With the mixer set on the lowest speed, blend in the almond extract, then the vanilla. Transfer half of the beaten egg whites to a clean bowl.

Fold the dry cocoa mixture into the beaten egg whites in one bowl, then pour this chocolate batter into the tube pan. Fold the remaining dry mixture into the beaten egg whites in the other bowl, and spoon the batter over the chocolate batter in the tube pan. Plunge a spatula down through both layers of batter, then bring it back to the surface with a twisting motion. Repeat this step at 1-inch intervals around the cake to marble the batter thoroughly.

Bake the cake for 45 minutes. Invert the pan and let the cake cool for 90 minutes. Run a knife around the sides of the pan to loosen the cake before turning it out. Sift the confectioners' sugar over the cake.

Honey-Glazed Buttermilk Cake

Serves 16
Working time: about 30 minutes
Total time: about 2 hours and 30 minutes

Calories **273**
Protein **3g.**
Cholesterol **9mg.**
Total fat **6g.**
Saturated fat **2g.**
Sodium **126mg.**

3 cups cake flour
1 tsp. baking soda
2 ⅓ cups sugar
4 tbsp. unsalted butter, cut into ½-inch-thick pats
4 tbsp. corn-oil margarine, cut into ½-inch-thick pats
2 tsp. pure vanilla extract
1 ½ cups buttermilk
4 egg whites
grated zest of 1 lemon
Honey glaze
¼ cup sugar
¼ cup buttermilk
¼ cup honey
½ tsp. pure vanilla extract

Lightly butter a 12-cup Bundt pan, then dust it with flour. Preheat the oven to 325° F.

Mix the flour, baking soda and sugar in a bowl. With an electric mixer on the lowest speed, cut the butter and margarine into the dry ingredients until the mixture has the consistency of fine meal.

Stir together the vanilla, buttermilk and egg whites. Mix half of this liquid with the dry ingredients on medium-low speed for one minute. Add the remaining liquid and mix it in at medium speed for one minute more, scraping down the sides of the bowl as necessary. Stir in the grated lemon zest.

Pour the batter into the prepared Bundt pan. Bake the cake until it begins to pull away from the sides of the pan and feels springy to the touch — about 55 minutes. Set the cake aside to cool in the pan.

To make the glaze, combine the sugar, buttermilk and honey in a small saucepan. Bring the liquid to a boil over medium heat, then continue boiling it, stirring occasionally, until it is a light caramel color and has thickened slightly — about 10 minutes. (Although the buttermilk in the glaze will separate when the liquid first comes to a boil, the subsequent cooking will yield a smooth, well-blended sauce.)

Remove the saucepan from the heat; stir in the vanilla and 1 teaspoon of water. Let the mixture cool completely — it should be thick enough to coat the back of a spoon.

Invert the cooled cake onto a serving platter. Lift away the Bundt pan and pour the glaze over the cake, letting the glaze run down the sides.

⅔ cup of the sugar, and the tangerine or orange zest and juice, and mix them thoroughly.

To prepare the meringue, beat the whites and cream of tartar together in another bowl until the whites hold soft peaks. Add the remaining ⅔ cup of sugar 2 tablespoons at a time, beating continuously until the whites are shiny and hold stiff peaks.

Stir one third of the meringue into the cake batter to lighten it, then fold in the remaining meringue. Rinse a 10-inch Bundt cake pan with water and shake it out so that only a few droplets remain. Spoon the batter into the pan and bake the cake for 50 minutes. Increase the oven temperature to 350° F. and continue baking the cake until a tester inserted in the thickest part comes out clean — five to 15 minutes more.

When the cake is done, remove it from the oven and let it rest for 10 minutes. Loosen it from the sides of the pan with a spatula and invert it onto a rack. Allow the cake to cool completely — about one and a half hours.

To prepare the lemon glaze, first sift the confectioners' sugar into a small bowl, then stir in the lemon juice and zest. Continue stirring until a smooth paste results. Stir in the sour cream and pour the glaze over the cake, letting the excess cascade down the sides.

Tangerine Chiffon Cake with Lemon Glaze

Serves 16
Working time: about 30 minutes
Total time: about 3 hours (includes cooling)

Calories **201**
Protein **3g.**
Cholesterol **69mg.**
Total fat **6g.**
Saturated fat **1g.**
Sodium **108mg.**

2 cups cake flour
1 tbsp. baking powder
4 eggs, separated, plus 3 egg whites
⅓ cup safflower oil
1 ⅓ cups sugar
2 ½ tbsp. finely chopped tangerine zest or grated orange zest
1 cup strained tangerine juice or orange juice, preferably fresh
½ tsp. cream of tartar
Lemon glaze
¾ cup confectioners' sugar
1 tbsp. fresh lemon juice
1 tbsp. grated lemon zest
1 tbsp. sour cream

Preheat the oven to 325° F.

To make the cake batter, sift the flour and baking powder into a large bowl. Whisk in the egg yolks, oil,

Lemon Cornmeal Cake with Blueberry Sauce

Serves 10
Working time: about 35 minutes
Total time: about 1 hour and 30 minutes

Calories **215**
Protein **4g.**
Cholesterol **68mg.**
Total fat **9g.**
Saturated fat **4g.**
Sodium **90mg.**

2 tbsp. sweetened dried coconut
½ cup sugar
¼ cup blanched almonds
1 cup stone-ground yellow cornmeal
½ cup unbleached all-purpose flour
1 ½ tsp. baking powder
½ cup buttermilk
grated zest and juice of 1 lemon
¼ cup unsalted butter
2 eggs
1 pint blueberries
⅛ tsp. ground cinnamon

Preheat the oven to 350° F. Cut pieces of wax paper to fit the bottom and sides of a 9-by-5-inch loaf pan. Line the pan with the wax paper.

Grind the coconut with 1 tablespoon of the sugar in a blender or food processor. Transfer the coconut to a small bowl. Grind the almonds with 1 tablespoon of the remaining sugar in the blender or food processor; transfer the almonds to the bowl containing the coconut, and set it aside.

Sift the cornmeal, flour and baking powder into a bowl. Combine the buttermilk, lemon zest and lemon juice in a measuring cup. Cream the butter and the remaining sugar in a bowl; the mixture should be light and fluffy. Add the eggs one at a time to the creamed butter and sugar, beating well after each addition. Alternately fold in the sifted ingredients and the buttermilk, adding a third of each mixture at a time. When the batter is thoroughly mixed, stir in the ground coconut and almonds.

Spoon the batter into the prepared loaf pan. Bake the cake until a wooden pick inserted in the center comes out clean — 30 to 40 minutes. Cool the pan on a rack for 10 to 15 minutes, then turn out the cake on the rack. Remove the wax paper; set the cake right side up to cool.

Just before serving time, prepare the blueberry sauce. Combine the blueberries and cinnamon in a small, heavy-bottomed saucepan over medium heat. Cook the blueberries, stirring occasionally, until they pop and exude some of their juice — about five minutes. Serve the sauce warm — do not let it cool — with slices of cake.

Oatmeal-Cocoa Kisses

Makes about 48 small cookies
Working time: about 30 minutes
Total time: about 4 hours and 30 minutes
(includes standing time)

Per cookie:
Calories **56**
Protein **1g.**
Cholesterol **0mg.**
Total fat **2g.**
Saturated fat **0g.**
Sodium **7mg.**

1 ¼ cups rolled oats
1 cup walnuts (about ¼ lb.)
¼ cup unsweetened cocoa powder
1 tbsp. fresh lemon juice
4 egg whites, at room temperature
¹⁄₁₆ tsp. salt
3 cups confectioners' sugar

Toast the rolled oats in a heavy-bottomed skillet over medium high heat, stirring constantly, until they are lightly browned — about five minutes. Scrape the oats into a food processor or a blender; chop them until they have the texture of fine cornmeal. Add the nuts and process until the nuts are finely chopped. Transfer the oats and nuts to a bowl.

Stir the cocoa powder and lemon juice into the oat-nut mixture. In a separate bowl, beat the egg whites with the salt until soft peaks form. Gradually beat the confectioners' sugar into the whites until stiff peaks form. Stir the oat mixture into the beaten egg whites.

Spoon the cookie batter into a pastry bag fitted with a large star tip. Pipe ½ teaspoon of the batter onto each corner of two baking sheets. Line each sheet with parchment paper or wax paper, pressing down on the corners so that they stick to the batter. Pipe the remaining batter onto the baking sheets in mounds about 1 inch across, spacing them 1 inch apart. (If you do not have a pastry bag, drop scant tablespoonfuls of the batter onto the baking sheets.) Let the mounds stand and dry out at room temperature for three to four hours so that they will be crisp when baked.

At the end of the standing time, preheat the oven to 300° F. Bake the kisses until they are dry and slightly puffed — 20 to 25 minutes.

Crisp Oatmeal Cookies

Makes about 48 cookies
Working time: about 30 minutes
Total time: about 1 hour

Per cookie:
Calories **56**
Protein **1g.**
Cholesterol **11mg.**
Total fat **1g.**
Saturated fat **0g.**
Sodium **51mg.**

2 eggs, plus 1 egg white
1 tsp. ground cinnamon
1 tsp. pure vanilla extract
¼ tsp. salt
1 tsp. baking powder
1 ½ cups sugar
2 tbsp. safflower oil
3 ½ cups quick-cooking oatmeal

Line a baking sheet with aluminum foil. Preheat the oven to 375° F.

Put the eggs, cinnamon, vanilla, salt, baking powder and sugar in a bowl. Beat the mixture until it forms a ribbon when the beater is lifted from the bowl — about three minutes. With a wooden spoon, stir in the oil, then the oatmeal. (The mixture is too thick to be combined with an electric mixer.)

Drop rounded teaspoonfuls of the cookie dough onto the prepared baking sheet, leaving about 2 inches between cookies. Bake the cookies until they are golden brown — 10 to 12 minutes. The cookies will puff up at first, then sink down — a sign that they have nearly finished cooking.

Let the cookies cool to room temperature on the foil before attempting to remove them. Store the cookies in an airtight container.

Banana Flan

Serves 8
Working time: about 45 minutes
Total time: about 3 hours and 15 minutes

Calories **158**
Protein **3g.**
Cholesterol **71mg.**
Total fat **2g.**
Saturated fat **1g.**
Sodium **36mg.**

½ cup plus ⅓ cup sugar
4 tsp. fresh lemon juice
1 cup low-fat milk
2 eggs
1 tbsp. dark rum
1 tsp. pure vanilla extract
¼ tsp. ground cardamom or cinnamon
1 cup banana purée (from 2 or 3 bananas)
2 bananas, peeled and diagonally sliced (optional)

Preheat the oven to 325° F.

Begin by caramelizing a 1-quart soufflé dish or a 6-inch-diameter cake pan: In a small heavy-bottomed saucepan, combine ½ cup of the sugar, 1 teaspoon of the lemon juice and 3 tablespoons of water. Cook the mixture over medium-high heat until the syrup caramelizes — it will have a rich brown hue. Immediately remove the saucepan from the heat. Working quickly, pour the caramel into the soufflé dish or cake pan. Using potholders to protect your hands, tilt the dish in all directions to coat the bottom and about one inch of the adjacent sides. Continue tilting the dish until the caramel has hardened, then set the dish aside.

To prepare the custard, put the milk into a heavy-bottomed saucepan over medium heat. As soon as the milk reaches a boil, remove the pan from the heat and set it aside. In a bowl, whisk together the eggs and the remaining ⅓ cup of sugar, then stir in the rum, vanilla, cardamom or cinnamon, banana purée, and the remaining 3 teaspoons of lemon juice. Stirring constantly to avoid curdling the eggs, pour the hot milk into the banana mixture. Transfer the custard to the caramelized dish.

Set the custard dish in a small roasting pan and pour enough hot tap water into the pan to come 1 inch up the sides of the custard dish. Bake the flan until a knife inserted in the center comes out clean — 20 to 30 minutes. (Take care not to insert the knife so deep that it pierces the caramel coating.) Remove the flan from the hot-water bath and let it cool to room temperature. Put the flan into the refrigerator until it is chilled — about two hours.

To unmold the chilled flan, invert a serving plate over the top of the dish, then turn both over together. The dish should lift away easily; if it does not, turn the dish right side up again and run a small, sharp knife around the top of the custard to loosen it. If you like, garnish the flan with a ring of banana slices. Cut the flan into wedges and spoon some of the caramel sauce over each one before serving.

Baked Apples Filled with Grapes

Serves 8
Working time: about 50 minutes
Total time: about 1 hour and 40 minutes

Calories **165**
Protein **1g.**
Cholesterol **11mg.**
Total fat **5g.**
Saturated fat **3g.**
Sodium **5mg.**

8 baking apples, cored
3 cups Gewürztraminer or Riesling
2 cups seedless grapes, picked over
½ tsp. ground mace
3 tbsp. unsalted butter

Preheat the oven to 400° F.

With a paring knife, cut a ring of semicircles in the skin at the top of each apple; as the apples bake, the semicircles will "blossom" in a floral pattern. Stand the apples upright in a 2-inch-deep baking dish and pour ½ cup of the wine over them. Put the apples into the oven and bake them for 30 minutes.

While the apples are baking, boil the remaining 2½ cups of wine in a saucepan over medium-high heat until only about 1 cup remains. Stir the grapes and mace into the wine, then reduce the heat, and simmer the mixture for 30 seconds. With a slotted spoon, remove the grapes from their cooking liquid and set them aside; reserve the liquid.

Spoon the grapes into the apples. Cut the butter into eight pieces and dot each apple with one piece of the butter. Pour the reduced wine over all and return the dish to the oven. Bake the apples until they are tender when pierced with the tip of a knife — 15 to 30 minutes more.

To serve, transfer the apples to individual plates. If necessary, use a knife to open up the "flower petals" you carved in the top of the apples.

Meringue Coffee Torte

Serves 12
Working time: about 50 minutes
Total time: about 2 hours and 30 minutes

Calories **165**
Protein **10g.**
Cholesterol **45mg.**
Total fat **6g.**
Saturated fat **1g.**
Sodium **220mg.**

2 tbsp. light brown sugar
2 eggs
½ cup whole wheat flour
½ tsp. baking powder
1¼ cups yogurt cheese (recipe, page 212)
4 tbsp. whipping cream
1 tbsp. honey
3 tsp. strong black coffee
18 walnut halves
confectioners' sugar to decorate
Walnut meringue
2 egg whites
⅓ cup light brown sugar
⅓ cup walnuts, finely chopped
2 tsp. cornstarch

Preheat the oven to 350° F. Grease an 8-inch round cake pan. Line the bottom with wax paper and then grease the paper.

Put the brown sugar and eggs in a bowl set over simmering water. Beat the mixture by hand or with an electric mixer until it is thick and pale. Remove the bowl from the heat and beat until the beater, when lifted, leaves a trail on the surface. Sift the flour and baking powder together over the mixture. Using a spatula or large metal or plastic spoon, fold in the flour. Pour the mixture into the prepared pan and level the top with a small spatula.

Bake the cake in the center of the oven until risen, lightly colored, and springy when touched in the middle—15 to 20 minutes. Leave the cake in the pan for five minutes, then turn it out onto a wire rack. Remove the paper and let the cake cool.

To make the walnut meringue, reduce the oven setting to 250° F. Line a baking sheet with parchment paper. Draw two 7½-inch circles on the parchment and invert the parchment. (The meringue circles are smaller than the pan in which the cake bakes, because meringue, unlike sponge cake, does not shrink as it cools.) In a large bowl, beat the egg whites until they hold stiff peaks. Add one-third of the sugar at a time, beating well after each addition. Mix together the chopped walnuts and cornstarch, and fold them into the meringue.

Divide the walnut meringue between the two circles and spread it evenly. Bake the rounds for one hour to one hour and 20 minutes, until the meringue feels firm and no longer sticky. Transfer the parchment with the meringue rounds to a wire rack. When the meringue is cold, peel off the parchment.

Beat the cheese and cream in a bowl with a wooden spoon. Stir in the honey and coffee. Put ¼ cup of the coffee cream in a pastry bag fitted with a medium-size star tip.

Place a meringue round on a plate and spread it with one-third of the remaining coffee cream. Slice the cake in half horizontally. Place one layer on the meringue and spread it with another third of the coffee cream. Top the coffee cream with the remaining layer of cake, the rest of the coffee cream, and finally the second meringue round.

Dust the torte with the confectioners' sugar. Pipe scrolls around the top edge of the torte and decorate it with the walnut halves.

Yule Log

YULE-LOG RECIPES USUALLY PRESCRIBE A SPONGE CAKE ROULADE COVERED WITH CHOCOLATE BUTTER FROSTING. THIS LOW-FAT VERSION IS CONSTRUCTED FROM A CHOCOLATE-FLAVORED EGG-WHITE BATTER WITH A CHESTNUT FILLING.

Serves 12
Working time: about 1 hour
Total time: about 2 hours and 30 minutes

Calories **175**
Protein **2g.**
Cholesterol **5mg.**
Total fat **4g.**
Saturated fat **2g.**
Sodium **25mg.**

6 egg whites
2 cups sugar
3 oz. semisweet chocolate, melted and cooled
½ cup all-purpose flour, sifted
cocoa powder to decorate
confectioners' sugar to decorate

Chestnut filling
1 cup chestnut puree
4 tbsp. light cream
1 tbsp. honey

Preheat the oven to 425° F. Place a small piece of parchment paper on a baking sheet. In addition, grease a 9-by-13-inch jelly-roll pan and line the pan with parchment paper. If possible, have ready two pastry bags fitted with ½-inch plain tips; one, however, will suffice.

Beat the egg whites in a large bowl until they hold stiff peaks, then beat in all but 1 tablespoon of the sugar, 1 tablespoon at a time. To make a crisp meringue for the mushrooms adorning the log, transfer ▶

about 3 tablespoons of the mixture into a smaller bowl, and whisk in the remaining tablespoon of sugar. Spoon the smaller quantity of meringue into a pastry bag, and pipe mushroom stalks and caps onto the parchment paper on the baking sheet. Place the baking sheet on the bottom shelf of the oven.

Return any meringue left in the bag to the bulk of the mixture. Quickly fold in the melted chocolate and the flour with a spoon. Transfer this mixture to the second pastry bag and pipe lines crosswise in the prepared pan. Bake the roulade for about 12 minutes, until risen and just firm to the touch. Remove the roulade and turn the oven off, but let the meringue mushrooms cool slowly in the oven.

Turn the roulade out onto a sheet of parchment paper and peel off the lining paper. Loosely replace the lining paper over the sponge cake, cover the cake with the pan, and allow the cake to cool completely.

To make the filling, beat together the chestnut puree, cream, and honey until smooth. Detach the mushrooms from the parchment paper and, using a dab of the chestnut mixture, attach each stalk to a cap.

Uncover the cake and spread it with the filling. Roll up the log carefully, starting at one short end; use the parchment paper to help you. Put the log on a serving plate and arrange the mushrooms on and around it. Dust both log and mushrooms first with cocoa powder and then with confectioners' sugar.

EDITOR'S NOTE: *To obtain 1 cup of chestnut puree from fresh chestnuts, slit 1 lb. of chestnuts down one side, parboil them for one to two minutes, shell, and peel them. Simmer the chestnuts in water for about 20 minutes, until they are tender. Drain and put them through a sieve.*

Christmas Garland

THE SWEETNESS IN THIS CAKE COMES FROM ITS ABUNDANT FRUIT. RICH AND MOIST WHEN FRESH, THIS CAKE WILL, HOWEVER, NOT KEEP AS LONG AS A TRADITIONAL FRUIT CAKE BECAUSE OF THE LACK OF BUTTER OR MARGARINE.

Serves 16
Working time: about 45 minutes
Total time: about 4 hours

Calories **270**
Protein **6g.**
Cholesterol **50mg.**
Fat **11g.**
Saturated fat **2g.**
Sodium **65mg.**

1 orange, finely grated zest and juice
⅔ cup chopped candied cherries
⅓ cup chopped mixed candied peel
3 tbsp. angelica or other green candied fruit, chopped
3 tbsp. candied pineapple, chopped
1 cup dried pears, chopped
½ cup dried apricots, chopped
½ cup golden raisins
½ cup currants
½ cup raisins
¾ cup walnuts, chopped
¾ cup Brazil nuts, chopped
⅓ cup almonds, chopped
1 cup whole wheat flour
¼ tsp. ground cinnamon
¼ tsp. ground allspice
¼ tsp. ground cloves
¼ tsp. grated nutmeg
1 tsp. baking powder
3 eggs, beaten
1 tbsp. molasses
Icing and decoration
1 cup confectioners' sugar
1 tbsp. brandy
8 walnut halves
4 candied cherries, quartered
holly leaves for garnish

Preheat the oven to 300° F. Grease an 8-inch ring mold. Put the orange zest and juice in a large bowl. Stir in the chopped cherries, mixed peel, angelica, pineapple, pears, apricots, golden raisins, currants, raisins, walnuts, Brazil nuts, and almonds. Sift in the flour, cinnamon, allspice, cloves, nutmeg, and baking powder, adding the bran left in the sieve. Pour in the eggs and molasses. Beat the mixture well with a wooden spoon. Transfer it to the greased ring mold and press it down.

Bake it for 45 minutes, or until it feels firm. Leave the cake in the pan for 10 minutes, then invert it onto a wire rack and set it aside until it is completely cool.

To make the icing, mix the confectioners' sugar with the brandy and a little water, if necessary, to give a thin coating consistency. Spoon the icing over the cake, then decorate the cake with the walnut halves, cherry quarters, and holly leaves.

Index

Picture Credits